Franz Heinrich Reusch

Nature and the Bible

Lectures on the Mosaic History of Creation in its Relation to Natural Science. Vol. 2

Franz Heinrich Reusch

Nature and the Bible
Lectures on the Mosaic History of Creation in its Relation to Natural Science. Vol. 2

ISBN/EAN: 9783337026691

Printed in Europe, USA, Canada, Australia, Japan

Cover: Foto ©Lupo / pixelio.de

More available books at **www.hansebooks.com**

NATURE AND THE BIBLE:

LECTURES

ON THE

MOSAIC HISTORY OF CREATION IN ITS RELATION TO NATURAL SCIENCE.

BY

DR. FR. H. REUSCH,
PROFESSOR OF CATHOLIC THEOLOGY IN THE UNIVERSITY OF BONN.

Revised and Corrected by the Author.

Translated from the Fourth Edition
BY
KATHLEEN LYTTELTON.

VOLUME II.

EDINBURGH:
T. & T. CLARK, 38 GEORGE STREET.
1886.

CONTENTS.

CHAP.		PAGE
XXIV.	The Theory of the Origin of Organic Beings by Spontaneous Generation,	1
XXV.	The Theory of Descent,	32
XXVI.	The Theory of Descent—*continued*,	65
XXVII.	The Theory of Descent—*Conclusion*,	95
XXVIII.	Man and Beast,	121
XXIX.	Man and Beast—*Conclusion*,	152
XXX.	The Unity of the Human Race,	181
XXXI.	The Unity of the Human Race—*continued*,	203
XXXII.	The Unity of the Human Race—*Conclusion*,	222
XXXIII.	The Duration of Life in the First Age. Old Testament Chronology,	246
XXXIV.	The Antiquity of the Human Race,	265
XXXV.	The Prehistoric Periods,	299
XXXVI.	Lake Dwellings and other Prehistoric Antiquities,	333
INDEX,		367

XXIV.

THE THEORY OF THE ORIGIN OF ORGANIC BEINGS BY SPONTANEOUS GENERATION.

THE first chapter of Genesis tells us that God created the vegetable world and the different kinds of animals, and lastly, created a man and a woman. In the account of the Flood it is further said that all men were destroyed on the earth excepting Noah and his family, and that all mankind is descended from the three sons of Noah. How do scientific doctrines concerning the origin of organic life, and the relations of the different organisms to one another, agree with these Biblical statements? And what does biology in particular say to the Biblical doctrine of the unity of the human race? I shall have to discuss these points in my next lectures. I begin with the *Origin of Organic Beings.*[1]

We here come to the question, whether organic beings, viz. plants and animals, can be produced only by reproduction from the germs and eggs of other plants and animals, or whether a so-called *generatio æquivoca* or spontaneous generation, or, as others say, Heterogeny

[1] Cf. Frohschammer, *Das Christenthum*, etc., p. 54 (*Der Ursprung des Organischen in der Natur*). Th. H. Martin, *Les Sciences*, etc., p. 91 (*L'Hétérogénie et l'origine de la vie sur la terre*). Huber, *Die Lehre Darwins*, p. 7. Reinke, *Die Organismen und ihr Ursprung* (*Nord und Süd*, vol. xviii., 1881, pp. 201, 213). T. von Nanstein, *Das Protoplasma*, Heidelberg 1880. Cf. Huxley's speech at the Meeting of the British Association at Liverpool: see *Athenæum*, 1870, 17th Sept., p. 374.

or Autogony,[1] *i.e.* the origin of plants and animals without germs and eggs from inorganic matter, is also possible. I will begin by surveying the history of the question; this history is interesting in itself, but it is also important to my object, because it shows that the theologian need not take a side in this question, but that, on the contrary, he may simply leave it to natural science to decide whether spontaneous generation is possible, and really can occur, or has occurred.

In the Biblical account of creation it is only said that the origin of the vegetable and animal world must be referred to the creative activity of God, and that God has taken measures for the reproduction and preservation of the species of plants and animals. We are not told how the first organic beings originated, and still less how thenceforth the separate individuals should come into existence; whether all plants should spring only from seeds or shoots, and all animals should come into existence by means of procreation or from eggs or germs, or whether there should be other ways also. The author of Genesis had no reason for entering into such scientific details.

S. Augustine,[2] in his explanation of the Mosaic account of creation, raises the question whether "certain small animals" were also created on the fifth and sixth days, or whether they originated later from putrefied matter. "For," he says, "many small animals originate from unhealthy vapours, from evaporations from the earth, or from corpses; some also

---

[1] On the expression *generatio aequivoca*, see Huber, *Op. cit.* p. 11.
[2] *D Gen. ad lit.* iii. 14, c. Faust, *M.*, vi. 8. *De Trin.* iii. 8, 9. Peter Lombard, *Sent.* ii. 15.

from decayed wood, herbs, and fruits. But God is the Creator of all things. It may therefore be said that those animals which spring from the bodies, and especially the corpses of other living beings were only created with them, *potentialiter* and *materialiter*. But of those which spring from the earth, or the water, we may unhesitatingly say that they were created on the fifth and sixth days." This passage from S. Augustine was included in the great dogmatic compendium of the Middle Ages, the Sentences of Peter Lombard, and the schoolmen maintained this view. S. Thomas,[1] no doubt, protests against Avicenna's theory that *all* animals could spring without seed from a certain intermixture of the elements, but he does not dispute the fact that certain animals spring from putrefied plants and animals.

The Fathers and the schoolmen did not derive this theory from the Bible, but as it was not opposed to the Bible they took it quite naturally from the ancient scientific writers, especially from Aristotle. We know that they not only assert that midges, fleas, lice, and other vermin sprang simply from the earth, but also frogs, serpents, and mice; the eel also, in which Aristotle could find no ovary, was supposed to have originated from slime. Even in the seventeenth century, the learned Jesuit, Athanasius Kircher, gives regular receipts for bringing animals into existence: "Take as many serpents as you like, dry them, cut them into small pieces, bury these in damp earth, water them freely with rain-water, and leave the rest to the spring sun. After eight days the whole will turn into

[1] Q. 71, a. 1; q. 72, a. 1.

little worms, which, fed with milk and earth, will at length become perfect serpents, and by procreation will multiply *ad infinitum.*" [1]

You see that theologians made no objection to the *generatio æquivoca* when it was assumed to a far greater extent than is ever the case now-a-days; and we need therefore certainly not dispute the principle of spontaneous generation from a theological point of view. If organic beings really spring from inorganic matter, we must simply suppose, with S. Augustine,[2] that God created some substances with the faculty of bringing forth certain classes of plants or animals according to the natural laws given by Him, and under certain conditions foreseen by Him from all eternity. No theologian—and, I think, no philosopher—ought to assert the *impossibility* of spontaneous generation. The fact that we do not understand *how* organic beings can spring from inorganic matter, is no proof that it cannot happen; we do not understand many physiological events which undoubtedly occur.[3] The question whether spontaneous generation takes place among certain classes of plants and animals, is one which can be decided only by means of observation. And the classes of organic beings, among which it was thought that spontaneous generation might exist, have become fewer and fewer under continuous observation, especially since the end of the seventeenth century.

The well-known saying, *Omne vivum ex ovo*, proceeds from the English savant Harvey, who is famous as the

---

[1] Quenstedt, *Sonst und Jetzt*, p. 229.   [2] Aug. *De Trin.* iii. 9.
[3] Martin, *Les Sciences*, p. 94.

discoverer of the circulation of the blood. But Harvey did not mean by this saying what is now generally understood; he only meant to assert that every living being originated in a small spheroidal portion of organic matter. He did not deny that such an egg could spring from inorganic matter by spontaneous generation. In his time, for instance, it was commonly believed that insects could spring from putrefied plants and animals. If a piece of flesh is placed in the sun and allowed to putrefy, maggots will appear in it, from which will proceed insects; and these maggots were generally believed, in the seventeenth century, to have come into existence by spontaneous generation. It was the Italian savant Redi who refuted this theory, in a very simple way, about 1690. He covered the piece of flesh with a very fine gauze, and then exposed it to the same influence; the result was that no maggots and insects were generated, and it was proved that the maggots in the uncovered piece of flesh proceeded from insects which came to lay their eggs in it, and the eggs were then hatched by the heat of the sun.[1]

The opinion that the so-called entozoa, intestinal worms and such like, originated by spontaneous generation from unhealthy juices in the bodies of men or animals, lasted longer. The extraordinary wanderings and changes of these parasites have only been detected in this century, principally by Van Beneden, and several German savants, Von Siebold, Küchenmeister, Leuckart, and others. There is no doubt that they do not originate by spontaneous generation, but

[1] Huxley, *On our Knowledge of the Causes and Phenomena of Organic Nature*, p. 73.

are reproduced like other animals, principally from eggs.[1]

Further, it was formerly assumed that the so-called mould fungi originated by spontaneous generation from germs which were, as it were, crystallized out of mouldy bodies, as the organized produce of decomposition. This opinion also is erroneous; at least A. de Bary says, "Hitherto we know of no demonstrated fact which would establish this theory; it rather appears, from many experiments made with great care, that the mould fungi in no way differ from other fungi with reference to their origin."[2] Neither do the so-called yeast fungi or ferment cells afford any proof of spontaneous generation. Yeast consists of very small vegetable cells, which, when they are placed in a liquid susceptible to the action, multiply by budding, and produce fermentation. The opinion that these cells originated by parentless spontaneous generation may be treated in the same way as that of the supposed spontaneous generation of mould fungi.[3]

A bitter controversy has been going on in France in recent years (since 1818), especially between the Academician Pouchet (ob. 1872) and Pasteur, about the so-called infusoria; the Abate Spallanzani in the last century, and in our century Ehrenberg, Balbiani, and others, having denied that they originate by

[1] Cf. C. O. Weber, *Ueber die Entstehung der Eingeweidenwürmer*, in the *Proceedings* of the Association of Natural History, Bonn 1863, xx. 95. M. Pertz, *Ueber den Parasitismus in der organischen Natur*, Berlin 1869, p. 18. Quenstedt, *Sonst und Jetzt*, p. 231. *Natur und Offenbarung*, 1864, p. 315.
[2] *Ueber Schimmel und Hefe*, Berlin 1869, p. 56.
[3] A. de Bary, *Op. cit.* p. 60. F. Hoppe-Seyler, *Ueber die Quellen der Lebenskräfte*, Berlin 1871, p. 15, 20 seq. F. Cohn, *Ueber Bakterien die kleinsten lebenden Wesen*, Berlin 1872, p. 18.

spontaneous generation. Pouchet maintained that small microscopic organic beings — they are called bacteria, and it is still uncertain whether they are plants or animals—originated by spontaneous generation if water was poured on to an organic substance, for instance, hay. Pasteur explained the appearance of these animals, by the precipitation of small germs which were floating in the air; and in order to substantiate this statement, he quoted the results of a series of ingenious experiments. He killed all the organic germs which were contained in the fluid with which he experimented, by boiling it; and then he either entirely stopped the access of air, or took precautions to ensure that all the organic germs contained in the air which he admitted should be killed,—for instance, by admitting the air through a red-hot tube, —or that they should be caught in cotton wool. In all these cases, no organic life was developed in the fluid.[1]

Many scientific men think that the doctrine of the

[1] "Pasteur fixed in the window of his room a glass tube, in the centre of which he had placed a ball of gun-cotton; ... one end of the glass tube was, of course, open to the external air; and at the other end of it he placed an aspirator, a contrivance for causing a current of the external air to pass through the tube. He kept this apparatus going for four-and-twenty hours, and the result was, that a very fine dust was gradually deposited at the bottom of it. That dust, on being transferred to the stage of a microscope, was found to contain an enormous number of starch grains. ... But besides these, Pasteur found also an immense number of other organic substances, such as spores of fungi, which had been floating about in the air, and had got caged in this way. Pasteur also took one of these vessels of infusion, which had been kept eighteen months without the least appearance of life, and, by a most ingenious contrivance, he managed to break it open and introduce such a ball of gun-cotton, without allowing the infusion or the cotton ball to come into contact with any air but that which had been subjected to a red heat; and in twenty-four hours he had the satisfaction of finding all the indications of what had been hitherto called spontaneous generation. ... He then took some decaying animal or vegetable substance, ... and filled a vessel

spontaneous generation of infusoria has received its death-blow, as Huxley says, by these experiments of Pasteur's. The famous Paris Academician Flourens said, as early as 1864, "No one thinks that insects are spontaneously generated since Redi (1688), that intestinal worms are spontaneously generated since Van Beneden (1853), that infusoria are spontaneously generated since Balbiani (1862), and since Pasteur it is not asserted of any animals."[1] This is going too far. No doubt most of the leading savants of the present age declare themselves decidedly against the assumption of spontaneous generation,[2] and one of the defenders of

having a long tubular neck with it. He then boiled the liquid, and bent that long neck into an S shape, or zig-zag, leaving it open at the end. The infusion then gave no trace of any appearance of spontaneous generation, however long it might be left, as all the germs in the air were deposited in the beginning of the bent neck. He then cut the tube close to the vessel, and allowed the ordinary air to have free and direct access; and the result of that was the appearance of organisms in it, as soon as the infusion had been allowed to stand long enough to allow of the growth of those it received from the air, which was about forty-eight hours. The result of M. Pasteur's experiments proved, therefore, in the most conclusive manner, that all the appearances of spontaneous generation arose from nothing more than from the deposition of the germs of organisms which were constantly floating in the air. To this conclusion, however, the objection was made that if that were the cause, then the air would contain such an enormous number of these germs that it would be a continual fog. But Pasteur replied that they are not there in anything like the number we might suppose, and that an exaggerated view has been held on the subject; he showed that the chances of animal or vegetable life appearing in infusions depend entirely on the conditions under which they are exposed. If they are exposed to the ordinary atmosphere around us, why, of course, you may have organisms appearing early. But, on the other hand, if they are exposed to air from a great height, or from some very quiet cellar, you will often not find a single trace of life."
—Huxley, *On our Knowledge of the Causes of the Phenomena of Organic Nature*, Six Lectures, London 1863, p. 78 seq. Cf. Aug. Müller, *Ueber die erste Entstehung organischer Wesen*, Berlin 1869, p. 9.

[1] *Examen du Livre de M. Darwin*, pp. 67, 121.

[2] Ehrenberg, Rudolf Wagner, Joh. Müller, Liebig, Brown, Virchow, Schleiden, Unger, Herm. Hoffmann (*Untersuchungen*, etc., p. 4), F. Cohn

this theory admits that those who agree with him form only a small and unimportant party, and that "almost all eminent men of science" are opposed to it.[1] But very thoughtful men, like Th. H. Martin,[2] are contented with asserting that no doubt the assumption of spontaneous generation has been made extremely improbable; but that all the conditions of a perfectly sure, inductive experiment have not yet been fulfilled. For the present we must be content with this statement, and the more so, as in recent times Pasteur's view has been decidedly disputed by many—in England, especially by H. Charlton Bastian;[3] and it has been said that experiments have proved that organisms can certainly originate in organic infusions, and that they may very likely originate in solutions of salts.

Therefore D. F. Strauss' observation: "It is certain that living beings still form themselves partly from inorganic, partly from dissimilar organic substances, under certain circumstances; the so-called infusoria forming themselves when water is poured not only on animal and vegetable, but also on mineral bodies, and

(*Bakterien*, p. 31), and others. In France, Flourens, Milne Edwards, de Quatrefages, Claude Bernard, Dumas, and others. Cf. Ulrici, *Gott und die Natur*, p. 366. Valroger, *La Genèse*, p. 38.

[1] Thus Giebel, *Tagesfragen*, p. 204. In France, besides Pouchet, N. Jolly and Ch. Musset believe in spontaneous generation; in Germany, Schaaffhausen. K. Vogt, who formerly did not believe in spontaneous generation (see *Natür. gesch.*, p. 148; cf. *Vorlesungen*, ii. 253), now says that he does not consider the subject as settled, even after Pasteur's experiments. (See his preface to Huxley's above-quoted book, p. viii.)

[2] *Les Sciences*, p. 97.

[3] *The Beginnings of Life*, London 1872. *Evolution and the Origin of Life*, London 1874. Cf. *Saturday Review*, vol. 34 (1872), p. 731; and for the controversy between Bastian and Huxley, see vol. 30 (1870), p. 550; vol. 32 (1871), p. 152. Other English savants have also declared themselves opposed to Bastian's theory; see *Popular Science Review*, April 1876. Zöckler, *Gesch. der Beziehungen*, etc, ii. 722.

entozoa forming themselves in animal bodies," was one of those which caused Humboldt to blame in very strong terms Strauss' "scientific levity;"[1] although he usually shows great sympathy for his theological opinions. Strauss expresses himself much more cautiously in his last book;[2] he only says there that the question of the *generatio æquivoca* has occupied natural science again recently, although, because of the difficulty of proof, no generally accepted decision has been reached.

A fresh attempt has been made by Hæckel to prove the spontaneous generation of organisms. He says that it is the case only with one class of organic beings, the so-called monera.[3] These are, he says, organic beings of the simplest description; their entire body, which is at most as large as a pin's head during life, is nothing more than a shapeless mobile lump of jelly (protoplasm). The monera cannot "exactly be called either animals or plants;" "strictly speaking, they do not deserve the name of organisms at all," for they are not composed of organs, but consist entirely of shapeless, simple, homogeneous protoplasm,—that same proteid carbon-containing compound which, in endless modifications, is found in all organisms, as the essential and never-failing basis of the phenomena of life. It propagates itself by subdivision. When such a little spheroid has attained a certain

---

[1] *Correspondence with Varnhagen von Ense*, p. 117: "There is one thing which displeases me in Strauss, and that is the scientific levity with which he treats the question of the formation of organic out of inorganic matter; he even apparently sees no difficulty in believing that man was formed from Chaldean primæval mud."

[2] *Der Alte und der neue Glaube*, p. 169.

[3] *Natürliche Schöpfungsgeschichte*, pp. 164, 305. *Das Leben in den grössten Meerestiefen*, p. 33. *Anthropogenie*, p. 377.

size by the assimilation of foreign albuminous matter, it falls into two or more pieces, which again, by simple growth, become like the parent body. "Perhaps the most remarkable of all the monera" have been found in the fine calcareous mud which has been dredged up in the course of the deep-sea researches so largely instituted of late years. They are sometimes roundish formless lumps of jelly, sometimes a gelatinous network covering fragments of stone and other objects. These "beings living in the deep sea,"—if these little lumps of jelly can be really considered as living beings,—were called Bathybius by Huxley in 1868, and in honour of Hæckel, Bathybius Hæckelii. Unluckily it is very likely, although Hæckel does not mention it, that the Bathybius will have to be removed from the list of living beings. At least Huxley asserted, in an English periodical in August 1875, that he feared "the thing to which I gave that name is little more than sulphate of lime, precipitated in a flocculent state from the sea-water by the strong alcohol in which the specimens of the deep-sea soundings which I examined were preserved;"[1] and Dubois Raymond says, "Since then the scientific existence of the Bathybius Hæckelii has become as precarious as that of its supposed fossil model, the Eozoon Canadense."[2] Johannes von Nanstein even says, "The Bathybius only exists in the dark depths of scientific superstition."[3]

[1] *Nature*, 19th Aug. 1875. Cf. *Annals and Magazine of Natural History*, ser. 4, vol. 16 (No. 95, Nov. 1775), p. 325. C. Semper, *Der Hæckelismus in der Zoologie*, Hamburg 1875, p. 30.
[2] *Ueber die Grenzen des Naturerkennens*, 4th ed. 1876, p. 43.
[3] *Das Protoplasma*, p. 178. Cf. K. A. Zittel, *Die Kreide*, Berlin 1879, p. 27.

Hæckel therefore thinks that the monera originate by spontaneous generation. He reminds us that chemists have recently succeeded in doing what was asserted fifty years ago to be impossible, that is, in producing carbon compound, or so-called "organic" substances, as urea, alcohol, acetic acid, and so on, from inorganic substances. Therefore there is every probability that sooner or later we shall succeed in producing artificially the proteid compounds, or protoplasm itself. We may therefore assume that in nature also there may be formed from inorganic substances first some simpler carbon compounds, and from these, protoplasm capable of life; if this exists, it only needs to individualize itself in the same way as the mother liquor of crystals individualizes itself, and the moneron is there.

But Hæckel himself admits that "this event must remain a pure hypothesis so long as it is not directly observed or repeated in experiments."[1] He adds that the process of the spontaneous generation of monera would in any case be very difficult to observe, and could hardly be verified with undoubted certainty, even if it still happened daily and hourly. But it cannot be difficult to repeat the process by means of an experiment, if it is as simple as Hæckel makes it. "The special conditions of existence," under whose influence the Bathybius originates, according to Hæckel, may be artificially produced; but yet he has not responded to the challenge to fabricate a Bathybius.[2]

We may concede this much to Hæckel; it has not

---

[1] *Natürliche Schöpfungsgeschichte*, p. 309. Cf. *Anthropogenie*, p. 377.
[2] *Ausland*, 1870, 1091.

been proved that the origin of monera by spontaneous generation is impossible; but looked at from a strictly scientific point of view, it is not in the least more likely than the similar origin of infusoria. Frohschammer rightly remarks with reference to this, "At any rate it is not yet proved that proteid matter forms itself anywhere in nature from inorganic matter without the mediation of organic forces. And even if we should succeed in producing such albuminous compounds by experiment, yet even then there is no proof that they also originate by themselves in nature, because in experiment there is still the systematic intelligent action of the investigator, a systematic action, which, if we do not fall back on the action of the Creator,"—and Hæckel is the last person to do this, —" cannot always be replaced in nature by chance or by the relations of things, even if all the substances and forces which the experimentalist has at his disposal are present. And supposing that albumen did at any time form itself in nature, it would not prove that germs or cells, single-celled organisms, however simple they might be, formed themselves from it of their own accord. Up to this time, so far as we know, no organism has been inorganically or empirically formed, even from albumen which itself has been formed in organisms. This is hardly likely to happen more easily or to be more possible in nature, for, on the contrary, general experience shows continually that albumen cannot even exist apart from a living organism, but dissolves and decays, instead of forming itself into cells or organisms."[1]

[1] *Das Christenthum*, p. 62.

Hæckel's theory that albuminous protoplasm could "individualize" itself into monera, in the same way as the mother-liquor of crystals individualizes itself in crystallization, is rather venturesome. The organic cells and the crystals are essentially different, in that "the cell does not only grow by additions to the outside, but primarily from within; that it does not lose its activity like the crystal at the moment of its formation, but creates from within itself new forms like itself, and that, alike in its dimensions, its extent, and its duration in time, it is limited by its own individual formative and living impulse."[1] "Organic bodies," says K. E. von Baer, "are not only changeable, but they are the only things that change themselves. The crystal and the rock are no doubt also exposed to final destruction, but the destruction does not come from within. Damp, heat, chemical and physical forces, in general help to wear them away. Were they placed in an isolated spot in the universe, they would last for ever; for what is lifeless cannot *die*, it is only *destroyed* by the outside world. On the other hand, organic bodies destroy themselves, they are not only subjected to constant change, but their whole development is a progress towards death."[2] Virchow also mentions some essential differences between the organic individual and the crystals, although he disputes the assumption of the so-called vital force. "The crystal can grow indefinitely if it finds the conditions and the matter for its growth. On the other hand, with the living being, the internal law of its

---

[1] Huber, *Die Lehre Darwins*, p. 14. Michelis, *Hæckelogonie*, p. 100.
[2] Reden, Petersburg 1857, i. 38; see Huber, *Op. cit.* p. 15.

destiny (innere Zweck) is also the limit of its external development. Space and time have a meaning and a value only for the living being; for only the living being carries within it the power of self-preservation and self-development, only the living being loses itself if it is not determined from within to attain to a certain development within a certain period. Thus the individual carries its aim and its measure within itself; thus it proves itself to be a *real* unity, instead of the merely notional unity of the atom."[1]

After what has been said, we may at all events consider that recent researches have shown that the theory of spontaneous generation has been proved to be not inadmissible only in the case of the simplest and smallest organic being; that, according to most scientific men, however, no organic being comes into existence by spontaneous generation. But if the idea of a contemporary spontaneous generation is inadmissible, or at least very problematical, may we not still assume that spontaneous generation did occur in the earlier periods of the earth's history?

"Now-a-days," says Burmeister, "when plenty of beings capable of reproduction exist everywhere, there is no need that new ones should form themselves from

[1] *Vier Reden über Leben und Kranksein*, p. 49 ; see Huber, *Op. cit.* p. 22. Semper, *Der Hæckelismus in der Zoologie*, pp. 29, 34, calls Hæckel's "carbon theory" "an entirely unjustified hypothesis," which, he says, seems to have originated because the modern name for organic chemistry is the chemistry of carbon compounds. The two supporters of this theory, Hæckel and Seidlitz, "forget that organic chemistry is not in the least synonymous with the chemistry of the living organism ; the former deals only with dead, the latter only with living organic bodies. Unfortunately we know at present very little of the latter, but we know enough to be able to say that its laws need by no means be identical with those of organic chemistry."

matter; and, perhaps, the original material from which they could form themselves is wanting, as by far the greater part of the organic substance now existing is already contained in living organisms, and the only provision for the existence of new individuals appears to be by means of procreation. But in the early ages of organization all this was different, and therefore the course of generation was probably different also."[1] Hæckel reminds us that at the time when, after the origin of water in a liquid state on the cooled crust of the earth, organisms were first formed, the immeasurable quantities of carbon which we now find deposited in the coal measures existed in a totally different form; they were probably for the most part dispersed throughout the atmosphere in the shape of carbonic acid. The whole composition of the atmosphere, including even its density and electrical conditions, was therefore very different from at present; and, in like manner, the chemical and physical nature of the primæval ocean, its temperature, density, saltness, etc., must have differed widely from that of the present ocean; so that we cannot, at least, contradict the supposition that at that time, under conditions quite different from those of to-day, a spontaneous generation, which now is perhaps no longer possible, may have taken place.[2]

We may admit the possibility, but the supposition is not scientifically probable. Frohschammer justly says with reference to this: "As in these days, according to our experience, cells and germs only originate in organisms, we have no right to suppose,

[1] *Gesch. der Schöpfung.* p. 287.   [2] *Nat. Schöpfungsgeschichte*, p. 303.

without certain proof and sure warrant, that it was different in early days, in the beginnings of organic nature. This is a principle which is generally insisted on in natural science in the present day, and which, therefore, ought not to be discarded in this case without very good reasons."[1] Men of science can make no objection to the following angry words of Quenstedt's,[2] "To the savant, to understand means to *see*, and he can only draw conclusions on this basis. If, now-a-days, even the smallest plant cannot come into existence without a germ, what thoughtful savant would venture rashly to assert that the whole beautiful vegetable and animal world, up to man, had been generated *only* in the dead earth? But to many the idea that the Creator has power to breathe life into the dead lump of clay is so unwelcome, that they would rather embrace the wildest dreams in order to prove themselves apparently right. Yes, they say, it is very easy to explain why the earth can *now-a-days* bring forth no living creature; now it is in its old age, but when it was young, *things were different*. It is amusing to see how these men, who usually subject to the sharpest criticism the slightest instinctive revolt of the mind against abstract laws of nature, tell us when they come to the beginnings of organic life, how then, in the bosom of the old formations, every speck of mud suddenly teemed with life, and describe the unwearied creative might of the dead earth. Here we have a specimen of the narrowness of man's spirit; he believes that nothing can exist but what he can conceive. When philosophers go this length we may perhaps

[1] *Das Christenthum*, p. 64.   [2] *Sonst und Jetzt*, p. 233.

pardon them; for if they could no longer think, what would be left to them? As students of nature, however, we may only draw conclusions from accurate observations, but we must always define the limits beyond which we cannot go. If Unger is right in saying that not the meanest plant can spring from our soil without a germ, must not a sober investigator conclude that what cannot occur to-day by existing laws of nature, can never have occurred? For it is upon this very fixity of these eternal laws that the whole structure of earthly knowledge rests."

The older savants, to whom Quenstedt is probably alluding in this passage, were much more liberal with suppositions that things might have happened formerly which do not happen now, than is held to be allowable or even possible in these days. There is a fantastic work by the well-known savant Oken, which is notorious in this respect, in it there is a description of how men might have sprung from the warm primæval ocean as boys of about two years old.[1] I was reminded of

[1] In a paper in the *Isis*, 1819 (cf. Wagner, *Gesch. der Urwelt*, ii. 270), with the motto, "Let us make man." "A child of two years old," he says, "would no doubt be able to preserve its own life, if it found nourishment close at hand, such as worms, snails, cherries, apples, turnips, potatoes, and even mice, goats, cows; for the child sucks without being taught, and at that age it had teeth, and could walk." The first man, therefore, must have originated as just such a "boy" as Oken has described above; he even gives us a drawing of him. But how? "The fact that everything living has come from the sea is a truth which no one who has any knowledge of natural science and philosophy—and no one else need be considered—will dispute. No doubt thousands of the embryos of these boys originated in the sea, if they did originate at all. Some were thrown on the shore before they attained to maturity, and were destroyed; others were crushed against rocks, others were devoured by fish. But what did that signify? Thousands remained who were thrown on shore at the proper time, soft and mature, who then burst open their shells, scratched out worms, and took the mussels and snails from their shells. If

Oken's idea by Hæckel. He does not actually quote its contents, but he ends a pamphlet, published in 1870,[1] with the observation that recent investigations might afford a striking confirmation of Oken's mystic prophetical sentence, "Every organic thing has arisen from slime, and is nothing but primitive slime in different forms. This primitive slime originated in the sea from inorganic matter." Hæckel, no doubt, does not say that boys of two years old originated from primitive slime in the deep sea, but only that the monera did so, and especially the Bathybius Hæckelii. But he considers these monera as his $\Delta \acute{o}s\ \mu o\iota\ \pi o\hat{v}\ \sigma\tau\hat{\omega}$; if they spring from the primitive slime of the sea depths, the origin of the whole animal and vegetable world up to man is explained; for the pedigree of all living things may be traced back to the monera. But I shall have to speak of this later. Let us confine ourselves to the question whether organic beings came into existence by spontaneous generation in the earliest periods of the earth's history.

we can eat oysters now, why could not the sea men have done the same? If the sea rose, the boy could escape, he got to higher land, and found plenty of plants, even if they were only toad-stools. There was no want, therefore, of food and nourishment, nor of things to while away the time, for probably dozens of other boys had been driven on to the same coast at the same time. Why should not this boy have been able to make sounds some of pain, others of joy, others when calling, others of disgust, others of tenderness, others in anger? Who can doubt all this for a single instant? Language therefore originates in man, as man does in the sea. We have thus shown that children develop in the sea, and can preserve life out of it. But how did they get into the sea? Not from outside, for everything organic must originate in water. They have therefore originated in the sea. How is that possible? No doubt just as other animals, at least infusoria and medusæ, have originated and still originate every day." In conclusion, Oken says that it is only for want of warmth that the sea cannot bring forth men now-a-days; formerly it was at blood heat, and therefore it was then possible for men to originate in it.

[1] *Das Leben in den grössten Meerestiefen*, p. 39.

It is one of the most certain discoveries of geology, that plants and animals have not existed from eternity,[1] and that organic life on the earth had a beginning. If the modern geological histories of the earth are not wrong in their most essential points, there was a period when there were no organic beings on the earth.[2] We may leave undecided the question as to the period in which the first plants and animals appeared; but all eminent geologists agree in asserting that there was some such period.

How did these first organisms come into existence? Let us for a moment put aside the answer given to this question by philosophers and theologians, and let us see what men of science answer from their point of view. All scientific men who have interested themselves in this question without allowing their philosophical and theological views to influence their opinion, would simply answer, "Natural Science cannot ascertain how the first plants and animals came into existence; as men of science, we do not know." Thus G. Bischof says, "In all our investigations, however far we may follow them up, we come at last to a point beyond which we cannot go. As men of science we know just as little of the manner in which the first plants came into existence on the earth, as we do about the origin of things."[3] And F. Cohn says:[4] "There is no (plant) cell which does not consist of the carbon compound albumen; this exact

---

[1] Zolbe, *Neue Darstellung des Sensualismus*, 1855. Cf. Zöckler, *Gesch. der Beziehungen*, ii. 726.

[2] Frohschammer, *Das Christenthum*, p. 72. Cornelius, *Die Entstehung der Welt*, p. 134.

[3] *Lehrbuch*, etc., 1st ed. ii. 101.   [2] *Licht und Leben*, Berlin 1869, p. 26.

substance is only generated in plant cells: every cell, therefore, presupposes a previous cell, in which its vital matter was prepared. Thus we find ourselves in a circle from which there is no escape. The question always remains, How did the *first* cell come into existence? Here, as always, when Science comes forth from the region of observation and experience, and ventures to inquire into the origin of things, the answer is wanting." In a work which appeared later, he says: "There is no doubt that life on the earth had a beginning; but there are now no analogous phenomena to show how the first living beings came into existence."[1] And although, agreeing with the English savant Sir W. Thomson,[2] he adds to this statement a supposition that organic life may have been carried to our planet from another, that the germs of the Bacteria or of a similar extremely small and simple being may have come from some life-supporting plant, and have been carried about in space like tiny specks of dust, whence they entered the earth's atmosphere, and thus brought organic life to the earth,—this is only, as Cohn himself says, "an idea which far outstrips the boundaries of exact science," and an attempt "to supplement by fancy, the gaps which sober inquiry cannot fill up." Nanstein says that the attempt is too absurd to require serious discussion,[3] nor is the question answered even by this supposition. It is only removed one step further, and it comes back in this form, How did organic life come

[1] *Ueber Bakterien,* Berlin 1872, p. 31.
[2] He brought forward this hypothesis at Edinburgh in 1871. Cf. Zöckler, *Op. cit.* ii. 723. Pfaff, *Schöpfungsgesch.* 2nd ed. p. 736.
[3] *Das Protoplasma,* p. 179.

into existence in the planet from which the Bacteria germs found their way on to the earth?

Huxley, one of the most enthusiastic and gifted supporters of the Darwinian theory, sums up a long discussion in these words: "The inquiry which we undertook, at our last meeting, into the state of our knowledge of the causes of the phenomena of organic nature—of the past and of the present,—resolved itself into two subsidiary inquiries; the first was, whether we know anything, either historically or experimentally, of the mode of origin of living beings. . . . The reply which I had to give to the first question was altogether negative, and the chief result of my last lecture was, that neither historically nor experimentally, do we at present know anything whatsoever about the origin of living forms. We saw that, historically, we are not likely to know anything about it, although we may perhaps learn something experimentally; but that at present we are an enormous distance from the goal I indicated."[1] Darwin himself did not enter into the question of the origin of organic beings. In the first edition of his first famous book, he said it was his task to trace back all organic beings geologically to some few primæval forms, into which he says "life was breathed." As this expression was ridiculed, he gave the following explanation of it in a London paper:[2] "Nor is there a fact, or the shadow of a fact, supporting the belief that these elements, without the presence of any organic compounds, and acted on only by known forces, could produce a living creature?

---

[1] *On our Knowledge*, etc., p. 82.
[2] *The Athenæum*, April 25, 1863, p. 554.

At present it is to us a result absolutely inconceivable. Your reviewer sneers with justice at my use of the 'Pentateuchal' terms of one primordial form into which 'life was breathed;' in a purely scientific work I ought perhaps not to have used such terms; but they will serve to confess that our ignorance is as profound on the origin of life as on the origin of force and matter."[1]

Burmeister closes the section of his *History of Creation*, in which he speaks of the first appearance of vegetable and animal life on the earth, with the following sentence, which is quite appropriate in the mouth of a scientific man: "Be then what thou wilt, thou first earliest day of life; we have no eyes now to see thee, no feeling to understand thee, and therefore no pen to describe thee according to thy nature."[2]

If the final result of natural science is that it can tell us nothing of the origin of the first organic beings,[3] it cannot of course object when to

---

[1] Cf. Zöckler, *Op. cit.* ii. 623. [2] *Gesch. der Schöpfung.* p. 354.
[3] "The appearance of vegetables, of animals, and of men on the surface of the globe is a fact; but we have not yet, and perhaps never shall have, knowledge enough to explain it, or even to point out its immediate cause. This fact no longer occurs in our time, and we have not been able to reproduce it even among the lowest species. On this subject, then, we are without those elementary data, which the study of the inorganic world supplies when we wish to explain the formation of minerals and rocks. In consequence of this, we have so far no means of understanding the mode in which these beings are formed. Can this want of information upon the causes and conditions of the appearance of organized beings be supplied by observation of what now occurs? No; for the phenomena that produce are very different from those that preserve. Observation can establish these, but those we have no means of guessing at. A man who is ignorant of metallurgy and its industrial processes, can acquaint himself with the mechanism of a watch, and become an excellent clockmaker. But so long as he confines himself to the study of his chronometers, the greatest intelligence, the most profound meditations will never teach him the origin of the metals of which the wheels are made; how they have been worked,

the question which it refuses to answer, the Bible replies that the origin of organic beings must be traced back to the creative will of God. And if, notwithstanding all this, savants inveigh against the doctrine, it is because unluckily not all men of science have such a distinct view, as those whom I have quoted above, of the work and the limits of their science; or are so careful to avoid mixing up the results of exact inquiry with their own personal philosophical or unphilosophical views. Let me quote one of the many who fall into this error.[1] Hæckel says: "The spontaneous generation of Monera has no doubt not yet been certainly observed; but it does not seem at all impossible in *itself*, and for *general reasons* it must be assumed as the beginning of the peopling of the earth with living beings, as the origin of the animal and vegetable world."[2] Even the expressions "in itself," and "for general reasons," show us that we are dealing with a philosopher, or whatever Hæckel may be called, but certainly not with a man of science. On another occasion Hæckel openly admits that "the question of spontaneous generation depends not upon empirical science, but upon philosophy."[3] The "general reasons" which, according to Hæckel, oblige us to assume that

---

or by what processes the iron has been transformed into steel, to manufacture the mainspring. The physiologist and the anthropologist, in dealing with animals and plants, or with men, are in the position of our clockmakers; and unfortunately they have not yet discovered any equivalent for the schools to which the clockmaker can go for instruction." Quatrefages, *Rapport*, etc., p. 242. *Histoire de l'Homme*, iii. p. 14.

[1] Burmeister, *Gesch. der Schöpfung*. p. 284. Rolle, *Ch. Darwin's Lehre*, p. 220. Preyer, *Der Kampf und Dasein*, p. 40. O. Schmidt, *Das alter der Menschheit*, p. 23.

[2] *Ueber die Entstehung*, etc., p. 10.

[3] *Das Leben in den grössten Meerestiefen*, p. 43.

the first organisms originated by spontaneous generation reduce themselves to these; he thinks that the idea of a spiritual being existing before and outside the visible world, a God who created the world, is inadmissible. Now if the first organic beings did not originate of themselves by spontaneous generation, we must suppose that they were produced by a force independent of matter; and as, according to Hæckel, this supposition would be absurd, there is no escape from the other supposition, the hypothesis of spontaneous generation.

An intellectual French writer, Th. H. Martin, makes a striking observation about this confusion between the hypothesis of spontaneous generation and atheism. By denying the divine providence and the creation, certain defenders of heterogeny who pretend to support the experimental method, commit two faults—first, they proceed from a still doubtful hypothesis as if it were a demonstrated truth, and secondly, and still worse, they draw therefrom a conclusion which could not be drawn even if the fact of heterogeny were undisputed. In this they proceed from the principle, either boldly asserted or cautiously implied, that as life began on the earth, it must necessarily have originated of itself by some natural development of inorganic matter, and therefore primitive heterogeny must be *certain a priori* in order to explain the first origin of all species and of the human race, because it is the *only possible hypothesis*. This is the triumphant argument with which people who talk a good deal about experimental science and its methods, would close the discussion about the origin of all species of plants and animals! But either this argument is strangely thoughtless nonsense, or those who bring it forward silently assume that the creation and organization of the world by Divine Providence are impossible hypotheses, as God does not exist, and matter alone is necessary and eternal. In trying therefore to prove atheism by heterogeny, they assume atheism as the basis of their proof.[1]

Hæckel no doubt tries to palliate the arbitrariness of this proceeding by saying that if we do not accept the hypothesis of spontaneous generation, we must "have recourse to the miracle of a supernatural creation" in this *one* point only; while in all other cases, the regular process of development of matter proceeds entirely without the interposition of the Creator.[2] By the "regular process of development of matter," Hæckel means this, the whole history of the earth divides itself into two great parts, whose line of separation is the origin of the first organic beings. In the first part, the earth formed itself into an igneous fluid ball, out of matter existing from all eternity, "under the exclusive dominion of invariable and necessary natural laws, the ἀνάγκη, which is in all times and in all places the same, and never changes,"[3] this ball then received a solid crust, continents, seas, etc.; and at last the form in which it was fitted to be the dwelling-place of organic beings. All the first half of the earth's history can be scientifically explained without its being necessary to have recourse to "the wretched

---

[1] *Les Sciences*, pp. 106, 120.
[2] *Nat. Schöpfungsgesch.* p. 309. Cf. *Anthropogenie*, pp. 367, 383.
[3] *Generelle Morphologie*, ii. 450.

expedient of a personal Creator," to use Hæckel's own words. The second half of the earth's history begins with the origin of the first Monera, the Bathybius Hæckelii, and similar organisms. This also occurs under the exclusive dominion of invariable and necessary laws of nature. The ἀνάγκη in nature has caused more perfect organisms to develop from the Monera, and from these still more perfect ones, and so on through millions of developments, up to and including man. By the theory of Descent, which I shall discuss in my next lecture, we can prove, according to Hæckel, that all the species of the animal and vegetable world proceed from the Monera, and in this history of development we need not once have recourse to any other force than that which lies in nature itself, to any other law than that of the ἀνάγκη which governs nature. Thus the whole history of the earth from the primæval mist dispersed in space to the first appearance of man, yes, even to the present day, runs its course evidently according to purely natural laws, and there is no necessity for the interposition of any Being existing outside the world. Only one chasm remains to be bridged over, the chasm which separates the two great parts of the earth's history from one another, and divides the organic from the inorganic world. Given the first Monera we are all right, these will suffice to explain all that follows. If their origin requires no creator, nothing requires one, and as we require one for nothing else, we surely shall not allow our argument to be disturbed for the sake of this one small animal, but rather calmly assert that the origin of the first organisms by spontaneous generation is a "necessary postulate of the theory of the world as a whole."[1]

In examining this argument, one might come to another conclusion. It is admitted that the origin of the first organisms by spontaneous generation cannot be proved. They did originate, and if they did not originate by spontaneous generation, we cannot, according to Hæckel's own confession, avoid the conception of an external creator. But if this is the case, there is a rock on which the whole theory is wrecked, and a rock is enough to sink a ship; a link is wanting in the chain, and one link wanting in the middle of a chain will make the whole useless.

Nor is it correct to say, as Hæckel does, that the origin of organisms is the only point in which there would be a question of assuming the supernatural interference of an external Being. I have already observed that the eternity of matter is by no means a scientific truth; it is rather an arbitrary philosophical or unphilosophical assumption; and whence comes this ἀνάγκη which has guided the development of original matter with such strict consistency, and such sure result, that the earth has been produced in its present form? Is this to be ascribed to chance? And if this is inconceivable to the philosopher, are we not driven to the supposition of an external plan, according to which the development of things has been guided? And who can have conceived and realized this plan but a spiritual Being superior to the material world?[2] Therefore the origin of the first organisms is not the first

---

[1] *Das Leben in den grössten Meerestiefen*, p. 43.
[2] Cf. Huber, *Die Lehre Darwin's*, p. 184 seq.

point in the earth's history at which Hæckel's mechanical or "monistic" theory is found wanting. Neither is it the last point, and we shall see later, that even the theory of Descent is not able to explain the origin of the whole animal and vegetable world by "the exclusive dominion of invariable and necessary laws of nature" by the ἀνάγκη, which Hæckel appeals to; but rather that even if the theory of Descent might be admitted of plants and animals, the origin of man at least cannot be proved, unless we have recourse to what Hæckel calls the miracle of supernatural Creation.

What I have said is sufficient to show you why Darwin's theory of the development of the whole world of organisms from a few original germs was received with such applause by the scientific men who support Hæckel's "philosophical views." Pfaff says: "Herein lies the great fascination of this theory, it affords to materialism a possibility of tracing back the origin and existence of all living beings to a casual combination of external physical and chemical processes; Darwin has brought the goal towards which materialism is striving with all its might, so temptingly near."[1] Only brought near, it is not said to be already reached. For the system, as stated by Darwin himself, still leaves one gap. In his first work, Darwin did not attempt to explain the origin of the first organic being. This called forth the following angry remark from H. G. Bronn, who translated the book into German:[2] "A personal act of creation is still necessary to produce Darwin's first organic being, and if this is necessary at all, it seems immaterial to us whether the first act of

[1] *Die neuesten Forschungen*, p. 107. [2] P. 516.

creation brought forth only one, or 10 or 100,000 species." To make the "monistic theory of the world" consistent, one more step was required; it was necessary to state that the origin of organic beings by spontaneous generation, as it could not be proved by strict scientific inquiry, is a necessary postulate.

I shall speak of the theory of Descent in my next lecture; after what has been said to-day, we may take the following statements as representing the conclusions of science as to the origin of organic beings:—

1. According to the present order of nature, it is most probable that no single kind of plant or animal originates by spontaneous generation. There are only a few very small animals of very low organizations of which scientific men think that there is no proof that they do not so originate.

2. Natural science is not justified in supposing that spontaneous generation, which does not occur now, ever did occur; or that matter formerly possessed a power of generation which it does not possess now.

3. Natural science is consequently not in a position to give any scientific opinion as to the origin of the first organic beings.

4. Therefore natural science cannot possibly make any objection to the statement in the Bible, that the first plants and animals were created by God.

Even if spontaneous generation were possible to the extent which older writers on science and theology believed it to be, still that would not prove that the doctrine of the creation of organic beings was scientifically untenable. Even if plants and animals can originate by themselves from matter, it cannot be proved that they really did so originate, and were not created by God. And if inorganic matter had organized itself into living beings, that would not be by virtue of an essential indwelling force working according to necessary laws, but according to laws which God had given, and under conditions which had been foreseen and prepared by God.[1] For this reason former theologians made no objection to the theory of the *generatio æquivoca*. But it is easy to see that the further development of natural science has more and more decreased the extent to which spontaneous generation was believed, and has shown it to be very problematical even to the small extent in which it is still believed by some; and for this reason it has approached more nearly to the Biblical doctrine, so that here also we may truly say that the Bible may look forward to the progress of scientific inquiry with hope rather than with anxiety.

[1] Th. H. Martin, *Les Sciences*, p. 99.

XXV.

THE THEORY OF DESCENT.

It is said in the Hexæmeron that God created the plants and animals "according to their kind," that is, not in one kind but in many kinds. This statement means practically that all the various classes of animals and plants which exist, are to be traced back to the creative activity of God. But we must not conclude from the statement that all the different kinds and species enumerated in the handbooks of Botany and Zoology, are said by the Bible to have been created as they are now by God, and that since they were created they have remained essentially unaltered, separate and shut off from one another. The Hebrew word *Min*, which is translated "kind,"—in the Vulgate it is sometimes given as genus, sometimes as species,—has not the exact technical meaning which belongs to "kind" or "species" in natural history; the word might also be translated "genus, sort, variety." The "trees after their kind" simply mean the different sorts of trees which exist. The Bible therefore does not prevent our supposing that the varieties of plants and animals were originally fewer, and that they have only gradually reached their present number. The different sorts of roses, pinks, and dahlias which grow in our gardens now, and the different sorts of chickens and doves which are to be seen in zoological gardens, or in the court-yards of poultry fanciers, did not exist 100 years ago—this variety owes its existence to human industry. In the same way the forms of plants and animals have been modified by natural conditions, by the differences in the soil, the food, and the climate, etc. The Bible says nothing about the extent of the variation of plants and animals; how many of the different kinds now enumerated in the handbooks of botany and zoology have been formed in the course of ages, and how many kinds God originally created, are purely questions for natural science.

The general opinion of scientific men hitherto has been that there exists a certain number of groups of organic beings, although it cannot be accurately determined how many, which are separate from and independent of one another and which have always possessed certain characteristic and distinguishing signs. These groups must therefore have originated singly and separate from one another; according to the Biblical teaching, their ancestors were created by God. These groups are called species, and Linnæus sums up the ordinary view in the sentence: "Species tot sunt diversæ, quot diversas formas ab initio creavit infinitum ens." "There are as many different species as there were different forms created in the beginning by the Infinite Being." Linnæus even thought, as I have mentioned before, that each species had been created in the shape of one pair, and that all individuals of one species had, like men, the same ancestors. I have already shown that the Bible does not say this; on the contrary, it is just as little in accordance with the Biblical account as it is scientifically conceivable. Neither does the Bible or history tell us, nor can it be discovered with certainty by scientific inquiry, *how many* species were originally created, and therefore how many species there are. But though it should appear that one group which constitutes one species in the Linnæan system should be divided into two or more species, or that several species of the Linnæan system must be considered as forming one species, yet Linnæus' main idea would not be affected.

Linnæus combined the species which are most nearly connected together into larger groups which he called genera, and since then it has become customary to connect the names of the genus and species together in the systematic enumerations of plants and animals. The domestic cat, *e.g.*, is *Felis domestica*, the wild cat, *Felis catus*, the tiger, *Felis tigris*, the lion, *Felis leo*, the panther, *Felis pardus*, the jaguar, *Felis onca*. These six beasts of prey are therefore species of one and the same genus, *Felis*. In botany in the same way seven kinds of pines are called species of the one genus, *Pinus;* the pine, *Pinus abies*, the fir, *Pinus picea*, the larch, *pinus larix*, etc. Linnæus includes the genera which are most like each other into the so-called order, *Ordines;* the orders which most resemble each other in classes. This division has been much modified by later writers, but we need say no more about it here, we are only concerned with the kinds or species.

Now men of science are at variance as to the meaning and the extent of the word "species." Individuals which spring from the same parents undoubtedly belong to the same species; but of course the genealogy of individuals can only be proved to a very small extent and in exceptional cases. Cuvier gives us the following definition, "All the individual animals and plants which can be proved to descend from one another, or from common parents, or which resemble the latter as much as the latter resemble each other, belong to the same species." The last part of this definition is unsatisfactory, because no criterion of likeness is adduced. Later writers, therefore, have given other definitions, and have especially laid stress on the fact that any qualities belonging to a species which are found in all the individuals of a group, and which are permanent and lasting, that is, which do not alter through all the generations of the animals and plants in question, must be held to be characteristic distinguishing marks of that species. Virchow says: "Species is the name generally given by scientific men to those living beings which reproduce themselves from generation to generation with similar qualities, with a certain sameness of internal constitution and of outward appearance, and in which, therefore, certain qualities and signs are hereditarily transmitted."[1]

---

[1] *Die Lehre Darwins, Deutsche Jahrbücher*, vi. 431. "In this question of species it does not signify whether the divergences are great or small, or whether they consist in so called essential or unessential details. From a practical point of view the decisive question is, whether differences of any kind are and remain *lasting*. If it is proved that these differences appear in the course of development, that is, where new individuals branch off, and that they remain and do not merge again, they must be considered as characteristic, and the individuals possessing them belong to a group of forms, they are one and the same kind, they constitute a genealogical unit. Individuals and groups in which the resemblance of the separate members is great enough to

Of course, besides the resemblances which characterize all the individuals of a species, we find individual differences. If one egg never completely resembles another, still less are two horses, two dogs, etc., exactly alike. There is conformity in the essential qualities which remain the same through all generations, and there is difference in the unessential qualities.

Those groups of individuals of the same species which resemble one another as to such unessential qualities, and which yet differ from the great mass of individuals, are called varieties; and if the peculiarities of these varieties become hereditary, there arise what are called races. Poodles, greyhounds, bull-dogs, terriers, etc., are, for instance, different races of the species dog; the dog, the wolf, the fox, etc., are different species of the genus *Canis; Canis domesticus, Canis lupus, Canis vulpus.* "The race," says Virchow, "forms a separate series within the species, which, however far we may go back, branches off once from the common root, and does not again amalgamate with it," but remains true to its own peculiarities; "the varieties, on the other hand, represent branches from the stem, which often repeat themselves, which occur as it were under the

warrant our *assuming* that blood relationship exists between them, can only be considered as belonging *provisionally* to one species. . . . It is evident that the larger number of the groups of individuals which are called species in books, can only be looked upon as such provisionally. The distinctive criterion of the species is blood relationship; individuals which can be proved to be related by blood form a species. Therefore those individuals who are *not* genetically connected, cannot be specifically connected. According to this, the essence of species is blood relationship, and those groups of forms which are related by blood, and can always be distinguished from other forms by characteristic signs, but which are not transition forms, constitute a species. These, therefore, show us the extent of a species." Herm. Hoffmann, *Untersuchungen,* etc. p. 21.

eyes of the observer, and sometimes produce progeny with the qualities of the original ancestry;"[1] as, for instance, we find that flowers which regularly produce white blossoms sometimes produce red; while from the seeds of the latter, after a few generations, white flowers will again spring. The varieties and races have therefore formed themselves in the course of time; the species, on the other hand, have existed from the beginning.

It is also a characteristic of species, that where an intermixture of animals of different species takes place the progeny does not remain fertile. For instance, horses and donkeys, which form different species of the same genus, can together bring forth mules, but these are sterile; and even where hybrids of different species are fertile, the power of reproduction dies out in the second or third generation, while the fertility of couples taken from different races of the same species undergoes no diminution. De Quatrefages says: "Crossbreeding shows us plainly the fundamental difference between the species and the race in animals and plants. The intercrossing of species, 'hybridation,' that is, the bringing forth of hybrids, occurs very seldom in nature. If it occurs by the interposition of man, the progeny is in most cases barren. If fertility lasts through some generations, it almost always diminishes considerably. On the other hand, the intercrossing of races," which de Quatrefages calls metissage in contradistinction to hybridation, "occurs often in nature, and is always just as productive as the intercrossing of individuals of the same race,—very often the fertility is markedly

[1] *Op. cit.* p. 341.

increased. The progeny produced by the intercrossing of species, *i.e. les hybrides*, hybrids, is almost always barren; the progeny produced by the intercrossing of races, *les metis*, mongrels, is always fertile. If the hybrids are fertile in the first generation, the fertility always ceases after very few generations; on the other hand, mongrels always remain fertile."[1] Of course the fertility and barrenness of these crosses has only been ascertained by observations made in comparatively few species and races—in most cases the theory rests on conclusion from analogy. But it must be generally assumed, as the great physiologist Joh. Müller says,[2] that, "The species of animals cannot possibly have been generated from one another. Judging by all that occurs now in the history of the animal world, they must have been created separately and independently of one another." In other words, all the individuals of the same species might possibly be descended from one pair of ancestors. I have already said that this is not actually the case, but the individuals of different species cannot possibly have had common ancestors.

It would in no way derogate from the truth of this theory were it to be discovered that some animals which are classed as different species of the same genus in reality had a common ancestry; that, for instance, cats, lions, and tigers could be traced back to a common stock. In such a case we should have to correct the details of the zoological system, and whereas we now put down *Felis domestica, Felis tigris,* and *Felis leo*, etc., as species of the genus *Felis*, we should, according to the

---

[1] Rapport, etc. p. 113. Cf. Th. Waitz, *Anthropológie*, i. 19–36.
[2] *Physiologie*, ii. 769.

above supposition, have to class them as races of the species *Felis*, just as bull-dogs, poodles, etc., are considered as races of the species *Canis domestica*. There would always be a limit to these alterations in our ideas of the species. No zoologist holding this theory would consent to consider the elephant, the mouse, the fly, and the whale as races of the same species, and as possible descendants from the same ancestor.[1]

Now this theory, that species is lasting and immutable, is in our day met by the Theory of Descent, of which Darwin is the principal expositor. This theory asserts that all forms of plants and animals which exist, or ever have existed, can be traced back to a few ancestral forms, perhaps to one primordial form. What we now call species were formed in the same way as varieties and races have been formed; variety, species, genus, order, are simply ideal conceptions, which may be useful for the classification of animals and plants, but are genealogically quite unimportant. All living beings are related, in the sense that all may be traced back through countless individuals to a common stock; just as the numerous varieties, *e.g.* of doves, may be traced back to one common ancestral form, from which in the course of time they have developed.

[1] Michelis, *Der Organismus und die Kirche*, Bern 1874, p. 18. He says, "The species may be quite rightly called a variety of the genus. In the genus the creative thought has reached an enduring form." Cf. p. 12. "The bounds of variability are at any rate fixed by the idea of the genus. In determining the species, there is always more space for variation; no alteration is possible in the genus." Even Linnæus was later on inclined to assume that the different species of a genus had originally only formed one species. Cf. V. Baer, *Studien*, p. 256. The Benedictine monk Augustine Calmet and others have supported similar views, in order to explain the housing of all the animals in the ark. Zöckler, *Gesch. der Beziehungen*, ii. 237.

Vixere fortes ante Agamemnona,—in a certain sense there were Darwinians even before Darwin, at least according to the title of de Quatrefages' book, there were "The Precursors of Darwin." It is not without interest to look back on these, if only because Darwin's reputation will lose nothing by the retrospect; on the contrary, a comparison between his theory and that of his predecessors will show the grandeur and genius of his system.[1]

As early as the last century Buffon (1707–1788) suggested that all the species of animals might perhaps be traced back to about forty original types; all the forms which we now call species had developed by degrees from these, not however, as Darwin supposes, by improvement, but, on the contrary, by degeneration; so that the present more imperfect animals are degenerate descendants of more perfect ancestors. Buffon's idea of the way in which this degeneration had taken place was somewhat naive. Bears, for instance, were obliged by certain unfavourable conditions to leave the land and take to swimming in the water; this naturally produced some effect on their bodily constitution, and by degrees they became seals. The seals gradually degenerated in the same way into dolphins and whales, and so on. Buffon himself afterwards retracted this opinion, and in his latter writings as in his earlier ones he maintains the usual theory of the immutability of species.

During Buffon's lifetime there appeared in Amsterdam in 1748 and 1756 an extraordinary French book,

---

[1] Cf. Quatrefages, *Charles Darwin et ses Précurseurs Francais*. Paris 870.

entitled *Telliamed, or Conversations between an Indian Philosopher and a French Missionary on the Diminution of the Sea.* The author's name was Benoit de Maillet—the name is written backwards on the title-page,—and he died in 1738. His secretary, a certain Abbé Lemascrier, edited the work. Parts of the book are said to be very reasonable, but the sections in virtue of which he is called a precursor of Darwin certainly are not among them. I will only quote one passage, in which he explains how birds sprang from fishes. He thinks that if the process did not take place every day before our eyes, it would be much more difficult to believe that a caterpillar can turn into a butterfly than that a fish can turn into a bird. Flying-fish might perfectly easily have been driven at some time by the wind from the sea on to the land, where they fell into the bushes or on to the grass. There they found nourishment, but were not able to return to the sea. By the influence of the air their fins split, became fluffy, and turned into long feathers, the skin was covered with downy feathers, the lower fins became feet, the body was changed, the neck and beak grew longer, and behold, the fish had become a bird.[1]

Jean Lamarck (1744–1829) in his *Zoological Philosophy*, which was published in 1809, takes the matter more gravely. He thinks that only two primordial forms existed, the infusorian and the worm, both of which originated by spontaneous generation. From these two primordial forms all species of animals have

---

[1] Tellamed, *ou entretiens d'un philosophe indien, avec un missionaire français sur la diminution de la mer.* Cf. Quatrefages, pp. 9, 19.

developed themselves gradually, on the whole progressing, but in a few cases retrogressing. From the infusorian spring the medusæ and their allies the molluscs, etc.; from the worm, the insects, fish, birds, mammals, and, of course, lastly man. In explaining the changes, Lamarck proceeds from the physiological fact, that use and exercise strengthens and developes the organs, whereas they are stunted by disuse. He assumes that if an animal is brought under new conditions, and is therefore obliged to conform itself to them, the efforts and exertions which it makes in consequence of this will ever develope new organs; while, on the other hand, the organs which it cannot use in the new conditions become stunted. For instance, a bird which is obliged to seek its food in the water, endeavours to move on the surface of the water, and for this purpose stretches out its toes. In consequence of the continued stretching out of the toes, the skin which unites them at their bases stretches, and at last becomes the membranous web. On the other hand, the strand snipe, which cannot swim, but only approaches the water in search of food, is constantly in danger of sinking into the mud. The bird, wishing to avoid this, stretches its legs as far as it can, and in consequence of this continual stretching of the legs of those birds, through many generations the legs become long and thin, as we see them in storks. One more example. A mollusc as it moves along tries to touch the bodies which lie before it. It endeavours to touch them with some of the more prominent parts of its head; in consequence of these efforts the juices of its body flow with peculiar strength to these parts. By this means the nerves then are gradually developed, and at last tentacula are formed at these parts of the head.[1]

I have spoken somewhat at length on Lamarck's theory, because in both Darwin's and Hæckel's systems there are some analogies to it. Of Darwin's other precursors, I will only mention Etienne Geoffroy St. Hilaire (1772-1844 ; we are not now concerned with his son Isidore Geoffroy, 1805-1861). The dispute between him and his famous colleague Cuvier in the Academy turned principally on the question as to whether the animals now existing were descended from the animals of the earlier geological periods. Cuvier disputed the genealogical connection between the recent and the fossil animals; Geoffroy maintained that the present animals are descended from the fossil animals, e.g. the crocodiles of the present day from the primæval Saurians. Geoffroy does not appear to have gone farther in assuming a possible mutability of species, at any rate not nearly so far as Lamarck and Darwin. It was this dispute between the two French savants, which reached its climax at a sitting of the Academy July 19, 1830, in which Goethe was so much interested that on August 2 he saluted an acquaintance in Weimar with the exclamation, "Well, what do you think of this great event ? The volcano has burst forth, everything is in flames, and there are no more negotiations behind closed doors." Goethe's friend in his innocence thought that the old man was talking of the revolution of July, the first news of which had arrived at Wiemar on that day. Goethe, however, cared

[1] *Philosophie zoologique* (nouvelle edition, *revue et précédée d'une introduction biographique, par* Ch. Martins. Paris 1873).

very little about it in comparison with the dispute at the Academy; and if Hæckel, who tells the story,[1] seeks at length to prove that Goethe also was a precursor of Darwin's, we must pardon it in a Jena professor.[2] A theory similar to Lamarck's was brought forward in England in an anonymous book,[3] which was translated into German by Vogt in 1849, and which I have already repeatedly mentioned. Vogt, who then held different views from those he has at present, says in his notes to the translation, that these speculations are quite absurd. Oddly enough, Charles Darwin's grandfather, Erasmus Darwin, held the same theory as Lamarck.[4]

I now come to the man who gives the name to the controversy which divides scientific men into two opposite camps. C. Darwin, who was born in 1808 and died in 1882, had already drawn up a sketch of his theory in 1844. But an outward inducement was necessary in order to persuade him to come forward

---

[1] *Natürliche Schöpfungsgeschichte*, p. 79.

[2] Semper, *Der Hæckelismus*, p. 34, says: "It is always represented to the public that Goethe was a conscious supporter of the Darwinian theory. O. Schmidt's protest against Hæckel's entirely false conception of Goethe's opinions is steadily ignored by the Jena savants." Dr. Kossmann, in a paper called "War Goethe ein Mitbegründer der Descendenz theorie?" (see the *Proceedings of the Heidelberg Ass. for Natural History and Medicine*, new series, vol. i., Heidelberg 1875) shows by carefully comparing the opinions stated by Hæckel to have been expressed by Goethe, and the real expressions of the latter, that the quotations from Goethe given by Hæckel are completely inaccurate. Cf. Zöckler, *Op. cit.* ii. 597. H. Zöckler, ii. 601. For Darwin's other predecessors in Germany, Treviranus, Oken, and others, see Hæckel, *Op. cit.* p. 83. Jean Paul criticizes these theories of development in the *Museum* (1814), iii. (*Sammtl. Werke*, Berlin 1827, vol. xlix. p. 58).

[3] *Vestiges of the Natural History of Creation.*

[4] Zöckler, *Darwin's Grossvater als Arzt, Dichter und Naturphilosoph. ein Beitrag zur Geschichte des Darwinismus*. Heidelberg 1880.

openly. In 1858 he received from an acquaintance who had travelled in India for many years—A. R. Wallace—a MS. with the request that he would have it published in an English periodical. To his surprise Darwin found that the paper contained a theory precisely similar to the one he had thought out.[1] He published his friend's paper in a periodical in August 1858, and with it a short abstract from his own MS., and in November 1859 he followed it up with the book which has at all events made his name immortal, *On the Origin of Species by Means of Natural Selection, and on the Preservation of Favoured Races in the Struggle for Life.*

Edition followed edition in England, and translations appeared in Germany and other countries.[2] Darwin himself said that this somewhat comprehensive work was only a preliminary extract from a more exhaustive work, which was to contain the whole mass of the observations which he could bring forward in support

[1] On Wallace's theory, see Huber, *Die Lehre Darwins*, pp. 45, 203 ; and Quatrefages in the *Journal des Savants*, 1870, Sept. p. 529. Zöckler, *Op. cit.* ii. 634.

[2] The American, Hudson Tuttle, published a book called, *Arcana of Nature, or the History and Laws of Creation*, Boston 1859, at the same time as did Darwin the *Origin of Species*. H. M. Achner, who translated it into German, says he did so " more as a curiosity than because of its intrinsic value." The author practically agrees in all essentials with the writer of *Vestiges of the Natural History of Creation*, but he is decidedly more atheistic. He is a "medium," through whom spirits communicate with man ; he has written several books on this subject, and " amongst other things he has depicted on a piece of linen stretched on cardboard, 3600 feet long, the whole process of formation which the earth's crust has undergone with all its palæontological attributes." " This," he says, " he painted, being himself passive, and guided by unseen powers." The same powers dictated to him his book on the Creation, as he acknowledges in his dedication of it to them, in which he declines the authorship for himself. Cf. Zöckler, *Op. cit.* ii. 612. See also his paper, "Die Speciesfrage," *Jahrb. für Deutsche Theologie*, 1860, p. 679.

of his theory. Up to 1868, however, only one portion of this work appeared, dealing with the most unimportant part of the system, that is, with the changes which are brought about in animals and plants through the artificial breeding of man. In the year 1871 a third work by Darwin appeared, called *The Descent of Man and Selection in Relation to Sex*. In one part of this work he completes and modifies his system by dealing with sexual selection in addition to the so-called natural selection; in the other part he endeavours to prove that his theory is applicable to man also, that he also has been evolved by natural development from low organic forms, a conclusion which in his first book he either passed over in silence or only just mentioned, but which most of his followers had at once seen and vociferously announced. Other books which have since appeared are of less importance to his theory.

There can be no object in recapitulating here the names of the several eminent men to have declared themselves for and against Darwin's theory.[1] The controversy has often become so lively that Pfaff is hardly exaggerating when he says, "There is no example in the history of natural science in which a hypothesis or anything connected with it has excited people's passions to such an extent as has Darwin's hypothesis on the origin of species."[2] The fact that the Darwinian theory has in many cases been discussed, not with the repose and objectiveness with which purely scientific problems are usually treated, but with

---

[1] Cf. Huber, *Die Lehre Darwin's*, p. 93. G. Seydlitz, *Die Darwin'sche Theorie*, Dorpat 1871, p. 9; *Zts. für Ethnologie*, 1871, p. 56.

[2] *Die neuesten Forschungen*, p. 115.

the eagerness which is generally reserved for political, religious, and party questions, is explained by the fact that such religious questions are very naturally raised by the Darwinian theory. Even if we put aside its application to man, if in reality, as Darwin says, all plants and animals spring by natural development from a few very simple forms, it is only necessary to suppose further that these simple primæval forms have originated by spontaneous generation from inorganic matter, to make the hypothesis of a Creator apparently unnecessary in the earth's history.[1] No doubt this is only apparent, it is not so in reality, as I showed in the previous lecture. But the belief that the Darwinian theory supports the atheistic and materialistic view of nature, although it is not actually the reason for which men like Hæckel and Vogt accept the theory,[2] is yet

[1] "We philosophers and critical theologians," says Strauss (see *Der Alte und der neue Glaube*, p. 176), "talked in vain when we decreed that miracles should disappear. Our assertions had no effect because we could find nothing to replace them, no natural force which could come in where miracles had hitherto seemed to be necessary. Darwin has found this natural force, this action of nature. He has opened the door through which a happier posterity will be able to drive out miracles for ever. Every one who knows all that depends on miracles will look on him as one of the greatest benefactors of the human race."

[2] In the *Lehrbuch der Geologie* (1854), Vogt defends the theory of the immutability of species. In the notes to his translation of *Vestiges of the Natural History of Creation* (1858) he overwhelms the supporters of the theory of spontaneous generation and transmutation of species with the most withering sarcasm. In the first volume of the *Vorlesungen*, p. 16, he says that he "cannot accept all the conclusions of the Darwinian theory," but that he is "not disinclined to support it as far as the more nearly related types are concerned." In the second volume of the same work, p. 255, he makes this reservation only, he thinks that the first cells from which the organisms were developed must have possessed different forms, must have been differently constructed, and must have had different powers of development; in everything else he is a true Darwinian. I quote the following passage from Ausland, 1867, p. 704: "Vogt belongs to the class of quarrelsome savants; he makes a vicious attack on any of his colleagues who dares to adapt scientific research to

the chief reason why they express themselves in its favour with an enthusiasm, I might almost say with a fanaticism,[1] which would be incomprehensible in a purely scientific question. On the other hand, this is also the reason why scientific men and philosophers who do not share the materialistic views of Hæckel and Vogt, and theologians especially, attack Darwinism as a philosophical and theological heresy. For the present let us put aside the application of the Theory of Descent to men, and let us first of all examine the proofs of this theory as stated by Darwin.

theological objects. No doubt it is a mistake to do this, for the scientific inquirer should confine himself strictly to his object, which is to describe, calculate, and compare, and to discover laws. It is the business of the theologian, not of the man of science, to harmonize these laws with the religious opinions of the present day. But Vogt is guilty of this very fault. He is almost more a theologian than a man of science, because he is always making incursions into theological regions, and trying to gain over converts to his own, that is, to atheistic opinions. For this reason, those who look in his works for information about Nature and her laws, and not for Vogt's own opinions, find that there is a purpose in them, and begin to suspect that in all scientific questions Vogt will take the side which is most decidedly antichristian and anti-biblical. Vogt formerly—although, considering his atheistic opinions, this has always surprised us—supported the theory of the immutability of species. Later on he eagerly embraced the Darwinian theory, and helped to extend it. Perhaps it may have attracted him, because, to use his own words, "we have now got rid of the Creator" ("es nun mit dem Schöpfer ganz vorbei sei").

[1] Hæckel puts Darwin next to Copernicus and Newton; he calls his theory "the morning star of a new period in the history of human culture;" and says that the opposition to it is "a storm whose raging will for a long time divide the educated world." *Ueber die Entstehung*, etc. p. 13. In the *Gen. Morphologie*, ii. p. 434, he says, "Many of the assertions made by the opponents of the Theory of Descent show such an astonishing want of natural, clear, and acute reasoning power that we should be warranted in placing those who make them lower than the more intelligent dogs, horses, and elephants. As these animals are mostly not hampered by the enormous mountains of dogmas and prejudices which pervert the thoughts of most men from their youth up, we often find that their judgment is more correct and natural than that of 'savants.'"

According to Darwin, all forms of plants and animals are descended from a few primæval forms, perhaps from one quite simple form. In order to establish this theory an unlimited mutability of organic forms must be supposed possible, in direct contradiction to the theory which obtained formerly, of the immutability of species in its essential qualities. Let us see, therefore, on what Darwin founds his theory.

It cannot be denied that the species of plants and animals are to a certain degree undefined and mutable. This is exemplified by cultivated plants and domestic animals, which separate into countless varieties and races. Take for instance the different races of dogs, cattle, horses, etc. ; the different sorts of fruit, grain, turnips, cabbage, and ornamental plants. These have originated by human selection ; the forms which were specially good were chosen out for reproduction, and these useful qualities were reproduced in the descendants and became hereditary. It was not in man's power to call forth these useful and pleasing qualities, but he had an opportunity of profiting by those which did exist, and of perpetuating them in the individuals which he bred.[1]

A pigeon, for instance, has a few supernumerary tail feathers, which give it a peculiar appearance. The owner wishes to multiply this kind, he therefore allows the eggs of that pigeon to be hatched. He selects those among the young pigeons who display the same peculiarity ; these he pairs, keeping the others away, and the peculiarity becomes a lasting one. He always selects those for breeding in whom the peculiarity is

---

[1] A. Müller, *Ueber die erste Entstehung organischer Wesen, und deren Spaltung in Arten*, Berlin 1869, p. 18.

strongest, and thus the race of fantailed pigeons is produced. Or a gardener wishes to make a white flowering plant produce red blossoms. He chooses out from the different seedlings of the plant those which show any approach to red, and sows their seeds. Most of the plants thus produced show an inclination to red, a few will be redder than the first lot, and only the seed of these is sown. In the following generation the red will show itself still more strongly in some of the plants. If the selection is carried on through several generations, the gardener will at length obtain only red flowering plants. This mode of proceeding presupposes the following facts,—1. That individuals of the same kind are more or less different, and that these individual differences are universally connected with the conditions of the life, nourishment, surroundings, etc., of each individual. 2. That not only the common qualities of the kind, but also, at least in many cases, individual peculiarities, are inherited by the descendants.

We can see how far it is possible for a species to vary by taking the case of the pigeons, which Darwin has specially observed. Some races of pigeons are remarkable for a tuft of feathers on the back of the neck, forming a kind of hood; others have a strangely-shaped beak or feet; others are distinguished by peculiar, often very strange, ornaments; for instance some have a great development of skin about the head, or very large heads; others have peculiar habits, like the laugher pigeon, turtle dove, tumbler pigeon, etc. The differences extend to the internal structure, to the muscles and the skeleton. We find differences in the number of vertebræ and ribs, in the size and shape of bones, etc.

And yet Darwin thinks he has proved that all the races of pigeons are descended from a single wild stock, the blue rock (Columba Livia). The fact that certain peculiarities can be produced to order, shows how powerful artificial selection is, if it be properly carried out. An experienced English breeder offered to produce a certain feather in three years; in order to produce a certain desired shape of the head or beak, he would, he said, require six years.

Taking these results of artificial breeding, Darwin says that something similar to this takes place among wild plants and animals in their natural state, and he gives to these processes the name of "natural breeding," or "natural selection." Nature proceeds like man. It selects the individuals for breeding frome normous numbers. Each kind of plant and animal multiplies at such a rate that there is not room on the earth for all the individuals. According to Malthus' well-known statement, man increases in geometrical progression, while the quantity of food increases only in arithmetical progression. Hence man's constant struggle for the means of supporting existence,—means which are necessary, but not attainable by all. A similar struggle for existence takes place in the animal and vegetable world. Many, nay most individual plants and animals are destroyed before they come to their full development and are capable of reproduction. The earth has not room for all. From the beginning of its existence every organism struggles with a series of hostile influences; it struggles with animals who live on it, and whose natural food it is; it struggles with the temperature, weather, and similar influences; above all, it struggles with other organisms like itself. Every individual of the animal and vegetable world struggles for the necessary means of existence with other individuals of the same kind which live with it in the same place. For instance, in a thickly-sown wheat field only comparatively few of the numerous young plants which stand on a square foot can remain alive. They struggle with one another for the space which every plant requires in order to extend its roots; they struggle for sunlight and moisture; and in this struggle for life a few only win, the others perish.

But in this struggle for existence it is clear that the position of the separate individuals is quite unequal, the prospects of all are not equally favourable. This is caused, on the one hand, by the individual differences between individuals of the same kind, and, on the other, by many external conditions. Those individuals whose peculiarities harmonize best with the special external conditions, are most favourably placed; and these favoured individuals will be successful in the struggle for existence, while the less favoured ones will be destroyed. For this reason Darwin employs the expression first originated by Herbert Spencer, the "Survival of the Fittest." But those individuals who are favoured, or who are most suited to the conditions, do not only survive, but are able to reproduce themselves, while the less favoured ones die without leaving progeny. But if the individuals who reproduce themselves are those who are favoured in the struggle for existence, we learn from the experience of artificial selection that the peculiarities of those favoured individuals will not only be inherited, but will gradually increase, and be strengthened in the following generations, and that at last a generation will appear which differs markedly from the original form. Let us suppose that a good many plants of the same kind are growing together in a very dry place. As the hairs on the leaves are very useful for drawing moisture from the air, it follows that in this unfavourable place where the plants are suffering from the want of water, and are struggling with each other to obtain water, the individuals with the hairiest leaves will be the most favoured. These only will survive, while the others with smoother leaves will die. The hairier kinds will reproduce themselves, and their descendants will be even more remarkable for having leaves with thick strong hairs than were the plants of the first generation. If this process is continued through many generations in the same place, this peculiarity will at length be so much increased, the number of hairs on the surface of the leaves will be so much greater, that the plant will appear to be a new species. And besides this, it must be remembered that all the parts of an organism are connected together, and that therefore, as a rule, no part can be altered without its affecting other parts also. For instance, if the number of hairs on the leaves of a plant increases, nourishment will probably be withdrawn from other parts of the plant; the material which might go towards forming blossoms or seeds is diminished, the blossoms or seeds become smaller, and this will be the mediate or indirect result of the struggle for existence, which at first only produced a change in the leaves.

I add an example quoted by Darwin from the animal world. Wolves obtain their prey partly by craft, partly by strength, partly by fleetness. Let us suppose that the fleetest prey—a deer for instance—had increased in number in a certain region, or that other prey had decreased during that season of the year when the wolf is hardest pressed for food. Under these circumstances those wolves are the most likely to obtain nourishment who are most qualified to hunt down the swift-footed stags, that is, those wolves who are swiftest and slimmest. These will remain alive, and will reproduce themselves, while the short-legged, heavy wolves will die out under the given conditions. So that in this case a slim, swift variety of wolf will be produced, and other structural alterations will occur owing to the influence of the separate parts of the organism on one another, which I have alluded to above.

In describing this struggle for existence, and the natural selection which it brings about, Darwin also notices the fact which, as I mentioned above, was first discovered by Lamarck, namely, that the organs are strengthened and perfected by use, and stunted by disuse. For instance, in consequence of the increase of insect-eating mammals in a certain region, the food of the latter becomes scanty. Only ants or termites are left in any quantity. Some of the insect-eaters who are thus forced to feed on ants become accustomed to it and suffer no want, while the others who cannot accustom themselves to this food die out. Ant-eating specially develops certain muscles of the tongue. The mouth need not be opened widely for it, and it therefore remains small. In the course of several thousand generations the whole organization of the animal accommodates itself more and more to the new way of life, and thus an animal is formed which is, as it were, made for ant-eating. Ant-eating has therefore produced the peculiar shape of the ant-eater. Or a bird of prey accustoms itself to seeking its prey by night, because it gets more booty by surprising animals in their sleep, or by catching night animals. In him and his descendants the eye accustoms itself to the darkness, and becomes keener by continual usage, and thus the owl's eyes are produced. On the other hand, just as the owl's eye becomes keener in darkness, the mole becomes blind, because he tracks his prey by smell. And in subterranean caves we find animals who have only stunted rudimentary eyes. As the eye was not used, it no longer attained to its normal development, and in later generations it became more and more stunted. According to this supposition the blind or short-sighted animals found in dark caves might be descended from animals like themselves in all but sight. The difference between them came about in the course of ages through the struggle for existence, and the gradual harmonizing of the organism to the conditions of life.

Darwin admits in his latter work that he ascribed too much to natural selection. He now seeks to find a new support for his theory by taking sexual selection to aid natural selection. Sexual selection, he says, depends on the advantage which certain individuals possess over other individuals of the same species exclusively with regard to reproduction. Males who have better organs of sense, and locomotive and prehensile organs, better means of attack and defence than their rival males, and males who are more attractive to the females by reason of their form, the colour of their plumage, their song, etc., pair more easily than do the less well-furnished males, and transmit the advantages they possess to their descendants.

For instance, it is well known that in the rutting season the male stag fights for the possession of the does. The principal weapons in these fights are the horns. Therefore those stags will always remain victorious, and will attain to reproduction, whose horns are best fitted for fighting, while those less well provided will not be able to pair. The individual advantage possessed by the stags who are able to pair will be inherited by their offspring, and will probably be increased in each generation according to the rule which I mentioned when speaking of artificial selection. If, therefore, we go back in the history of stags, we may assume that the present shape of the horns has been formed by degrees; that the ancestors of the present stags many thousand years ago had only quite small horns, and therefore in this matter were not different from roes and goats; and that the present difference is the work of time and continued sexual selection. The mane is an important weapon of protection to the lion, as it preserves him from wounds on the head and neck while fighting with rivals. The lion who has the thickest mane is therefore in a position of advantage while fighting for the female, and therefore the formation of the lion's mane, like that of the stag's horns, may be a result of sexual selection.

In these cases the combat lies between individuals of the male sex; they seek to kill or drive away their rivals, while the females remain passive. In other cases the struggle takes place in a different way, the males vieing with one another to excite or charm the female, and the female then chooses the pleasantest companions. It has been observed that at pairing times the males of certain kinds of birds display their plumage and other ornaments in the presence of the females, that the males of other kinds compete together in song, and that the female canary, for instance, always selects the best singer, and that in the natural condition the female finch chooses out of hundreds of males the one whose song pleases her most. Individuals, therefore, who excel others in one of these respects have an advantage over them, inasmuch as they pair more easily. They transmit their individual advantages to their progeny, and in this way sexual selection conduces to differentiation and perfection. If during a long series of generations the individuals of one kind prefer to pair with individuals of the other sex who have some peculiar characteristic, the descendants will slowly but surely be modified in the same way.

It is therefore possible that the differences which we now find in the organic world are not original, but have been gradually developed. The different varieties of roses and pigeons have evidently been produced by artificial selection, and may be genealogically traced back to one single original simple form; and if the result which has been produced by artificial selection in plants and animals when domesticated has also been produced in the condition of nature by natural and sexual selection in the manner which has just been described, we are justified in assuming that the differences which we now find among wild plants and animals are not more important than the differences between cultivated plants and domestic animals, consequently there is no essential difference between species and variety. From this it follows that we must not speak of species as strictly separated and divided from each other as having existed without essential change from the beginning, but that we may assume a boundless mutability of organic forms, and that the forms which are now reckoned as different species in the ordinary botanical and zoological systems have been developed gradually in the course of time from more simple forms by a process of differentiation and perfection. Hence the title of Darwin's first book—*The Origin of Species by Means of Natural Selection,*—we should now say by means of natural and sexual selection,—"*or the preservation of favoured races in the struggle for life.*" According to this theory each variety, if it becomes permanent, can develop into a race, and every race is the beginning of a species, or rather, if the differences are comparatively small, we may speak of races. These races may be called species when the differences have become greater. The distinction is artificial and subjective, not natural and objective, as the schoolman would say not a *distinctio a parti rei* or *rationis ratiocinatæ*, but only a *distinctio a parte intellectus* or *rationis ratiocinantis*.

Let us pause here for the present. It appears to me that no one can deny Darwin's deserts. He has raised again the question of the origin and mutability of species, and probably the consequent investigations will show that we have been too narrow-minded in this matter hitherto, that our ideas of the mutability of organic beings have been too limited in many cases, that many groups of plants and animals which are now considered as separate species must be regarded only as varieties or races, and that therefore the number of species which existed originally—let us for the present say the numbers of species originally created—is smaller than the number of species which are enumerated in our zoological and botanical systems. I say that investigations will probably lead us to this conclusion; at present we have certainly not reached such a conclusion, for in order to attain to it, we require wider and more fundamental investigations than can be instituted by a single man, even although that man be a Darwin, or even by a single generation of students. But if this conclusion is reached, it will be a great gain for natural science; it does not signify if several of the theories about the determination of species, and the classification of plants and animals, which obtained universally before Darwin, have to be given up; on the contrary, it is well that more important and better founded theories should be put in their place. The theologian may look on quietly at *this* controversy; it does not matter to him whether the number of the species of plants and animals is reduced or not. The Bible does not say how many species were originally created. And the theologian need not care whether the number of original species is reduced by science to a hundred or to ten. The Bible only says, that God created plants and animals after their kind; that all existing plants and animals, which may be divided into genera, species, varieties, or any other groups, must be traced back to the many or to the few forms of plants and animals which came into existence through the creative activity of God.

I may observe that in one way it can only rejoice the theologian that the limits of the mutability of species should be as wide as possible, and that men of science should unanimously conclude that even organic forms which differ widely may be descended from a common stock. The more this is acknowledged the less there is to be said against the Biblical doctrine of the unity of the human race. If cats, lions, and tigers not only belong to the same genus but to the same species, and are possibly descended from the same or similar ancestors, it is clear that no objection can be made to the common ancestry of negroes and Europeans.

On the whole I think there is nothing objectionable in the assertion which Vogt made in the year 1863, when he held other views than he does at present. It was to the effect that he must decline the last conclusions of the Darwinian system, but that he believed in it so far as the question of the near relation of types was concerned. With this limitation I myself could become a Darwinian without ceasing to be a theologian and a believer in the Bible; no objection, theologically speaking, can be made to the idea that the more nearly related types of the vegetable and animal world are descended from a common ancestry.

No doubt, looked at from a scientific point of view, the question is at present by no means so unobjectionable as this. Darwin's theory, that the same results which are produced by man by means of artificial selection could be produced by plants and animals in a wild state by means of what he calls natural and sexual selection, is *à priori* improbable. In artificial selection, the thought, the experience, and the judicious treatment of the breeder must be considered; if in the so-called natural selection we do not fall back on a design carried out and guided by the Creator,—and this is not included in the system, and is by no means the belief of most Darwinians,—everything must be left to chance; for "nature" is not a person who can reflect and act, and when we say that "nature selects," we are only speaking figuratively.[1] The breeder is obliged, and is able, carefully to choose out those animals whose pairing will probably transmit and increase certain peculiarities; he will therefore ascertain that these peculiarities exist in both males and females. In nature it is left to chance to decide whether two individuals who suit in this respect will come together; and as the characteristics which are requisite in order to form races for the most part only appear occasionally, it will be a very fortunate chance if they are found in the individuals who pair. But if these characteristics are to be fixed and increased, not only must a suitable pair come together *once*, but throughout a series of generations suitable pairs must *always* come together; if once an unsuitable pairing takes place, the advantage which was gained is in a great measure lost. Therefore a long and unbroken series of lucky chances is necessary. And there is yet another difficulty, if experienced breeders are correct in saying that at any rate among the more highly organized mammals the intercrossing of closely related animals is not advantageous;

---

[1] "The breeder has an object, an end in view; the struggle for existence has only a result, no object." Baer, *Studien*, p. 424.

that if such animals are continuously intercrossed, that is, if the so-called incestuous breeding takes place, a race degenerates and dies out.[1] In order to accomplish the results, therefore, which are essential to the Darwinian theory, it is not only necessary that throughout a series of generations just the right pairs should come together by chance, but also it is essential that these animals should not, at least as a rule, be related to one another. This again greatly diminishes the probability.[2]

Further, in artificial selection it is possible and even necessary that the individuals who are to produce a new race should be isolated so that they only pair together; for if a cross takes place, and the new race pairs with the original stock, the progeny easily reverts to the old stock.[3] For instance, if fantailed pigeons pair with common pigeons, the race degenerates. As I have said, this isolation can be produced in artificial breeding, but who is to take care that in the natural state the races are kept pure, as is necessary if the result contemplated by Darwin is to be attained. Is it chance? It is a difficult task, so difficult that a German Darwinian, M. Wagner of Munich, thinks it necessary to come to his master's rescue with a new hypothesis. He thinks that if the pairs who are to form a new race are not isolated, the formation of the race is very difficult and almost impossible. Therefore we must see how such isolation can be brought about in the natural state, and so Wagner hits on what he calls

---

[1] Cf. Huber, *Die Lehre Darwin's*, p. 342.
[2] Cf. Huber, *Op. cit.* p. 249.
[3] Cf. Baer, *Studien*, p. 348.

"The law of migration of organisms."[1] Individuals of the same species which live in one place, he says, compete with one another as to food and reproduction. This competition causes single individuals to overstep the boundary of the original place of abode, that is, to emigrate. Besides these active migrations, there are also often passive migrations,—that is to say, separate individuals are often carried away from the original dwelling-place by currents of air or water, or by other casualties. The changed conditions of life in the new home cause changes in those individuals who have emigrated, and in their descendants; and if the emigrants are separated from the original home by streams, mountains, and other obstacles, they are sufficiently isolated from the rest of their kind who have remained to form a new race.

It cannot be denied that such cases do occur in nature. But it is only in exceptional cases that all these favourable conditions coincide. In many cases the individuals who have emigrated or lost themselves will not be able to exist in the new home; if the climatic and other natural conditions are *very* different, they will die out; and if they are not different enough to cause the emigrants to die out, the peculiarities which appear in them will not be very important. Further, it will be very fortunate if the isolation is lasting. In most cases the very places to which former individuals have migrated will be reached later on by other individuals; then the isolation is not complete.

[1] *Die Darwinische Theorie und das Migrationsgesetz der Organismen*, Leipzig 1868. Cf. A. Weismann, *Ueber den Einfluss der Isolirung auf die Artbildung*, Leipzig 1872. Hæckel, *Nat. Schöpfungsgeschichte*, p. 238. Huber, *Die Lehre Darwin's*, pp. 162, 257, 294.

At any rate Wagner's law of migration is only calculated to explain a few single formations of race ; and if it is to produce extended effects we must suppose that numberless migrations and numberless fortunate chances have occurred which may very well be imagined and described on paper, but which by no means take place so often in reality.

After all that has been said we may conclude, and I will go no farther to-day, that it is arbitrary to assume, as Darwin does, that natural selection can be compared to man's power of artificial selection, and that whatever is proved to have been accomplished by the latter, can without further ado be ascribed also to the former. As a matter of fact, too, we find that among cultivated plants, garden and pot flowers, vegetables and grains of different kinds, and also among domestic animals, countless varieties and races have developed, whereas in the realm of nature, among the wild plants and animals, the varieties are much less numerous, and far more rarely remain fixed and develop into races.[1] This seems to support the theory that although the species possess more or less mutability, this mutability is not unbounded, but is confined to certain limits.

[1] A. Wigand (*Der Darwinismus*, i. 47) shows at length that "variability in domestic races and variability in nature are such different things, that it is out of the question to draw any analogy from the former, or to conclude anything from it as to the variations from which the natural species, races, etc., are supposed to proceed."

XXVI.

THE THEORY OF DESCENT—*Continued.*

Darwin has modified the theory of descent in several ways since the year 1859, and many of those who became believers in this theory, in consequence of the impulse which he gave to it, have sought to support it by other hypotheses in addition to the working of natural and sexual selection.[1] But all those who support the theory of descent unanimously assume that the separate species of plants and animals are descended from a few simple forms, that is, that there exists an unlimited mutability of species.

All the careful observations which have been made hitherto go to prove that species is more or less variable, but not that its variability is unlimited. The Giessen botanist Hoffmann made experiments for years with garden plants. He gives the following as the result: " 1. There are some very strong varieties which may be made permanent. They are connected with the common stock by sports, intermediate forms, or genealogically. But it has not yet been ascertained whether these varieties can be made permanent in such a manner as to prevent a return to the original form. 2. There are other varieties which cannot be made permanent, and this is

[1] Huber, *Zur Kritik*, etc., pp. 4, 23. A. Weismann, *Bericht uber die Weiterentwicklung der Descendenz-Theorie im J.* 1872. *Archiv. fur Anthr.* vi. 119-144.

the commonest case. 3. The extent of the varieties is limited, but it differs with different plants." And Hoffmann gives this as the general result of his observations, "Experience strengthens the belief that transmutation through the formation of varieties is extensive, but not unlimited; on the contrary, it is contained within clearly defined limits."[1] An eminent breeder, Settegast, says the same of domestic animals. There are races which are specially variable, and are therefore well suited for breeding, because their form and qualities adapt themselves easily to the objects of the breeder, which vary according to the varying requirements. On the other hand, there are races which resist all change, and which, as Settegast expresses it, receive all the efforts made by the breeder to vary them with wooden obstinacy. Everywhere the breeder finds a limit; for instance, in the case of pigs, as Settegast asserts, the strongest influence of breeding, climate, etc., has not been even able to transform diverging rows of teeth into parallel ones, or a long lachrymal bone into a short one.[2]

The observations which have been made about artificial breeding may not yet be complete enough to justify a final conclusion; but so far as they extend at present, they tell much more against than for the supposition of an unlimited mutability of species. But if even artificial selection can only produce limited effects, we must expect, according to what I said in my last lecture, that natural selection and similar influences will produce results still more limited.[3]

---

[1] *Untersuchungen*, pp. 25, 26. [2] Cf. Huber, *Die Lehre Darwins*, p. 227.

[3] Baer (*Studien*, p. 383; cf. pp. 245, 298) thinks that a limited mutability, a development of " the separate species of a genus, or at most of very closely related genera, from a common ancestral form " is likely.

But this holds good not only of the present, but also of the past, so far as we know it. Ancient figures and sculptures on Egyptian and Assyrian monuments show that the domestic races of Africa and Asia entirely resembled the present ones. The Ibis which exists now exactly resembles the Ibis of the time of Pharaoh, as Cuvier and Humboldt have ascertained from the mummies that have been preserved. In the Egyptian pyramids and in the Swiss Lake dwellings, wheat and barley corns have been found, which cannot be distinguished from the present grain. "The barley," says Humboldt, in his *Geography of Plants*, "which fed the horses of the Atridæ was undoubtedly similar to that which we now gather in, in harvest. All the plants and animals which now exist on the earth do not seem to have changed their characteristic form for many thousands of years."

In face of these facts Darwin no doubt maintains that a few thousand years is much too short a time to produce great changes; *many* thousand years would be necessary for this, as according to his theory they only develop very gradually. But to this it has been replied with perfect justice, that the mere length of time will not help us at all. Time in itself has no effect on the changes; these can only be produced by physical processes in the course of time, and if these processes cannot be discovered by observation within a limited time, it is arbitrary to assume that they might take place in a longer period.[1]

---

[1] The transmutation hypothesis in its usual form assumes unlimited mutability ; by so doing it contradicts the positive facts of our empirical knowledge, and in order to conceal this weakness it vainly has recourse to

And further, if species only originate by the reproduction and increase of small varieties, and as these varieties occur in every possible manner, we should expect to find in the present animal and vegetable world a mixed diversity of forms without rule or order. But in reality the species of plants and animals differ plainly and sharply from one another. There are no doubt species which display many varieties and transitional forms; but they are the exception, and in these single cases the classification of species may perhaps be faulty. But generally speaking we do not find the quantity of transitional forms that Darwin's theory would lead us to expect.[1] Darwin endeavours to meet this fact by assuming that as the new varieties are formed with extreme slowness, the intermediate and common forms which were destroyed in the struggle for existence, and were removed by natural selection, would be found as a rule in the fossils, and not existing now. But, as a matter of fact, we find only sharply defined species among the fossils, and not the countless transitional forms which must have existed according to Darwin's theory.[2] One of the most eminent palæontologists, Professor Göppert of Breslau, ends a paper,[3] "On the Darwinian theory of transmutation in its bearing on fossil plants," with these words, "This theory finds no support among the fossil flora, nor among the fossil fauna; this has in my opinion been proved in the most convincing manner by Reuss." Darwin has no doubt pointed out that some æons, just as the hypothesis of autogeny has recourse to the primæval age, and "the conditions which once were different."

[1] Baer, *Studien*, p. 291.   [2] Pfaff, *Grundriss*, p. 283.
[3] *Neues Jahrbuch*, etc., von Leonhard und Geinitz, 1865, p. 297.

transitional forms have been found, but these are exceptions which occur comparatively seldom,[1] and here again his principal argument is a purely negative one. It is this; our knowledge of the extinct organisms is said to be very imperfect, and it will always remain imperfect, because many organisms have been entirely destroyed by geological processes. But we can hardly suppose that by some accident only the pure species have been preserved, or have been found up till now, and that the transitional forms have been destroyed or are still unknown.[2] At any rate in this respect also the facts as known at present tell much more against than for the Darwinian theory. It is of course possible that the further progress of research will put many things in a more favourable light; but such possibility is no proof.

I have already said that many scientific inquirers believe the fertility and sterility of the crosses to be a sure test of the species and the variety; this no doubt is not exactly decisive, but at any rate the facts as regards this also, so far as they are at present known, are rather against than for Darwin. I must admit that it is doubtful whether this holds good in the case of some animals. Hæckel, for instance, asserts that permanently fertile hybrids have been bred since 1850 from hares and rabbits in France; and that he himself possesses specimens of this new species, which he calls "Lepus Darwinii."[3] But of this intercrossing of hares

[1] Baer, *Studien*, p. 375.
[2] Pfaff, *Grundriss*, p. 397. A. Wigand, *Der Darwinismus*, i. 295 : " Where the materials for comparison exist, we are told the time has been too short for change (see above, p. 67); when we grant long periods of time, we are told that the materials for comparison do not exist; a capital seesaw."
[3] *Naturliche Schopfungsgeschichte*, p. 131.

and rabbits, which is a regular industry in France, Quatrefages says:[1] "The descendants of these hybrid breeds, Leporidæ, do no doubt reproduce themselves; but it has been observed that after a few generations they degenerate, and again become pure rabbits if they are crossed with one another, and if the race is not renewed from time to time by intercrossing with hares." Therefore, and this fact is very awkward for the Darwinian theory, Hæckel's Lepus Darwinii does not constitute a new species or distinct race, standing between hares and rabbits; it is an intermediate form which can be produced by crossing, but which does not last, and eventually goes back to the original form. This seems to support the theory that the species are real and lasting, and that the varieties and intermediate forms which arise in the progress of time do not become distinct species, but disappear again. Again Darwin's assertion, that the sterility of hybrids and the temporary character of hybrid races is only a difficulty at first, and that it may be overcome in time, just as in acclimatizing plants and animals success is often only reached after repeated efforts, is simply an assumption and an appeal to possibilities. It may be so; one of the good results of the Darwinian theory is that it stimulates us to continual careful experiments and observations, which, whatever may be their final result, will advance our knowledge of nature. Therefore Darwin has the merit of having reopened a question which was believed to be decided, and of having made it a subject for scientific observation. But he and his followers have no right to

[1] Quatrefages, *Ch. Darwin*, etc., p. 253.

anticipate the results of these indispensable observations, and to say that because it is possible that they may lead to a conclusion favourable to the theory of descent, therefore this theory may be considered as correct, although the results of inquiry have been hitherto unfavourable to it.[1] The least we may expect is that the supporters of the theory should admit that it is not yet proved; that, on the contrary, there are still weighty objections to it ; and we can only wait to see whether the progress of research will remove these objections, and give us better reasons for believing in the theory than we have at present.

Huxley, who is one of the most learned and acute supporters of the theory of descent, openly acknowledges the difficulty which lies in the fact of the fertility of races, but the sterility of species, that have intercrossed. He says, " There is, in fact, one set of these peculiarities which the theory of selective modification, as it stands at present; is not wholly competent to explain, and that is the group of phenomena which I mentioned to you under the name of Hybridism, and which I explained to consist in the sterility of the offspring of certain species when crossed one with another. It matters not one whit whether this sterility is universal, or whether it exists only in a single case. Every hypothesis is bound to explain, or at any rate not be inconsistent with 'the whole of the facts which it professes to account for ; and if there is a single one of these facts which can be shown to be inconsistent with (I do not merely mean inexplicable by, but contrary to) the hypothesis, the hypothesis falls to the

[1] J. B. Meyer, *Philos. Zeitfragen*, p. 73.

ground,—it is worth nothing. One fact with which it is positively inconsistent is worth as much, and is as powerful in negativing the hypothesis, as five hundred. If I am right in thus defining the obligations of an hypothesis, Mr. Darwin, in order to place his views beyond the reach of all possible assault, ought to be able to demonstrate the possibility of developing from a particular stock by selective breeding, two forms, which should either be unable to cross one with another, or whose cross bred offspring should be infertile one with another." For in this case only would it be proved that new *species* could be formed whose intercrossing is not lastingly fertile, whereas so long as the intercrossing remained lastingly fertile, there would be nothing but new races. Huxley continues, "Now it is admitted on all hands that, at present, so far as experiments have gone, it has not been found possible to produce this complete physiological divergence by selective breeding. . . . So far as we have gone yet with our breeding, we have not produced from a common stock two breeds which are not more or less fertile with one another." Huxley then observes that he does not know of any fact which could justify the assertion that such sterility cannot be produced by proper experimentation, and that he himself sees every reason for believing that it may and will be so produced. And he ends with these words : " So that though Mr. Darwin's hypothesis does not completely extricate us from this difficulty at present, we have not the least right to say that it will not do so." [1]

[1] On our Knowledge, etc. Lect. vii. p. 149 seq.

Qui vivra, verra. At any rate Darwinians have no right to assert that their leader's hypothesis is proved. On the contrary, the way in which we are continually put off with possibilities when we compare the theory with actual facts, raises well founded doubts as to the theory itself. Even with reference only to what I have spoken of—and the principal point is still to come,—I think we may say with J. B. Meyer,[1] that "Darwinism is not condemned because it sets up hypotheses, but because these hypotheses are bad. No science can exist without hypotheses, and good hypotheses may be of great service to a science. But we can only admit them in order to explain existing facts; and we cannot admit those hypotheses which require for their support not only other hypotheses, but also facts which are entirely unproved. Now the Darwinian theory requires many such hypotheses, and therefore it is scientifically wrong and inadmissible."[2]

The explanation of undoubted facts is here rightly said to be the object of scientific hypotheses. The more completely and simply a hypothesis explains the facts in question, the more plausible it is. I have shown by several examples that the Darwinian theory does not explain many important facts, or at least cannot explain them without having recourse to further hypotheses. There are no doubt certain groups of facts in the face of which the Darwinian theory appears to a superficial observer an attractive, and according to its supporters the only satisfactory hypothesis. The

[1] *Philos. Zeitfragen*, p. 103.
[2] Cf. Hæckel, *Nat. Schöpfungsgeschichte*, p. 126. *Anthropogenie*, pp. 86, 692.

existence of the so-called rudimentary organs belongs to these. By the rudimentary organs are meant those parts of the body which are intended for a special purpose, and yet have no functions. In some animals which live in caves or under the earth, and which therefore can never use their eyes, we find hidden under the skin real eyes, or something resembling real eyes, but these eyes cannot perform their functions because they are covered with an opaque membrane, and therefore cannot be reached by the light. It is supposed that in the ancestors of these animals, which lived in the daylight, the eyes were well developed, were covered by a horny transparent capsule, and actually served the purpose of seeing. As the animals accustomed themselves by degrees to an underground mode of life, and withdrew from the light of day, they no longer used their eyes, the latter then deteriorated more and more from generation to generation, so that at last only the rudiments of eyes remained.[1] Darwin explains that the wings of those birds and insects which live in islands, and therefore need not fly much or far, grow stunted in this way. He goes farther, and assumes that those kinds of birds which are called running birds, whose legs, like those of the ostrich and cassowary are strongly developed, and whose wings are very slightly developed, are descended from birds which had stronger wings, that they had got out of the habit of flying, had thus lost the use of their wings, and had therefore preserved only rudimentary wings.

The stunting of the wings among birds and insects

According to Baer, however, this is doubtful. See *Studien*, p. 437.

which lived on islands is explained in this manner; those that flew well and much were while flying blown by the wind into the sea; those that flew ill therefore had in this case an advantage in the struggle for existence, they were not so easily blown into the sea, and remained alive longer than individuals of the same kind that flew well. And therefore, in the course of of several generations, the wings became gradually stunted by the process of natural selection. For instance, in the island of Madeira, out of five hundred and fifty kinds of beetles, two hundred had no wings, or wings so imperfect as to make flying impossible. No doubt it is not unlikely that a gradual stunting actually took place among many species of birds, but it is rather hazardous to generalize from this, and to explain all the so-called rudimentary organs in this way. It is possible that among many species the rudimentary form of the organ is the original one, and that it stands in its proper relation to the whole organization. If organs which are not used not only gradually grow stunted but at last disappear,[1] we cannot understand why several of the so-called rudimentary organs, if they are really useless to the animal, have not disappeared altogether; as, for instance, the nipples in male mammals, and the rudimentary toes at the side of a horse's foot.[2] It does not follow that because the ostrich has wings like all other birds, therefore it ought to have equally useful wings, and that its ancestors must have had wings as useful as those of the eagle. If we assume this, we are suppos-

---

[1] Hæckel, *Nat. Schöpfungsgeschichte*, p. 223.
[2] Huber, *Zur Kritik*, p. 14. Michelis, *Hæckelogonie*, p. 80.

ing the very thing which has to be proved, namely, that *all* differences between animals must have arisen by gradual transformation. This may be assumed where it can be proved by observation or induction, but if we go farther, we are leaving the region in which hypothesis is justifiable, and we find ourselves believing startling things, such as Hæckel and Darwin sometimes tell us, as, for instance, that in the so-called tail vertebræ, man has a rudimentary tail, and that during the two first months of the development of the human embryo this stands out, and only grows in later. "This rudimentary little tail of man is," as Hæckel says," an irrefutable proof of the fact that he is descended from tailed ancestors."[1] Or, most men are not capable of moving their ears at will, although the muscles for moving them exist. By means of continued practice some men succeed in accomplishing the feat of moving their ears at will. Therefore the muscles which accomplish this exist in man, only they are stunted, therefore man is descended from ancestors who had moveable ears, like many animals.

It would be far more important if the Darwinian theory professed to explain not only the stunting of separate organs, and their gradual perfecting, but also the growth of new organs. For instance, how did the eyes originate which do not exist in animals of low organization, and according to the Darwinian theory did not exist in the ancestors of the more highly organized animals.[2] Hæckel thinks that comparative anatomy and the history of development shows us in the

[1] *Nat. Schöpfungsgeschichte*, p. 258.
[2] Hæckel, *Nat. Schöpfungsgeschichte*, p. 11. *Anthropogenie*, p. 563.

animal kingdom such a gradual perfecting of the eyes, that it is quite possible to imagine from it what must have been the gradual development of these organs in the course of ages, through all stages of perfection. In the lowest animals the eye appears as a simple spot of colour, which cannot reflect any picture of outward objects, and is at most sensitive to the different rays of light. To this is added a sensitive nerve. Later on, the first beginning of the lens is gradually developed inside this spot of pigment, a refracting body which is able to concentrate the rays of light, and to reflect a distinct picture. But all the complicated apparatus for focussing and moving the eye is still wanting, the additional refracting media, the highly differentiated membrane of the optic nerves, etc., which make the eye such a perfect organ among the higher animals. Comparative anatomy therefore shows in a series of unbroken steps all the possible transitions from the simplest possible organs to the most complete apparatus, and we can therefore quite well imagine the gradual development, even of so complicated an organ as this. If any one does not understand this, and in contemplating these most perfect organs still believes that an external Creator is necessary, he resembles the savages,—Hæckel loves such comparisons as these,—who seeing for the first time a ship of war, or a locomotive, thought that these objects must be produced by supernatural beings, and could not understand that such an apparatus could be produced by a man, organized as they were.[1]

---

[1] *Nat. Schöpfungsgeschichte*, p. 634; cf. *Anthropogenie*, p. 547. A. Müller, *Die erste Entstehung*, etc., p. 24.

In spite of comparative anatomy, the matter is not quite so simple as this. According to the Darwinian theory, the origin and development of the eye must be conceived of in this manner. First of all, cells form themselves in the skin of an animal, which react on light by expanding and contracting. In later generations a sensitive nerve was gradually connected with these cells, and by this means the animal could distinguish between light and darkness. A drop of fluid in the epidermis was the beginning of a refracting medium. This fluid gradually thickened in the centre, and this was the beginning of the lens. Besides this, the apparatus of motion, the additional refracting media, the membrane of the optic nerve, have been gradually evolved in the course of countless generations. In all this we must not forget the concurrence of millions of chances which must have been necessary in order first to produce and then to preserve each small improvement, to reproduce them in the descendants, to fix them and to increase them, etc. All this would be easily explicable if we were to assume the existence of a power which guided all these chances according to a design; but then it would be simpler to assume the existence of an external Creator. In Darwin's theory both are inadmissible, everything must be the result of fortunate chance, and blind forces of nature working without aim or plan.

The discussion on this point is one of the best parts of Frohschammer's criticism on Darwinism.[1] He says, very strikingly, "Therefore eyes *with* crystalline lenses must have been evolved by natural selection from

[1] *Das Christenthum*, etc., p. 513.

imperfect eyes *without* crystalline lenses and all the rest. This could only happen if this perfect eye were contained in the most imperfect eye as in a germ which need only develop itself; but this would involve an *internal* principle of development, and the *external* principle of development by means of natural selection assumed to exist by Darwin would be superfluous, or at least no longer the primary and special cause. Or else the faculty for the further development, or the origin of the crystalline lens, was not present in the most imperfect eye ; and in this case its formation from its first beginnings could only have taken place either by *generatio aequivoca* or chance, or by a special Divine creative activity. As Darwin assumes neither of these, the thing simply remains unexplained, that is, the possibility of the transformation is not proved, the difficulty therefore not removed. Darwin no doubt compares the perfect eye to the telescope, and the effects produced by natural selection on the perfecting of the eye to the efforts of the human intelligence for the improvement and completion of the telescope. But this is clearly wrong, unconscious nature can no more imitate or perform the systematic actions of the optician than she can imitate or replace the actions of an artist, for instance a painter or a watchmaker. The material conditions necessary for producing works of art are no doubt all present in nature ; but in spite of this no one would say that nature could of itself through natural activity produce a picture or a watch. In dealing with this point Darwin falls back on a regular personification of natural selection, in order to prevent his explanation of the origin of the perfect eye from coming to a standstill altogether. Natural selection must "narrowly observe" and "carefully choose," and must "find out with unerring tact every improvement in order to produce further perfection." If we are to understand this literally, Darwin himself would appear to be introducing into nature a power acting according to design, which would make all his other attempts at explanation superfluous. But Darwin evidently does not mean it to be understood literally, and in this case such expressions are quite inadmissible. Natural selection, as an aggregate of mere efficient causes, *cannot* observe, choose out, and act according to a plan, but must take everything as it comes, and can only make use of and preserve the favourable conditions or changes; or to put it more correctly, these changes, if they once occur, preserve themselves because they have occurred. Natural selection therefore cannot strive after more perfect eyes, it can only preserve them and make use of them when they are there, that is to say, if they have in any manner come into existence. Darwin himself admits that if any composite organ could be pointed out which could not have been perfected by countless small successive modifications, his theory must undoubtedly break down. The existence of the perfect eye really cannot be explained by countless small successive modifications; for it is distinguished from the imperfect eye by having essentially *new* parts; new parts which *cannot* proceed from the former ones by gradual development, unless they have been contained in them from the beginning according to a plan, and which therefore can only have originated by a sudden bound, and that is by an unexplained and mysterious occurrence, not by natural selection. What holds good of the eye holds good also of other organs, especially of the sexual differences which are found in the more perfect organisms.[1]

A. Wigand rightly lays stress on the fact that Darwin is not able to explain the existence of those organs which only become functional when they are completely developed. So long as the proboscis of the bee is not long enough to reach the nectary of the flower, so long as the tendril of the creeper is neither able to twine itself, nor long enough firmly to entwine a support, so long this organ is of *no* use to the individual; the insect will not compete with other individuals whose proboscis is more imperfect than its own, but will simply starve; the creeper with a relatively more perfect tendril, is not the least in a more advantageous position, if the tendril has not reached the proper stage of development.[2]

"Natural selection," says Huber, "is according to Darwin's theory not a creating principle, but only a process starting from a given basis, originating with a new state of things. This new state of things is not itself the result of natural selection, neither are variations caused by artificial selection, the latter can only deal with those variations which already exist. If a new organ appears in a rudimentary state in any living organism, and if this variation is of advantage to the organism in the struggle for existence, then, according to Darwin, the process of natural selection will begin in this

---

[1] Frohschammer, *Das Christenthum*, p. 517; Pfaff, *Die neuesten Forschungen*, p. 102.
[2] *Der Darwinismus*, i. p. 131.

organ, and act indirectly on the whole organism. But if natural selection only acts in the case of a given variation, and on that variation, and does not create the new organ, but only helps to develop it after the material for this development is provided, natural selection cannot by itself cause one stage in the organic world to develop into another, because the higher orders of organisms are provided with organs which do not exist in the lower ones. Progress beyond any organic stage which has been reached can therefore only be caused by the appearance of a new form, by the spontaneous tendency towards a new organ, and this is an event which is not explained by Darwin's theory of development."[1] It is therefore a bad hypothesis, because it does not sufficiently explain facts which it should explain.

As I am speaking of the hypothesis as to the origin of new organs, I will mention Darwin's explanation of the origin of animal instincts, and I will give you an abstract of Frohschammer's excellent criticism on this point.[2] Of course we must not assume that any of this psychical power and activity existed in the earliest animal forms; it only began with the gradual progress of the bodily organization, and it was itself very gradual, because small variations were formed which gradually accumulated and were inherited. Here also Darwin falls back on artificial selection in order to explain the way in which natural selection works. The faculties, for instance, which dogs obtain by training are often inherited; even before they are trained, young pointers are specially qualified for their work in consequence of the inherited tendency; and young

[1] *Die Lehre Darwins*, p. 364. [2] *Das Christenthum*, pp. 469, 522.

sheep dogs show a disposition to run round the flock instead of running by its side.

The cuckoo is one of the examples brought forward by Darwin in order to illustrate the origin of instinct by natural selection. The American cuckoo makes its own nest and hatches its own eggs. Let us suppose that the ancestor of our European cuckoo had the same habits as the American, but yet occasionally laid an egg in another bird's nest. If the old bird profited by this occasional habit, or if the mistaken instinct of the strange mother caused the young bird to become stronger than he would have become through the care of his own mother, either the old cuckoo or the young cuckoo who was fed at the expense of strange birds gained by it. The young cuckoo inheriting this tendency was even more inclined to imitate the accidental exceptional action of the mother, and to lay its eggs in strange nests in order to obtain stronger descendants. Darwin thinks that by a continual process of this kind, that which originally only occurred as an accidental exception might have become the usual habit among cuckoos, and that the peculiar instinct of cuckoos originated in this way. But whence came the cuckoo's power of perceiving the advantage to be gained by using strange nests, of making such clever use of this insight, and also of entrusting its eggs only to certain birds, and not to any and every kind?

Again, bees, as is well known, construct their combs in an ingenious manner out of regular hexagonal wax cells, this construction ensures that the greatest quantity of honey shall be stored with the least possible expenditure of expensive material, that is, of wax, and all the bees work in the dark hive according to this system. The ancestors of the present bees did not practise this art, just as their kinsmen the humble-bees do not practise it now. At first they built irregularly, but the swarm which stored the most honey, and used the least wax in the process, succeeded best in the struggle for existence; they transmitted the knowledge of perfect construction which enabled them to attain this result to other swarms, and so at last those bees which had gradually attained to the present perfect mode of structure conquered in the struggle for existence, while all the others died out. But how do we explain the fact that these bees noticed and made use of every advantage of structure which appeared by chance? And above all how can we explain the fact that the *constant* power of building in this manner, with this regularity and order, originated and maintained itself among millions of individuals. Natural selection does not explain this, because other kinds, for instance the humble-bees, who do not possess this instinct, this talent, have survived in the struggle for existence. Besides, many other things are unexplained with regard to the bees; for instance, the instinctive hatred of the queen-bee, which impels her either to kill her daughters, the young queens, or to perish herself in the conflict with them.

Again, according to Darwin, the instinct of migration in certain animals was not originally inherent in these kinds, but it arose from an experience which had become hereditary and second nature, a want which had originally been felt from without and had been satisfied by chance. The birds which migrated to the south before the winter were preserved, while those who remained behind died out. As the migration was of advantage in the struggle for existence, the habit became fixed, and was transmitted as a hereditary instinct. But does this explain why the migratory birds always fly in the right direction and reach the right goal? In this case a geographical knowledge and experience must have become natural, and we do not find that in the case of man, to whom Darwin's theory certainly should apply, historical and geographical knowledge is ever inherited from the parents. But if we ascribe the direction of the migration to natural causes, currents of air, or the action on these birds of agencies which are unknown or inaccessible to us, Darwin's explanation as to the origin of instinct must be given up.

The cunning of the fox also is, according to Darwin, the result of gradually won experience, a gradually gained cleverness which became hereditary. But if the conditions were favourable to the fox, no special mental effort was necessary on his part in order to to satisfy his wants, and he would hardly have exerted his brains without such outward necessity; while, on the other hand, no mental progress would be possible without exercise and effort. But if the conditions were unfavourable, and lastingly so, it was much more likely that the fox should grow stunted in body and mind than that he should develop under these conditions, and should transmit his mental attainments to his progeny. Even savage tribes in a needy condition always remain at the same stage of mental development, and if Darwin's theory of the gradual development of the fox's cunning were correct, ought not many other animals to have removed or supplemented their bodily weakness by mental attainments, and the hereditary facility produced by them? and yet we do not find that this is so. On the other hand, we find comparatively high mental attainments even in animals whose bodies are so favourably organized that the former are not necessary. For instance, the intelligence which is ascribed to the elephant cannot be traced to the desire to make up for bodily incapacity by mental perfection.

It may be true that faculties, which are originally imparted to animals by training, may to a certain degree become hereditary. But at any rate this only occurs in the case of certain peculiarly constituted animals, and then only to a moderate extent, and under human supervision and foresight. It is hardly conceivable that even this is possible in the natural state. A faculty does not become hereditary in a short time, and a prolonged continuous similar activity in similar animals under similar and different conditions presupposes the very thing which is to be obtained; the instinct and the power of always doing the same thing, and always exercising some particular faculty in the same way.

You see that wherever the details of Darwin's theory are compared with facts, unsurmountable difficulties arise. One of its opponents, Hoffmann, says, "The weak side in the Darwinian hypothesis is that it rests on premises which are not based on experience; on the other hand, its strength, to the impartial observer of nature, consists in its grandeur and simplicity."[1] The

[1] *Untersuchungen*, etc. p. 28.

first statement is indisputable, and is partly admitted by the Darwinians themselves. But the simplicity of the hypothesis could only be a recommendation if it sufficed to explain the different facts which have to be considered, and this is not the case. Grandeur is no proof of truth; for even a mere fancy may be grand.

Darwin himself describes the theory of descent very well under the following image: "The affinities of all the beings of the same class have sometimes been represented by a great tree. I believe this simile largely speaks the truth. The green and budding twigs may represent existing species, and those produced during former years may represent the long succession of extinct species. At each period of growth all the growing twigs have tried to branch out on all sides, and to overtop and kill the surrounding twigs and branches, in the same manner as species and groups of species have at all times overmastered other species in the great battle for life. The limbs divided into great branches, and these into lesser and lesser branches, were themselves once, when the tree was young, budding twigs; and this connection of the former and present buds by ramifying branches may well represent the classification of all extinct and living species in groups subordinate to groups. Of the many twigs which flourished when the tree was a mere bush, only two or three, now grown into great branches, yet survive and bear the other branches; so with the species which lived during long past geological periods, very few have left living and modified descendants. From the first growth of the tree, many a limb and branch has decayed and dropped off; and these fallen branches of various sizes may represent those whole orders, families, and genera which have now no living representatives, and which are known to us only in a fossil state. . . . 'As buds give rise by growth to fresh buds, and these, if vigorous, branch out and overtop on all sides many a feebler branch, so by generation I believe it has been with the great tree of life, which fills with its dead and broken branches the crust of the earth, and covers its surface with its ever-branching and beautiful ramifications."[1]

Hæckel has imitated the genealogical trees of families which have spread widely from their origin from a single ancestor, by making a regular genealogical tree of all organic beings, in which the moneron stands at the beginning as the original ancestor, and all the species of plants and animals which have existed, or still exist, have found their place.

Darwin may well say, "There is grandeur in this view of life, with its several powers, having been originally breathed by the Creator into a few forms or into one ; and that, whilst this planet has gone cycling on according to the fixed law of gravity, from so simple a beginning endless forms most beautiful and most wonderful have been and are being evolved."[2] The hypothesis is grand, no doubt, but is it admissible, that is, does it suffice to explain all the facts which have to be considered, and does it not come into conflict with assured facts?

I have enumerated a series of objections to the Darwinian theory of descent, and I have specially laid stress on the fact that the observations which have

[1] *Origin of Species*, pp. 104, 105.　　　[2] *Ibid.* p. 429.

been made up to the present time show that the effects produced by artificial selection cannot, without further ado, be also ascribed to what Darwin calls natural and sexual selection; further, that although we may admit that organic forms are variable, and that certain changes and variations may be transmitted and become hereditary, yet that up to the present time all observations show that this is confined within certain more or less narrow limits; also that in order to account for the changes of organic forms which Darwin assumes to have occurred, we must suppose that an endless series of fortunate chances took place throughout an endless number of generations, and that the theory cannot explain the origin of entirely new organs, such as the eyes, etc. In order to make our review easier, I have purposely up to this time confined myself to the application of the Darwinian theory to the more nearly allied species. But the more we follow it out the more problematical it becomes. We might, for instance, at any rate think it possible that the cat, the lion, the tiger, and the other animals belonging to the genus *Felis* really were allied, that is, were descended from common ancestors, that a *Felis* had at one time existed whose descendants in the course of ages, after countless generations, had gradually differentiated into domestic cats, lions, tigers, etc., just as the descendants of the first men have differentiated into Europeans, Mongols, Americans, and negroes. There is greater difficulty in assuming the common ancestry, for instance, of the lion or elephant and the mouse, and it becomes still greater if we are to believe that the elephant and the humming-bird, the eagle and the earth-worm, the butterfly and the whale had common ancestors; and according to Darwin this is what we must believe. Hæckel, in his genealogical tree, traces the descent of the elephant on the one hand, and the butterfly on the other, from the same moneron, or if not exactly from the same, yet from precisely similar individuals. But how many intermediate forms must there not have been between the elephant and the moneron, and again between the moneron and the butterfly? And as Hæckel could, of course, only set down the principal forms in his genealogical tables, we must multiply the intermediate forms which he has set down by thousands or millions. For every change which occurs and is perpetuated by natural selection is quite unimportant in itself, and hardly perceptible. The difference which exists between the elephant and the butterfly—and that of size is by no means the only one—is therefore the sum of millions of tiny differences, and each one of these originated quite gradually of itself, each one required, in order to perpetuate itself, not only a long time, but also the concourse of a great many fortunate circumstances. And how did all these small differences begin, and how were all these fortunate circumstances which perpetuated them brought about? Let us call the thing by its right name—by chance.

Darwin no doubt warns us against this expression, and says that chance is only the expression of our ignorance, or our want of discernment. This is in a certain sense true. "A chance," says Frohschammer, "in the sense of an event which occurs without sufficient cause acting according to law, is no doubt impossible;

every event in nature must have a certain cause, and must, if it occurs, occur according to fixed and definite laws. But still we may talk of chance if by it we mean events whose occurrence the known course of the laws of nature does not lead us to expect; whose reason and whose law is hidden from us, and which on this account we do not recognise as belonging to any plan, and cannot foresee and calculate, and ascribe to a certain cause. The origin of some small useful or harmful change in an organism, even when it is produced by some cause or other, is a chance in this sense,"—for the change *need* not occur, and does not occur in many cases. " Natural selection only begins to work when this chance variation has taken place," and here again it is affected by the occurrence of circumstances which need not occur, and in fact do not always occur; and whose actual occurrence in any given case is therefore also a matter of chance. " So that at last the Darwinian theory gives us a principle whose reason, law, and necessity, that is, whose true essence is unknown to us, and which we therefore cannot well consider as a certain principle of knowledge or of interpretation." [1]

This objection no doubt would vanish if we were to suppose that the Creator, who, to use Darwin's expression, breathed life with its several powers into one form from which the endless forms of the organic world have been evolved, that the Creator gave to this original form the power and tendency to develop, and that according to design He brought about the conditions favourable to this development. But Darwin cannot assume this, and still less can his followers, for then

[1] *Das Christenthum*, p. 495.

the Creator, Preserver, and Guider of the world, whom, to use Vogt's expression, they have turned out at one door, would come in again by another, and in a grander form than before; for the power and wisdom of God would be shown much more overwhelmingly if He had caused the whole organic world to be evolved, as the Darwinian theory describes it, from one primordial form than if He had created it at once. But if the designed and provident action of a higher Power be denied, and consistent Darwinians must deny it, nothing is left but chance.

And again, on the one hand Darwin is obliged to assume that changes in organic beings occur easily and often, on the other hand that the changes which have occurred are often and easily perpetuated and become hereditary. But these two principles of mutability and of inheritance and perpetuation do not as a matter of fact usually co-operate, but, on the contrary, are often antagonistic. In proportion to the facility with which changes occur is it difficult for the changed organisms to become distinct species, and while, on the one hand, by assuming that the existing species can be modified we produce a likelihood of change, on the other hand it is difficult to stop these changes, because it is only in rare cases that the outward conditions of nature are so fixed and unchangeable as not at once to give occasion for fresh changes.[1]

Darwin no doubt relies on the enormously long period, on the millions of years which must have elapsed before these accumulated small changes can have produced differences of species which are clearly distinguish-

[1] Frohschammer, *Op. cit.* p. 496.

able before the differences in species become as fixed and lasting as we see them now;—so lasting that at the present time artificially produced varieties easily sink back into the regular species if they are no longer looked after. But, as Frohschammer rightly observes,[1] "these millions of years at most explain the accumulation of changes, the growth of differences in species, and their confirmation. They do not explain how it came about that first the gradual slow change went on for an immeasurably long period, then ceased, and in another immeasurably long period became established, and then how, lastly, fresh slight changes and gradual transformations took place after so long a period of rest for no apparent reason. These enormously long periods, with which Darwin is so lavish, only make the process *possible* in time, but they do not explain why it took place; nor do they give the reason for the alternation in the process which accordingly appears to be casual, without principle or law. However immeasurably long we may suppose this period to be, its length alone cannot have caused a series of evolutions to take place, then to pause, and then to begin again. If two lines are really exactly parallel, they will not approach each other by a hair's breadth, even if they are prolonged to all eternity. And so also immeasurable periods cannot produce what time, whether short or long, cannot cause. Be it long or short, we want another cause to explain the beginning and continuation of a process of evolution. And further, it is uncertain whether we are justified in assuming that these long periods of time have passed during the development of the organic world; and for

---

[1] Frohschammer, *Op. cit.* p. 497.

this reason they are not sufficient to explain the phenomena." We are moving in a circle, we assume immeasurable periods of time, because we think by this means to explain the origin of the multiplicity of organic beings, and we then support the assumption by saying that without it we cannot account for the origin of this very multiplicity.

It is also rather hazardous to assume that small imperceptible changes have originated in organisms, and that these changes can only become really noticeable differences of species by accumulation in an immeasurably long period of time. "If these changes were so small as to be imperceptible, natural selection could not well make use of them in order to preserve and further to develop those organic forms to which they were peculiar, and therefore no sufficient foundation exists for natural selection. But if we were to suppose that these changes were great enough directly to afford a real advantage in the struggle for existence, their origin becomes more difficult to understand, and according to the Darwinian theory it is totally inexplicable."[1]

[1] Frohschammer, *Op. cit.* p. 499.

XXVII.

THE THEORY OF DESCENT—*Conclusion.*

It is of course impossible to give in a few lectures an exhaustive account and criticism of the theory of descent, and of the explanation of it given by Darwin and his followers. I have been obliged to confine myself to its main outlines, and to a few details chosen as examples. You will find in the works which I have so often quoted of Frohschammer, Huber, J. B. Meyer, A. Wigand, and Pfaff, more detailed discussions in a form which can be understood by every educated man.

To-day I wish shortly to discuss two general considerations, much relied on by Hæckel, who, as you know, likes general, or, as he calls them, philosophical arguments. The first consideration is connected with the so-called natural system of the animal and vegetable world. Animals—of whom alone we will speak—were divided by Cuvier into four great divisions (branches), the vertebrata, articulata, mollusca, and radiata. Later zoologists have substituted for the radiata the two groups of the echinoderma and the cœlenterata or zoophytes; and for the articulata the two groups of the arthropoda and the vermes; and have formed another group, the protozoa, out of the infusoria and the spongiadæ, so that in all there are seven great divisions. Each of these is further divided into several principal classes, and each principal class into lesser classes. For instance, the mammals form one class of the vertebrata. Hæckel divides the class of mammals into three inferior classes, each inferior class into legions, the legions into orders, the orders into inferior orders or sections, the sections into families, the families into genera. Each genus comprises, according to the ordinary view, as we have already seen, several species, and a species again may comprise several varieties. Now this natural system, with its divisions and subdivisions, can very well be drawn out in the form of a genealogical tree; first of all comes the general term animal, then follow the principal divisions, the vertebrate animals, molluscs, etc., under the vertebrate animals come the principal classes, and so on down to the varieties. This representation shows the greater or lesser resemblance of the separate groups, or figuratively speaking, their relationship. So far all is undisputed. But then Hæckel comes in and says, the expression "related" has not only a figurative, but a literal meaning; the ideal relationship rests on a genetical relationship, the species related in form are related in blood, the pedigree of the so-called natural system, in which men of science have placed the different forms according to their greater or lesser degree of resemblance, is the real pedigree of organisms.[1] All the different forms of the domestic cat are descendants of one primæval ancestor who represented the species *Felis domestica*. The genus *Felis* comprises besides

---

[1] *Natürliche Schöpfungsgeschichte*, pp. 364, 400. *Über die Entstehung*, etc. p. 15. *Anthropogenie*, p. 88.

the domestic cat, the lion, the tiger, etc. All these different species of the genus *Felis* resemble one another so much in the shape of their bodies, in the form of the jaw and of the foot, that we may suppose that they have all sprung from one single ancestral cat. In the same way we consider that the genera cats and hyænas which we combine in the family of cat-like wild beasts, *Felina*, are descendants of one single cat-like beast of prey, which lived at a much earlier period of the world's history than the ancestral cat. In the same way all the dog-like wild beasts, *Canina*, are descended from one primæval dog-like ancestral form; the *Ursina* from a bear-like form, and so on.

Now we find that all these cat-like, dog-like, bear-like, and other animals resemble one another in some important zoological parts, principally in the form of the jaw and the foot; and, on the other hand, they differ quite plainly from all other kinds of mammals. For this reason all these families are included in one larger group, the order of the beasts of prey, or flesh-eaters, carnivora. According to Darwin's theory, these beasts of prey are all descended from one common ancestral form, and naturally this primæval beast of prey, the ancestor of the whole order of beasts of prey, must have existed much earlier than did the ancestors of the separate families of beasts of prey.

The other orders of mammals, the rodents, the apes, the marsupials, must have had a common ancestor, like the beasts of prey. All these orders of the class of mammals resemble one another in the fact which gives them their name, that the young are fed by the mother's milk; and also in several important portions of their internal structure. These common characteristics separate the mammiferous animals from the other classes of vertebrate animals, the birds, reptiles, amphibious animals, and fish. Thus all the mammiferous animals, however different they may be, resemble one another more nearly, *i.e.* they are more closely related, than any mammal resembles a bird or a reptile. In the same way all birds on the one hand, all reptiles on the other, resemble each other much more than any bird resembles a reptile. In all zoological systems these differences and resemblances are expressed in this way—all the orders of mammals are included in the class of mammals, all orders of birds in the class birds, all orders of reptiles in the class reptiles. According to Darwin, this systematic arrangement is founded on the fact that all the mammals have sprung from a common primitive mammalian ancestor, all birds from an ancient ancestral bird, all reptiles from a common reptile form.

If we go a step further, we see that all mammals, birds, reptiles, amphibious animals, and fish may be brought under the common head of vertebrate animals. The vertebrata resemble one another in several important particulars, for instance in the peculiar formation of the skeleton and the nervous system, while they differ in the same ways from the mollusca, articulata, etc. Consequently we must also assume a common form for all vertebrata, and also for all mollusca, etc.; so that at some period—no doubt a very long time ago—there were only seven different forms of animals, a vertebrate, a mollusc, etc. These seven are all descended from a moneron which came into existence by spontaneous generation.[1]

[1] See above, pp. 9 and 10.

According to this view, not only does the natural system of animals and plants "arrange the different forms in parallel or consecutive groups, according to their greater or lesser degree of resemblance, and by this means facilitate the survey of the enormous number of forms; nor is the natural system of organisms only intended to give us a short summary of our anatomical knowledge concerning the forms of the various groups; it also reveals to us the blood relationship of the organisms, and displays their real and actual pedigree." Or in other words, "the natural system of organisms is only the expression of the phylogeny of organisms; of the gradual branching out from the first simple ancestral form into the multiplicity of individual forms."

So says Hæckel.[1] It sounds very simple. But is this analogy between the genealogical arrangement of the system and the pedigree given in the Darwinian theory really a proof of the latter? Not in the least. The explanation I have just quoted is really intended to show us that *if* all animals are in reality descended from one single form, or from a few primitive forms, we must suppose that the genealogy of the animal world is something of this kind. Surely we must not *assume* this to be really the case, for this is just what has got to be *proved*. If the pedigree is to take rank as a real genealogical pedigree, it must be possible to prove in detail that the individuals which are put down in it as allied by blood are really descended from common ancestors, or may possibly be so descended; and to show not only that the cat, the lion, the tiger,

[1] *Ueber die Entstehung*, p. 20.

etc., may possibly be descended from a primitive cat, but also that this primitive cat, the primitive dog and bear, etc., are descended from the same primitive carnivorous animal, and the primitive mammal, bird, and fish, etc., from one primitive vertebrate animal. I have shown in the preceding lectures what great objections there are to this supposition, and how little the facts bear it out.

Further, if a pedigree is to be considered genuine, it must at any rate be proved that those individuals which are set down as members of it and as ancestors of other members, have really existed. Hæckel himself says, "For if the theory of descent is really true, if the petrified remains of formerly living animals and plants really proceed from the extinct primæval ancestors and progenitors of the present organisms, then without anything else the knowledge and comparison of fossils ought to disclose to us the pedigree of organisms."[1]

But he at once admits that this is still only very imperfectly the case, and that "we are still dependent upon very many uncertain hypotheses, when actually endeavouring to sketch the pedigree of the different organic groups."[2] We must not allow Hæckel's very detailed and elaborate pedigree to impose upon us; no doubt no single member is absent; everything is given just as accurately and completely as the pedigree of the royal house of Germany in a historical work. But if we look more closely at the way in which Hæckel has obtained all the names, we soon see

[1] *Nat. Schöpfungsgeschichte*, p. 335.
[2] P. 361.

that many of them are simply manufactured, that he has introduced organisms with suitable names, for whose existence no proof can be offered, but which *must* have existed if the system is correct; and which therefore, as the system is correct, have, as Hæckel says, really existed. Thus during the Laurentian period "there existed" a common primary form of the six higher animal tribes, which, as Hæckel says, "we shall call the Gastræa," and he then proceeds to describe it as accurately as if he had seen it.[1] In the same period the Protascus, the primary form of all zoophytes, "must" have existed; and "the Gastræa and Protascus were probably represented in the Laurentian period by countless different genera and species which we may include in the class of Gastræadæ,"[2] etc. But there is no more palæontological evidence for the existence of these primæval forms than there is historical proof that Teut or Thuiscon were the ancestors of the Germans.

No doubt palæontology shows us that generally speaking the lower classes of the animal world appeared first, and the higher classes later; and that the organic beings of the later periods are more nearly related to the present ones than are the earlier organic beings. But we do not find anything like the gradual progress of organization which is required

[1] *Nat. Schöpfungsgeschichte*, p. 445.
[2] *Nat. Schöpfungsgeschichte*, pp. 453, 454. On p. 596 the "chain of the animal ancestors of man" is given in twenty-two stages. "Comparative anatomy and ontogeny gives us a sure proof" of the existence of eighteen of these stages. The assumption of the first stage is "necessary for most important general reasons." The proof of the existence of the fourteenth stage "lies in the fact that it forms a necessary and intermediate link between the preceding and succeeding stages."

by the theory of descent and Hæckel's pedigree.[1] A close examination of the oldest fossiliferous formation, the Silurian, has afforded a result specially unfavourable to Hæckel. F. Römer thus sums up the results of these investigations.[2] "The condition of the Silurian fauna in no way confirms the statement that the first organic life on the earth was quite imperfect, and consisted of the lowest and simplest forms. For even if this assertion is apparently confirmed by the almost entire absence of all vertebrata, the condition of the other classes of animals is most decidedly opposed to it. The molluscs rank comparatively highly in the animal world, and among the molluscs the cephalopods are undoubtedly the highest; it is this very section of the molluscs which preponderates in the Silurian age. Again, the crustacea are the most perfect of the articulata, and the trilobites which belong to this class are found in great quantities in the Silurian strata. If the assertion that organic life must have begun with the lowest and simplest forms were correct, sponges, polythalamacea, and similar animals would form the Silurian fauna, and this is precisely what does not occur." No doubt it might be said that this assertion might yet be true, that still older fossiliferous deposits, whose fossils had possibly hitherto escaped observation, might be found under the Silurian strata. Römer proves in detail that these strata have been examined in many widely separated regions, Bohemia,

---

[1] See above, vol. i. p. 285. Pfaff, *Grundriss*, pp. 380, 395.
[2] *Ueber die ältesten Formen des organischen Lebens auf der Erde*, Berlin 1869, p. 22. Cf. the report on J. Barrande, *Trilobites*, Prague 1871, in the *Neue Jahrbuch für Mineralogie*, etc. Leonhard and Geinitz, 1871, p. 962. Baer, *Studien*, p. 304.

Scandinavia, and North America, and that it is hardly likely that earlier fauna should be found. For we find universally that under the earliest known fossiliferous strata there lie widely extended strata which evidently would have been very well fitted to preserve the remains of animals, had the seas which deposited these strata contained any such. They consist of very regular fine masses of slate, and show no signs of having been affected by any later influences, they are constituted just like the more recent strata, which are very rich in fossils, they have been dug up and laid bare in many quarries and walls of rock, and no sign of any animal has been found in them.[1]

In the deposits of the Laurentian period, in which, according to Hæckel, "the countless different genera and species of Gastræadæ must have lived," we find, with the exception of the *very* problematical Eozoon Canadense,[2] no fossils at all, and in the strata of the following periods also, several organisms, which, according to Hæckel, must have existed in those periods, are not found. Hæckel gets over this difficulty by saying that the organic beings which lived earlier were for several reasons only very imperfectly preserved in the fossiliferous strata; but still it is singularly unfortunate that the very forms which are necessary in order to make Hæckel's pedigree authentic are those which have not been preserved, and that, as he says

[1] Pfaff, *Die neuesten Forschungen*, p. 100.
[2] See above, vol. i. p. 286. "Some time ago there was great rejoicing among Darwinians; it was said that the primitive animal, or at all events a very near cousin, had been found in Canada, and it was named Eozoon Canadense. But the joy was soon clouded, for grave doubts as to the animal nature of this being were soon entertained, and it was pronounced by competent judges to be an inorganic formation."—Pfaff, *Op. cit.* p. 113.

himself, "if we had to compile the history, say, of the evolution of the vertebrate animals from the fossils alone, we should be rather badly off."[1] Perhaps we might say that it would be much the same as if we were actually to expect a historian to compile his history from authentic sources only, and when these sources fail, to refrain from asking his readers to accept his own additions as historical truths.

The fossils then, "the earliest, most irrefutable records," are not sufficient to authenticate the pedigree of organic beings. The philosopher must come to the help of the man of science, for as Hæckel says, "Without the necessary combination of empirical knowledge with the philosophic understanding of biological phenomena, it is impossible to gain a thorough conviction of the truth of the theory of descent."[2] "It is therefore not to be wondered at," he adds,[3] "that the deep inner truth of the theory of descent remains a sealed book to those rude empiricists. As the common proverb justly says, they cannot see the wood for the trees. It is only by a more general philosophical study, and especially by a more strictly logical training of the mind, that this sad state of things can be remedied. When we hear acknowledged specialists, teachers in zoology and botany, who certainly ought to possess a general insight into the whole domain of their science, or who are actually familiar with the facts of those scientific domains, observing that the theory of descent certainly is a scientific 'hypothesis,' but that it still requires to be 'proved,' then we are

---

[1] *Ueber die Entstehung,* p. 32.
[2] *Nat. Schöpfungsgeschichte,* p. 637.   [3] *Ibid.* pp. 641, 642.

really at a loss what to say. Those who are not satisfied with the treasures of our present empirical knowledge of nature as a basis on which to establish the theory of descent, will not be convinced by any other facts which may hereafter be discovered."

This is a bad prophecy, for even men of science who are not in the least suspected of any theological tendencies, or of a dislike on principle to the Darwinian theory, are not moved by Hæckel's warning words. The anatomist Aeby says: "The theory of descent, which has been lately so ably developed by Darwin, is a most splendid acquisition, and is calculated to be of immense service to science. It is for this very reason that we must protest against the assertions that this theory no longer requires proof, and against the way in which a blind faith in its truth is made the test of a trustworthy man of science. A theory is only useful when it opens up a free course to inquiry; it is harmful if it limits the free course of inquiry. The facts themselves must always be the test of the theory, not the theory the test of the facts. To our mind 'philosophical natural science,' as it calls itself in these days, fails here; it succeeds admirably in fashioning the facts according to its hypotheses, and in making up for the lack of the former by the number of the latter."[1]

[1] *Die Schädelformen*, etc. p. 71. "Although there is no proof that in any single kind of animal or plant any permanent form has changed into any other, and although years may be required before such a proof could be obtained, not only does 'philosophical natural science' give us complete pedigrees, as Hæckel has done, but it also lavishes its theories on the public. It is true that men of science only consider these theories to be clever hypotheses, but they are received by the public as welcome teaching, as real coin, and they thus become part of their lives, and are used as weapons to controvert our science which is said to teach false doctrines."—G. Lucæ. See *Archiv für Anthr.* vi. 14.

Hæckel no doubt would protest against the accusation that the lack of facts is made up for by the number of hypotheses, and that he resembles the historian who fills up the gaps in his historical records by assumptions or suppositions. He does admit that he considers the "records of creation, as shown in the fossils," to be "extremely deficient and incomplete," and that he therefore thinks that many additions are necessary in order that he may fill up his pedigree. But he does not admit that these additions only owe their existence to his own penetration and fancy, and he says, "We fortunately possess, besides fossils, other records of the history of the origin of organisms, which in many cases are of no less value, nay, in several cases are of much greater value, than fossils. By far the most important of these other records is without doubt ontogeny, . . . and to the invaluable records of creation furnished by palæontology and ontogeny are added the no less important evidences for the blood-relationship of organisms furnished by comparative anatomy."[1]

Now, if we look more closely at these two records, it appears, first, that comparative anatomy can only give direct evidences as to the form relationship of organisms; it can only give evidence as to their blood relationship if it is a fact that form relationship involves blood relationship; and as this is just the point which is to be proved, according to the rules of ordinary logic it may not be assumed in the proof itself. No doubt it is strange that "in the hands or forepaws" of nine different mammals of which Hæckel gives drawings, we find that although "the external forms are

[1] *Nat. Schöpfungsgeschichte,* p. 361. Cf. p. 367 seq.

very different, there exist the same bones, and that these bones are in the same number, position, and connection, from the hand of man to the breast-fin of the seal and dolphin, and to the wing of the bat; and that even the wings of birds, and the fore-feet of reptiles and amphibious animals, are composed of essentially the same bones as the arms of man and the fore-legs of other mammals." These facts, and others which have been discovered by comparative anatomy, form the foundation of the natural system of the animal world, as it has been propounded by Cuvier and K. E. von Baer, but when Hæckel assures us, referring to the facts which have been mentioned, that "We can, from this circumstance alone, with perfect certainty infer the common origin of all these vertebrate animals; here, as in all other cases, the degree of the internal agreement in the form discloses to us the degree of blood relationship;"[1] this is a conclusion which must be proved in order to be justified, and is not proved by the mere repetition of the assertion.[2]

It is just the same with what Hæckel calls ontogeny, the history of the development of the organic individual.[3]

Every animal organism which is produced by sexual generation is, at the beginning of its individual existence, a simple egg, a single cell. Now, according to Hæckel, up to a certain stage of their existence, during the first state of the germ or embryo which springs from the egg, vertebrate animals are either quite indistinguishable from invertebrate, or can only be

[1] *Nat. Schöpfungsgeschichte*, p. 363.   [2] Michelis, *Hæckelogonie*, p. 78
[3] *Nat. Schöpfungsgeschichte*, p. 264; *Anthropogenie*, p. 6.

distinguished by their size or by unessential differences of form, and by the formation of the egg membranes.

In a later stage of development there is formed within the embryo a cylindrical tube, which is the foundation of the spinal marrow. At first it is pointed both before and behind, and it remains so for life in the lowest brainless vertebrate animals, while in all other vertebrate animals the fore end of the marrow tube becomes dilated, and changes into a' roundish bladder. This foundation of the brain is alike in all Craniotæ, that is, all vertebrate animals possessing skulls and brains. It is only at a later stage of development that a difference appears between the brains of mammals, of birds, and of reptiles, and at a later stage still that the brains of the different orders of mammals differ. It is the same with the other parts of the body. In short, Hæckel says, "All vertebrate animals of the most different classes, fishes, amphibious animals, reptiles, birds, and mammals, in the first periods of their embryonic development cannot be distinguished at all, and even much later, at a time when reptiles and birds are already distinctly different from mammals, the dog and the man are almost identical."[1]

On these observations Hæckel founds the "biogenetical law," that "ontogenesis, or the development of the individual, is a short and rapid summary of phylogenesis, or the development of the tribe to which it belongs; that is to say, the ancestors which form the chain of progenitors of the individual concerned." So that just as in the history of the development of the

[1] *Nat. Schöpfungsgeschichte*, p. 275.

individual there is a time at which the separate species of mammals resemble one another, and also a time when the separate kinds of vertebrata cannot be distinguished, in like manner there has been a time in the history of the earth when all kinds of animals, and another when what are now the separate kinds of vertebrata, existed not in different, but in similar forms, from which the later different forms were gradually developed.

In this "intimate connection of ontogeny and phylogeny," Hæckel "sees one of the most important and irrefutable proofs of the theory of descent." "For," he says, "if the development of the tribe were not the reason, the *causa efficiens* of the development of the germ, there would be no reason why the individual organism should develop at all, and should not be born at once in a complete condition."[1] We will let this "philosophical" argument stand on its own merits, and only inquire whether the analogy between ontogeny and phylogeny is really as perfect as Hæckel must wish it to be.[2]

Karl Ernst von Baer — to whom Hæckel has dedicated his last work, *Ziele und Wege der heutigen Entwicklungsgeschichte*, and whom he calls in that dedication "the honoured master of the History of Development," who fifty years ago gave to morphology its genetic foundation—expressly says that the statement that ontogeny is a short summary of phylogeny is "not substantiated." An individual, while it is being developed, does not go through a stage corresponding

---

[1] *Anthropogenie*, p. 291.
[2] Cf. E. von Hartmann, *Wahrheit und Irrthum des Darwinismus*, Berlin 1875, p. 11; J. B. Meyer, *Philos. Zeitfragen*, p. 110; Max Schasler, *Materialistische und idealistische Weltanschauung*, Berlin 1879, p. 27.

to every animal in the whole series, but proceeds from a general character to a more special one, and so on to the most special of all. "The progress of development," he says, "has four different stages, which I have called types, and which correspond very nearly to Cuvier's "Embranchements." All animals are developed in this way; first of all the original type is decided, and in this stage the histological and morphological difference is very slight, and only just beginning. As this difference increases, the embryo emerges from its first form into a variation of it, that is, from a class of animals into an order or a family, then it becomes still more limited, and so on, till at last the peculiarities of the individual make their appearance. At one stage the embryo has only the general characteristics of the vertebrata ; a little later it becomes evident to which class of animals it will belong, whether it will be a reptile, a bird, or a mammal ; later still the order appears, then the family," and so on. "Besides," adds Baer, "the original resemblance between the embryos of all vertebrata is exaggerated by Darwinians, those embryos which will possess gills (fish and amphibious animals) cannot be confounded with those which are to develop lungs (reptiles, birds, and mammals); the latter no doubt resemble one another, but are quite distinguishable by the difference in the egg membranes." At any rate, according to Baer, "the course of the development of all animal forms can only be very generally compared to the development of the single individual, and there is no detailed agreement between them."[1]

[1] *Studien*, pp. 244, 426.

Even Hæckel cannot adduce any more facts. He calls ontogeny a "short summary" of phylogeny, that is to say, if the different animal forms, which according to the theory of descent form the ancestral line of a higher organism, are called A B C D, etc., we find in the development of the individual only a fragment of this series of forms, perhaps A B D F H, etc., or B D H L, etc. Many evolutionary forms have therefore dropped out.[1] These "numerous and perceptible gaps" would be of less importance if at least "the succession of the forms remained really the same." But "the historical record" of an order or a family "which is contained in the history of the individual's development" is not only "erased by abridgement," but is also often "falsified by changes."[2] Baer says of these "falsifyings of development:" "They pass my comprehension, since I feel convinced the manner of nature's operations is a subject for investigation, falsifying can have no part in it, and if there appears to be such, it is because nature is wrongly understood."[3] At any rate in what he says about "erasure" and "falsification," Hæckel confesses that the desired analogy, and a similar succession, does not exist everywhere, and therefore he is forced to admit that even this "record of creation," which is "the most important of all to special phylogeny," is not "less incomplete" than palæontology, and that it has "great defects, and often leaves us in the lurch." "The ontogenesis of the higher animal forms of the present day gives us a very faint and false picture of the original mode in which

---

[1] *Anthropogenie*, p. 7.   [2] *Ibid.* p. 293; *Ziele und Wege*, etc. p. 76.
[3] *Studien*, p. viii.

their ancestors developed. It is only by proceeding very carefully and critically that we can argue directly from the history of the germ to that of the race. Besides, the history of the germ is as yet known to us only in the case of very few species."[1] This admission is certainly not calculated to weaken the charge that Hæckel has sometimes moulded the facts according to his own ideas, and has made up for the deficiency of the first by the number of the last. And it seems at least very doubtful whether Hæckel has really always employed the great care and criticism which he declares to be necessary. As regards this point, the gravest objections are made to a whole series of details by many eminent savants.[2]

In his *History of Creation* Hæckel places side by side drawings of the embryos of man, of the dog, the chick, and the tortoise. Rütimeyer[3] says bluntly that Hæckel has evidently taken the discoveries of other investigators and generalized from them for speculative purposes. And of another passage in which Hæckel compares the embryo of the dog, the chick, and the tortoise, Rütimeyer observes that it is simply the same woodcut reprinted three times with three different names. Now, he says, such a proceeding is simply "joking with the public and with science." He adds, "We pass over such things in second or third hand compilations, but when they occur in a history of creation, written by one well conversant with the microscope, and when, besides this, we find that Hæckel does not call these drawings rough designs, but says, 'If

[1] *Anthropogenie*, p. 375.
[2] Cf. Huber, *Zur Kritik*, etc. p. 31; Semper, *Der Hæckelismus*, pp. 30-35.
[3] *Archiv für Anthr.* iii. 301.

these embryos, figs. 9, 10, and 11, are compared, you will not be able to detect any difference between them,' it is time to protest. Fortunately the time has gone by when knowledge was prescribed according to the beliefs of a caste; but we do still believe that an earnest inquirer is bound not by a written obligation, but by an internal sense of duty, to consider himself not under the censorship of a congregation, but in the presence of the highest attainable standard of truth, and this under all circumstances and without any reservation, even when employing the microscope." [1]

His's opinion of the drawings in the *Anthropogenie* is not more favourable.[2] He says, "I have no hesitation in asserting that the drawings, in so far as they are original drawings of Hæckel's, are partly extremely inaccurate and partly simply invented." Semper assures us that he could add a great many examples to those given by His. Thus, for instance, the pictures of the embryo of an earthworm copied from Kowalevsky are completely falsified, those of the amphioxus are partly so; and besides this, the first is made use of as completely to reverse Kowalevsky's account of it. On one occasion Hæckel gives a picture of a very early stage in the development of human life as if he had seen it; as a matter of fact no biologist has as yet done so.[3] "Hæckel's mode of proceeding," says His, "is a frivolous trifling with facts, and it is even more

[1] In the later editions of the *Nat. Schöpfungsgeschichte* the drawings have been replaced by others, and the text on p. 272 slightly changed. Hæckel has also endeavoured to excuse himself in his pamphlet *Ziele un l Wege*, p. 37.
[2] *Unsere Körperform und das physiologische Problem ihrer Entstehung*, Leipzig 1875, p. 170.
[3] *Der Hæckelismus*, pp. 35, 32.

dangerous than the trifling with words which was previously condemned. The latter can be criticized by every intelligent thinker, but the former can only be detected by the specialist, and it is the more unpardonable in Hæckel because he is well aware of the widespread influence which he possesses."[1]

Considering the overbearing and positive manner in which Hæckel states his views, it is not superfluous occasionally to remind people how inaccurate and inexact he is in his treatment of facts; and to show that Rütimeyer is quite justified in saying that the "History of Creation," and the paper, *Ueber die Entstehung und den Stammbaum des Menschengeschlechts*, are " a kind of fancy literature which reminds us of times long gone by, when observations were employed only as mortar for the stones given us by fancy, whereas now-a-days we are accustomed to the opposite state of things." You will find in Michelis' *Hæckelogonie* a detailed scientific and philosophical criticism of Hæckel's pedigree.

But if men of science object to the reasons adduced by Darwin, Hæckel, and others in proof of the theory of descent, it does not follow that they oppose that theory on principle. Even Pfaff does not dispute the assumption of a genealogical connection between

[1] His adds these words, and Semper says that he entirely agrees with them. "I myself grew up in the belief that among all the qualifications of the scientific inquirer, trustworthiness and an absolute reverence for truth were the only ones which were indispensable. And I am still of opinion that if these qualifications are wanting, all the others, however brilliant they may be, are useless. I therefore leave others to admire in Herr Hæckel the active and reckless leader, *I* think that the way in which he has conducted the dispute entirely shuts him out from the ranks of sober and earnest inquirers."—Cf. Pfaff, *Schöpfungsgeschichte*, 2nd ed. p. 709.

the earlier and later fauna and flora, that is, the principle of descent as such; he only objects to Darwin's attempt to solve the problem, and he would "rather wait for the correct theory which will correspond to the facts, and seek for it, than be content with a false theory which distorts the facts."[1] And although philosophers and theologians oppose Darwin and Hæckel, it does not follow that they are opposed on principle to the theory of descent, or that they assert that it is impossible to harmonize the theory of descent, rightly understood, with the theory of creation. "It would be quite possible to suppose," says Michelis, "that the Creator had purposely chosen the method of developing the organic form genetically as the way of attaining to the perfect organization which in man was united to intellectual development. . . . The difference between this ideal conception of the theory of evolution, which does not deny the idea of creation, and Hæckel's pseudo-empirical, pseudo-philosophical monistic conception, which is essentially materialistic, would lie primarily in this, that in the one case the idea of the human organism as the end of the whole organization is supposed to be included in the plan of the Creator, in the other the organization perfects itself as if by chance without any guiding thought."[2] At any rate the assumption

---

[1] *Grundriss*, pp. 393, 399.

[2] *Hæckelogonie*, p. 42; cf. p. 55; cf. Huber, *Die Lehre Darwins*, p. 204; Zöckler, *Geschichte der Beziehungen*, ii. p. 714; Warington, *Week of Creation*, p. 109. Even in the *Dublin Review*, N. S. vol. xvii. (No. 33, July 1871), p. 4, it is not only admitted that the theory of evolution does not contradict the doctrine of the creation, but it is also said that the theory that all plants and animals have been developed from a single primordial form in no way contradicts the Bible (pp. 9, 15).

that the theory of descent is true, even if we include in it spontaneous generation, no more excludes the assumption of a Creator than does the assumption that the earth has been developed from a gaseous ball.[1] "If science could make us really understand," says Lotze,[2] "how the hard part of the earth's crust and the atmospheric air first separated themselves from the fiery ball; how at every step of this separation the elements, joined in elective affinities, found scope for new action; how, then, under the favourable conditions which were produced by the blind necessity of nature's course the first germ of a plant and of an animal originated, still simple and unformed and little suited for wide development; how at last, under favourable conditions brought about in part by this simple individual life, the organic being gradually grew nobler, and in the course of countless centuries how species developed into higher species until at last man came forth, not in the image of God, but as the last link in the chain of necessary events;—if science could make us understand all this, what would be gained? The miracle of the immediate creation would only be pushed back to an earlier period, in which endless Wisdom had implanted in this unsightly chaos the wonderful capacity for this ordered development. By describing the whole series of stages and epochs of development through which the original formless matter has passed during its evolution, it would only increase the splendour and multiplicity of the scenes in whose outward pomp our fancy could wonderingly lose itself; but it would not explain the wonderful

[1] See above, vol. i. p. 240.   [2] *Mikrokosmus*, i. p. 420.

spectacle any better than does the acquiescent faith which traces back the origin of living creatures to the immediate creating will of God. We may fearlessly wait until science, with its impartial love of truth, has decided these questions in so far as science ever will decide them; whatever may have been the method of creation chosen by God, none will make the world more independent of Him, or knit it more closely to Him."[1]

I now come to the point which has really attracted the attention of the public to the Darwinian theory of descent, and to the controversy which has arisen on it, that is, to the question whether this theory can also be applied to man, or to make use of the popular expression, whether man is descended from the ape.

To-day I will confine myself to one point only, which, according to Hæckel, is the most important, and that is the "Pithecoid Theory," as he calls the theory that man is descended from the ape. Hæckel calls it the "philosophical confirmation of the human pedigree." I think

---

[1] "From Aristotle down to Humboldt men of science thought that the primary causes of the phenomenal world, the beginning of existence, the creation, lie outside man and before any observation, and therefore are without the limits of exact natural science. We cannot lay too much stress on this irrefutable truth, for all the materialistic attacks of modern natural science are only possible because this truth is steadily ignored, and because the axioms of natural philosophy are made use of instead of the exact results of research. No one can find fault if the inquirer says, For me and for my scientific researches there exist only secondary causes; the primary causes lie outside and before all observation. But if in describing the secondary causes which are seen at work in the creation the man of science thinks that he has found the primary causes, and by this means has solved the problem of creation, he is encroaching on other territory, and only displays his folly."—Fabri, *Briefe gegen den Materialismus*, Stuttgard 1864, p. 246.

that when I have discussed this "philosophical confirmation," I may in future leave aside all that Hæckel calls philosophical, and spare you the criticism of any more of such philosophical confirmations. He says, "As all the general series of appearances in the lives of animals and plants which are known to us, completely correspond to the theory that all organic beings are descended from a single form, or from a few quite simple common forms, and as no single appearance contradicts this assumption, we are quite justified in placing the theory of evolution or descent, as a great general *law of induction*, at the summit of all sciences of organic nature — at the summit of zoology and botany. But if the theory of evolution is in truth a necessary and general *inductive law*, its application to man is also a necessary particular *deductive law*, it is a theory which necessarily and inevitably follows from the first."[1] Hæckel explains the philosophical expressions, induction and deduction, on whose meaning, as he says, everything here depends, by the following example. Comparative anatomy enabled Goethe to confirm the general inductive law, that all mammals possess a pair of median upper jawbones—lying between the two halves of the upper jaw and (the premaxillaries) holding the upper incisors,—and from this fact he drew the deductive conclusion that man, who in all other bodily conditions does not differ essentially from other mammals, *must* possess such a bone; he asserted this without having seen a human premaxillary bone, and only proved its existence afterwards by observation.

[1] *Ueber die Entstehung*, etc. p. 27. See *Nat. Schöpfungsgeschichte*, p. 646; *Anthropogenie*, pp. 83, 371; cf. Michelis, *Hæckelogonie*, p. 103.

Parenthetically, I may say that I am not sure whether men of science would have been actually much impressed by Goethe's deductive conclusion that man *must* have a premaxillary bone, if it had not been possible actually to prove that he does possess one. "Deduction therefore," continues Hæckel, "is an inference from the general to the particular; induction, on the other hand, is an inference from the particular to the general. If from the resemblance of all vertebrata in form, structure, development, and phenomena of life, we infer that all vertebrata are descended from a single common form, this is an inductive inference. But if we go on to postulate a like descent for man, who resembles the other vertebrata in all essential points, this is a deductive inference. This deductive inference from the general to the particular is surer and more certain just in proportion as the inductive inference, which lies at its base, is sure and certain. But as the latter really rests on the broadest inductive basis, we may look upon the former as quite as certain. We must lay the greatest weight on the philosophical confirmation of the human pedigree," and therefore Hæckel repeatedly comes back to this "philosophical confirmation."

I think that this might be much more simply expressed according to the old scholastic logic, *per modum syllogismi*.

"All vertebrate animals are descended from one common ancestral form; man is a vertebrate animal, therefore man also is descended from this common ancestral form." There is nothing to be said against the conclusion, it is only the premisses which are in question. If the major and minor are right, the thing is settled; if either the major or minor are wrong, the argument comes to nothing. The correctness of the major stands and falls with the correctness of Hæckel's theory of development. I have spoken of this in sufficient detail. We will now more carefully examine the minor premise, namely, that man is a vertebrate animal, like all other vertebrate animals.

XXVIII.

MAN AND BEAST.

LINNÆUS begins his division of the animal world in this way: *A*. Mammalia; I. Primates: (1) Homo, *a*. diurnus—man; *b*. nocturnus—orang-outang and chimpanzee; (2.) Simia; (3) Lemur; (4) Vespertilio, etc. More modern zoologists give the following division: *A*. Vertebrata; I. Mammalia; (1) Man; (2) Apes, etc.

This division is as objectionable as possible. Man does not form a species which is co-ordinate with the apes, and which can be classed with these and other animals as units of the higher terms mammals and vertebrata. The only higher term in which both man and animals can be comprised is animal in the sense of a living visible being. The first division which can be made according to this theory is animal, rational and irrational; for the fact that man is a being gifted with reason is undoubtedly more fitted to be used as *differentia specifica* than the fact that he has a vertebral column and brings forth living young.[1] It is much

---

[1] "Very eminent zoologists think that because the children of men come into the world alive, and are suckled, and because man's anatomical structure resembles that of the mammals, he is nothing but a mammal with two feet and two hands. There lies between man and the most reasonable (?) animal an immensurable gulf which can never be bridged over by any other creature. The spiritual power which certainly forms part of the organization is nowhere displayed more clearly in man than in his recognition of the all-powerful Creator, in his power of investigating the laws of the immense universe, and of using the forces of nature for his

more correct to say, with Isidor Geoffroy St. Hilaire, A. de Quatrefages,[1] and others, that man forms a special province in nature which is distinguished from the animal world just as clearly as and even more clearly than the animal world is distinguished from the vegetable or mineral worlds.

But the question as to man's rightful place in the system of nature is comparatively unimportant when we consider the efforts which have been made to connect man genealogically with animals in general and with apes in particular. I need not discuss the earlier efforts to prove this, made by Lamarck, the author of *Vestiges of the Natural History of Creation*, and others, because this question has been more fully and in a certain sense more fundamentally debated recently than was even possible in former times. The theory that man is related to the ape has not only received fresh support from the development in the theory of descent which has taken place since it was first promulgated by Darwin, but has also been apparently strengthened by the fact that in the last few decades we have acquired more knowledge of the apes which most resemble man, the so-called anthropoid apes— the gibbon and the orang in South-eastern Asia, the chimpanzee and the gorilla in Western Africa.[2]

---

service."—H. von Meyer, *Die Reptilien*, etc. p. 115. Giebel, *Tagesfragen*, p. 50, says: "According to his essential zoological characteristics man is a mammal, and a mammal with nails, whose little toe is furnished with a nail;" but on p. 58 he adds: "The essential part of man is his spirit, and in comparison with this the zoological characteristics lose their importance. Things can only be compared with their equals, stones with stones, plants with plants, animals with animals, and man with man."

[1] *Unité de l'espèce hum*, p. 15 ; *Rapport*, p. 71.

[2] R. Hartmann, *Die Menschenähnlichen Affen*, 1876.

Darwin himself, as I have said before, only extended his theory of descent specially to man in his later work " The Descent of Man," which appeared in 1871. His followers propounded this development of his theory even before he did.[1] Huxley discussed the question in 1863 in a very learned book, which, as we must acknowledge with praise, is written without any of the frivolity so disagreeable in others; on the contrary it is earnest and, in so far as is compatible with its tendency, exalted in tone. After him Vogt discussed the subject in his *Vorlesungen über den Menschen*. A writer in criticizing this book[2] observes: " Any one who knows Karl Vogt will guess even before he has cut the two volumes that he seizes on this relationship to the ape with great gusto. And in fact he sometimes seems to have a cannibal delight in it. But," adds the writer truly, " one could not be prepared for his really admirable portrayal of the differences between men and apes. We have never read anything more exhaustive on this question; we have never felt more deeply the enormous gulf which divides us from

[1] At first man was only included in the circle of observation in order to make the theory consistent; but it was very natural that when once this step had been taken, efforts should be made to justify it by facts. In a short time so many observations were forthcoming, all of which seemed so undoubtedly to prove that the lord of creation was descended from the mammals most nearly related to him, that a great deal of prejudice and stupidity seemed to be required in order to dispute this new doctrine. Some even went so far as to assert that no real difference existed between man and the ape. The more decided these statements are, the more are we justified in inquiring whether they are founded on fact. No doubt in doing this we occasionally get rather strange notions of the proceedings of exact science, for we find that in reality what it gives us as proofs of the most startling conclusions are really only unconnected and sometimes simply contradictory fragments. Aeby, *Die Schädelformen*, p. 71.

[2] Ausland, 1864, p. 697.

the most highly organized animals, than in reading the pages of this atheistic cynic." This is not a joke, but sober earnest, and although a little exaggerated is on the whole correct. I shall often make use of Vogt's description in what follows. But, as we have seen, Hæckel is the most enthusiastic preacher of the doctrine of man's relationship to the ape. Many writers of lesser note and bookmakers have joined these three principal allies of Darwin.

Most of those who defend the theory of man's relationship to the apes think it well to begin or to end their argument by assuring us that there is nothing lowering or disgraceful to man in their theory. Hæckel even says that it will "everywhere have an enlightening and ennobling effect, and thus will lead men more and more towards their eternal goal through the light of truth to the joy of liberty."[1] "There is one thought," says another apostle of this doctrine,[2] "which reconciles us to the conclusions of science so startling to human feeling; man is not descended from the ape, this form was the last he broke through, the last veil he threw off, the mark beneath which the finer form developed, as the butterfly from its chrysalis, which came from the caterpillar as did the caterpillar from the egg. Thus everything in nature becomes a parable, because one law governs the whole."[3] Natural science places man just as high as do the

---

[1] *Entstehung*, pp. 35, 36.

[2] Schaaffhausen in the *Archiv für Anthropologie*, ii. 336, 340; cf. Darwin, *Descent of Man*; Strauss, *Der alte und der neue Glaube*, p. 194.

[3] "The frog is but a humble offshoot of the main line terminating in the Primates. There is something more like a lineal predecessor of the order in the Labyrinthodon of Owen, that massive batrachian which leaves its hand-like footsteps in the new red sandstone, and then is seen no

philosopher and the poet; but natural science alone can trace the way by which he has attained to this height. When we see at the height of his fame a man who was born in a poor cottage, and has attained to might and happiness through his own efforts, do we not admire him much more than the man who boasts of his inherited riches. So it is with our race. For this reason we are not ashamed to look back into the past; it is our surest proof of a better future. We have ideals beyond our own nature, but we try to reach them, and we can in reality approach them. Is not the golden age, which our poets sing of as a lost good, as a past splendour, and also as an undeserved happiness, is not that golden age more beautiful if it lies before instead of behind us, if we must first win that which we have never possessed?"

No Christian at any rate will be able to tranquillize himself with such edifying thoughts as these, and if it were as true as it is false that man's descent from the beast is "a scientific conclusion," with this would vanish, as Frohschammer[1] and others have well said, not only the poets' descriptions of the Golden Age, but also the Christian doctrines of the creation, and the original state of man. Theologians therefore have every reason, not to " become enthusiastic about the

---

more. Not for nothing is it that we start at the picture of that strange impression,—ghost of anticipated humanity,—for apparently it really is so. In these things the superficial thinker will only see matter of ridicule; the large-hearted and truly devout man, who puts nothing of nature away from him, will, on the contrary, discover in them interesting traces of the ways of God to man, and a deeper breathing of the lesson that whatever lives is to him kindred."—*Vestiges of the Natural History of Creation*, 6th ed. p. 217.

[1] *Das Christenthum*, p. 126.

results of natural science," but to try and prove scientifically that the theory of the genealogical connection between man and beast is *not* a "scientific conclusion." It is more than foolish to attempt to set them at rest by asserting that S. Augustine gave "an encouragement to free inquiry," when he said that "it is childish to suppose that God formed man from the dust of the earth with bodily hands and breathed on him with His throat and lips."[1] As if any theologian who was worthy of the name had ever imagined that the creation of men took place in this way, and as if S. Augustine by combating such an idea had become an advocate of the "Pithecoid Theory."

Let us now consider the proofs for the doctrine of man's descent from the animals. Hæckel has carried back the pedigree to the monera;[2] from these in the Silurian age the tube-hearted skullless vertebrata had developed, a class of animals whose sole survivor in the present day is the Lancelet (Amphioxus), which therefore we must regard with special veneration as the only animal now existing which can enable us to form an

---

[1] "Theologians who are anxious about the conclusions of natural science should remember what one of the greatest of the Fathers, S. Augustine, has said about the creation of man. In his work, *De Genesi* (*ad lit.*) i. 6, c. 12, he says: "It is childish to suppose that God formed man from the dust of the earth with bodily hands;" and in another place, i. 7, c. 1 and 17, he says: "As God did not form man with bodily hands, so neither did He breathe on him from His throat and lips. . . . It is said that God breathed into man's face, because the fore part of the brain where the senses are situated is in the forehead." This is an encouragement to free inquiry, which is the more honourable to him who gave it when it is remembered at what time these words were written. *Archiv für Anthr.* ii. p. 340; cf. above, vol. i. p. 149.

[2] *Entstehung*, p. 40 seq.; *Nat. Schöpfungsgeschichte*, p. 578; *Anthropogenie*, p. 494.

approximate conception of our earliest Silurian vertebrate ancestors.[1] In the later Silurian age "man's ancestors were real sharks, or at any rate resembled them very nearly." The sharks developed into mud-fish, "vertebrata which stand midway between fish and amphibia;" these into gilled Batrachia, "Amphibia like the celebrated Proteus anguineus, which inhabits the grotto of Adelsberg;" these again into tailed Batrachia, "resembling the present salamanders and newts;" then in the beginning of the secondary period the beaked animals (Ornithostoma) appeared, "mammals of the lowest class resembling the beaked animals in Australia and Tasmania" (Ornithorhyncus paradoxus and Echidna hystrix); after them the Marsupialia, "resembling the kangaroos," and after them in the beginning of the tertiary period came the semi-apes (Prosimiæ), then the tailed apes (Catarrhini) with narrow noses, without cheek pouches, and with tails, and then man-like apes (Anthropoids) without tails. Formerly Hæckel asserted that the ape-like man, or primary man, resembling the woolly haired Papuan negroes but of a lower class, had developed directly from these anthropoid apes. Now he says, " Although the ancestors of the stage immediately preceding are already so nearly akin to genuine men that it is scarcely necessary to assume that an intermediate connecting stage existed, still we may consider the speechless primæval men (Alali), or ape-like men (Pithecanthropi)

---

[1] Hæckel defends this observation in the *Anthropogenie*, p. 337, and he there repeats that "the Amphioxus is flesh of our flesh and blood of our blood." It is also, as he assures us twice over in the *Anthropogenie* (pp. 176, 298), "the most interesting of all vertebrate animals after man."

as such." And directly afterwards he says, "There is certain proof that such primæval men without the power of speech, or ape-like men, must have preceded man possessing speech, in the results obtained by an inquiring mind from comparative philology."[1]

You will allow me to pass over the earlier stages of the pedigree, and only to speak of our supposed nearest relatives, the anthropoid apes. Most of the supporters of the Pithecoid theory say with Hæckel,[2] that man is not descended from any of the now existing kinds of apes; on the contrary, they assert that the human race is descended "from a branch of the group of Catarrhini, long ago extinct, which, under favourable conditions, probably in Southern Asia, perhaps in a continent, Lemuria, now sunk under the Indian Ocean, became by natural selection, in the Pliocene or Miocene Age, the ancestor of the human race."

Let us therefore first ascertain whether the resemblance between the bodily constitution of man and the highest class of apes now existing is great enough to make it necessary to assume scientifically that both are descended from common ancestors.

---

[1] *Nat. Schöpfungsgeschichte,* p. 590; *Anthropogenie,* p. 491.

[2] *Entstehung,* p. 42; *Nat. Schöpfungsgeschichte,* p. 577. Hæckel is not right in saying that it is self-evident that none of the apes now existing could be the ancestors of the human race, or in assuring us that this opinion had *never* been held by thoughtful supporters of the theory of descent, but had been attributed to them by their thoughtless opponents (see also Virchow, *Menschen und Affenschädel,* p. 22). Schaafhausen says (see *Archiv für Anthr.* ii. 336): "Several zoologists have asserted recently that man is not descended from any of the existing species of apes, and they assume without sufficient reason that both apes and men had a common ancestor." He thinks that possibly this is done in order to make the relationship less repulsive, as fancy might paint these unknown apes in more attractive colours.

H. Burmeister says,[1] "Man is distinguished from the ape in his bodily form, by the greater development of brain, by the structure of the skeleton, which is intended for an upright posture, by the greater development of the pelvis, and by the striking typical difference in the extremities, for whereas in man the fore extremities, never the hinder, are the only true hands, in the ape, on the contrary, the hinder extremities are hands, and the fore extremities are more like paws, sometimes even having no thumbs."

I will let Vogt give us a commentary on these assertions. I shall keep to his own words[2] all through, of course leaving out as far as is possible the bad jokes and other irrelevant scurrilities with which he interlards his style.

Man is absolutely distinguished from the ape by his upright position which the ape only assumes, or is taught to assume, occasionally, but which he does not possess as a natural bodily quality. Man's arms and hands, which hang unfettered by his side, are left unhindered in their movements, and are suited to the several actions for which they are required by being detached from the ground, and by being entirely freed from the necessity of serving as supports to the body. On the other hand, even in the most manlike apes, the forehand is used for climbing just as much as the hinder; if the ape is moving on even ground, he always after a few steps supports himself on his closed hand, and by this means assumes a position which is more or less horizontal, according to the length of his arms. The arm in man is comparatively shorter, the leg longer

[1] *Geschichte der Schöpfung.* p. 371.   [2] *Vorlesungen*, i. 169 seq.

and stronger than in the ape. If man is put in the position which is natural to a quadruped, he is obliged to straighten out his arms, and to bend his knees considerably if the vertebral column is to be brought into a horizontal position parallel with the ground. In apes, on the other hand, either both limbs are equally long, or the leg is shorter than the arm, which in some apes is of immense length. A man standing quite upright can touch the middle of the upper part of his thigh with his fingers, the chimpanzee can touch the knee-cap, the gorilla can reach even farther, the orang can, without bending, even touch his ankles. If we look at the proportions of the different parts of the arm the difference is even more apparent. Supposing the length of the bone of the upper part of the arm to be 100, the length of the forearm is 75·5 in white men, in the chimpanzee 90·8; the length of the hand in the white man is 52·9, in the chimpanzee 73·7; in the other apes, especially in the orang, these differences are still more striking. The upper part of the arm is therefore comparatively shorter in the ape than in man, the forearm and hand longer. The difference in the leg is still more pronounced. If we take the length of the thigh bone as 100, we find that in the European the shinbone is 82·5, the foot 52·9; while in the chimpanzee the shinbone is reckoned at 80, and the foot 72·8. Here then it is the extremity which reaches a far greater length. But look at the difference between this extremity and the human foot. It is a real hand. The fingers no doubt are rather shorter and broader, the thumb larger and thicker than on the forehand, but still it is a real hand with a flat under surface, well separated, moveable long fingers, with thick opposable thumbs, and a long narrow deeply-furrowed palm. If we compare the print of this hand to a human foot, we see how right Burmeister was when he said in his excellent paper in the *Geologische Bilder*, that the foot was the real characteristic of man.[1]

Hæckel no doubt remarks, appealing to Huxley for confirmation, that all real apes are just as much two-handed animals as man, or to put it the other way, that man is just as much a four-handed animal as the ape; he says that many tribes of negroes can use their feet as a "hinder hand," and when they climb trees grasp boughs with it just like the "four-handed apes," etc.; of course, too, Hæckel gives us a picture in which a chimpanzee, a gorilla, an orang, and a negro are seen sitting on a tree together.[2] But it has been proved that these statements about the prehensile foot in man are totally incorrect;[3] Huxley's statement, to which Hæckel still refers, was contradicted years ago by several anatomists, and the saying that "only man

---

[1] "Der Menschliche Fuss als Character der Menschheit," *Geol. Bilder*, i. pp. 63-142. Recent investigations have confirmed this. A. Ecker the anatomist says, "I have shown that the special characteristics of the hand are the opposable thumbs, the long prehensile fingers fitted for grasping, and the general mobility of the whole, while those of the foot are the arched shape, the short and unprehensile toes, and the impossibility of stretching the bone of the great toe far from the others; the reader will therefore see clearly that the foot in noway resembles the hinder extremity of the ape, but that the latter is much more like a hand, and therefore should be called a hind hand. It is only in man that the foot is exclusively a means of support, and the hand exclusively a prehensile organ. Man alone has hands and feet."—*Correspondenz-blatt der deutschen Gesellschaft für Anthropologie*, 1881, p. 91.

[2] *Anthropogenie*, p. 480. *Nat. Schöpfungsgeschichte*, p. 569.

[3] Gerland, *Anthropolog. Beiträge*, Halle 1875, i. p. 185; cf. Huber, *Zur Kritik*, etc. p. 36.

has an upright gait, the four-handed animal is suited to an arboreal life, and moves on even ground very imperfectly on all fours,"[1] has received fresh confirmation. "All apes are more or less climbers; trees are their natural home; not one can walk in the proper sense of the word."[2]

As regards the head,—Vogt goes on to say,—and the development of the two parts which compose it, the skull and the face, in man the upper part is predominant, the lower, or rather the hinder part, in the ape. The (anatomical) face, comprised between the eyebrows, the chin, and the ear, is only a small appendage to the human skull,[3] which overlaps it on every side, projecting over the eyebrows in the forehead, over the side in the temples, over the neck at the back of the head, and by this means affording space for the unproportionably large brain; whereas in the apes the brain case is less apparent, the forehead is quite flat, or entirely disappears behind the overhanging eyebrows, and the occipital foramen is so far back that in the lowest apes it is situated almost entirely in the posterior face of the skull; in the others it is mostly at the back of the skull. (In apes the occipital foramen is situated in the posterior

---

[1] Lucæ in the *Archiv. für Anthr.* vi. 15, 27.

[2] Virchow, *Menschen und Affenschädel*, p. 27. Cf. Huber, *Zur Kritik*, etc. p. 35. Rauch, *Einheit des Menschengeschlechts*, p. 396. Baer, *Studien*, p. 312.

[3] "The history of the development of the face is exactly the opposite of that of the cranium; the higher stages of development are characterized by a decrease, not by an increase in its size. . . . Man possesses the smallest face, if not absolutely, at least in comparison to the size of the cranium, and this peculiarity exists everywhere, in spite of the difference in the prognathism, and in the length of the hinder skull."—Aeby, *Die Schädelformen*, etc. pp. 77, 80.

third of the base of the skull, in man it is usually in the centre, or even a little more forward.) In spite of the fact that the gorilla and the Australian negro (the lowest race of men) are of about the same height, the skull of the latter is one and a half times larger, and this is even more remarkable when we remember that the legs of the gorilla are comparatively shorter, and the trunk therefore bigger and more powerful. The smallest cranium measured by Morton, belonging to a man who was not an idiot, measured 63 cubic inches, the largest gorilla skull yet measured is $34\frac{1}{2}$ inches. If we compare the size of the cranium with the facial bones, and if we take the whole length of the skull as 100, and ascertain the proportion of the length of the cranium, that is, of the brain itself to the skull, we have the following figures:—European, 89·1; Australian, 78·7; orang, 47·7; gorilla, 45·9 : the proportions of the facial bones are consequently, European, 10·9; Australian, 21·3; orang, 52·3; gorilla, 54·1. Whatever we may say, and however we may look at the facts, we shall always find this important difference in the formation of the skulls of men and the apes which is shown by the comparison of the cranium and the facial bones. As we have seen in the case of the anthropoid apes, the length of the cranium never equals half the whole length of the skull, whereas among the lowest men the length of the facial bones is only an unimportant part of the whole, and even in the Australian it does not attain to even a quarter of the whole.

Thus far Vogt. Huxley's comparisons give us the same results. I will therefore quote only a few of the more general statements. "The differences between a gorilla's skull and a man's are truly immense." "The structural differences between man and even the highest apes are great and significant; every bone of a gorilla bears marks by which it might be distinguished from the corresponding bone of a man."[1]

As regards the brain, that of man is, no doubt, not absolutely the largest, for the brains of the elephant, the whale, and the narwhal are far larger. But as Huxley says, it must not be overlooked that there is a very striking difference in absolute mass and weight between the lowest human brain and that of the highest ape,—a difference which is all the more remarkable when we recollect that a full-grown gorilla is probably pretty nearly twice as heavy as a Bushman, or as many a European woman. It may be doubted whether a healthy human brain ever weighed less than 31 or 32 ounces; or whether the heaviest gorilla brain has exceeded 20 ounces.[2] The rule that man's brain is the largest in proportion to the weight of his body is not, however, without exception, for some of the smaller birds probably possess a brain which is relatively larger.[3] But still there is no doubt that the human brain differs very markedly from the animal brain, a conclusion which has been arrived at by many anatomists, however widely they may differ as to details.[4]

---

[1] *Evidences as to Man's Place in Nature*, pp. 76, 104.
[2] *Evidences*, p. 102. [3] Tiedemann, *Das Hirn des Negers*, p. 14 seq.
[4] Cf. Moleschott, *Der Kreislauf des Lebens*, 4th ed., p. 413 seq. Th. Bischoff in the *Wissenschaftlichen Vorträgen* held at Munich, Brunswick 1851, p. 313. Peschel, *Völkerkunde*, p. 63. J. B. Meyer, *Philos. Zeitfragen*, p. 173. Huber, *Zur Kritik*, etc. p. 39.

In addition to this anatomical difference there is a still greater difference with respect to bodily development. "Apes," says Virchow, "have generally a short life and a rapid development; they are born in a condition of bodily and spiritual maturity which occurs in animals but never in man; their farther development takes place in a few years, and an early death brings their life to a close. Although we are not fully informed as to the absolute duration of life among the anthropoid apes, it is questionable whether any one of them attains to the age at which the growth of man ceases; and it is at any rate certain that even the highest apes have reached their full development when man is still in early youth. They have arrived at sexual maturity at an age when man has not outgrown childhood. Still more characteristic is the difference as to the time when the various parts of the body develop. The brain of the ape grows less than any other part of his body; it is usually completed before the change of teeth takes place, whereas in man the real development only begins then. In the ape, directly after the change of teeth, there begins the quick growth of the jaws and facial bones, and the enormous increase in the outer parts of the skull, which are the distinguishing marks of the bestial character." [1]

[1] Virchow, *Menschen und Affenschädel*, p. 25. "Their hairiness and the position of the hair, their body of three feet in length, their far greater limitation as to climate and food, their life of only thirty years, are other important characteristics which show the difference between apes and men. The slow growth, long childhood, and late arrival at puberty, the absence of any special breeding time, and of all strongly developed instincts, menstruation, a great many special diseases, the power of speech, laughter and tears,—these are other physiological characteristics of man which separate him from the ape and have the greatest influence on the whole development of his life."—Th. Waitz, *Anthropologie*, i. 104.

In spite of all these differences between man and the ape, Huxley thinks that we may assume that they are descended from a common stock, because the anatomical differences between man and the gorilla, or any other of the highest apes, although great, are not so great as those between the highest apes and several of the lower apes. He says: "The pelvis, or bony girdle of the hips, of man is a strikingly human part of his organization, the expanded haunch-bones affording support for his viscera during his habitually erect posture, and giving space for the attachment of the great muscles which enable him to assume and to preserve that attitude. In these respects the pelvis of the gorilla differs very considerably from his. But go no lower than the gibbon, and see how vastly more he differs from the gorilla than the latter does from man even in this structure. Look at the flat narrow haunch-bones, — the long and narrow passage, — the coarse outwardly curved, ischiatic prominences on which the gibbon habitually rests, and which are coated by the so-called 'callosities,' dense patches of skin, wholly absent in the gorilla, in the chimpanzee, in the orang, as in man. In the lower monkeys and in the lemurs the difference becomes more striking still, the pelvis acquiring an altogether quadrupedal character." It is the same with the jaw. "Thus while the teeth of the gorilla closely resemble those of man in number, kind, and in the general pattern of their crowns, they exhibit marked differences from those of man in secondary respects, such as relative size, number of fangs, and order of appearance. But if the teeth of a gorilla be compared with those of an ape, no farther removed from it than a baboon (Cynocephalus), it will be found that differences and resemblances of the same order are easily observable; but that many of the points in which the gorilla resembles man are those in which it differs from the baboon; while various respects in which it differs from man are exaggerated in the former. . . . Passing from the Old World apes to the monkeys of the New World, we meet with a change of much greater importance than any of these. In such a genus as Cebus, for example, it will be found that while in some secondary points, such as the projection of the canine and the diastema, the resemblance to the great ape is preserved, in other and most important respects the dentition is extremely different. Instead of twenty teeth in the milk set there are twenty-four, instead of thirty-two teeth in the permanent set there are thirty-six, etc. . . . Hence it is obvious that greatly as the dentition of the highest ape differs from that of man, it differs far more widely from that of the lower apes and lowest monkeys."[1]

Thus Huxley comes to the conclusion that the anatomical differences which separate man from the gorilla and the chimpanzee are not so great as those which separate the gorilla from the lowest monkeys.[2] Darwin thinks that Huxley has proved this,[3] and Hæckel refers again and again to this "law" which has been proved by Huxley in a "masterly, convincing, and final" manner; and which "translated into the language of phylogeny is synonymous with the popular

---

[1] *Evidences*, pp. 76, 83 seq. [2] P. 104.
[3] *Descent of Man*, i. 191. Strauss, *Der alte und der neue Glaube*, p. 195.

saying, man is descended from the ape."[1] He calls the opposition which Huxley's law still encounters in many quarters "entirely unfounded and ineffectual." He does not even mention the names of those who opposed it, much less the reasons on which they founded their opposition, and yet those who after careful investigations have contradicted Huxley's statement, which has been converted by Hæckel into a "law," are eminent savants.

Lucæ has proved circumstantially, after examining several of the apes belonging both to the Old and to the New World, that the form of the bones of their hinder and fore extremities does not bear out Huxley's statement,[2] and that part of the statement which deals with the important point of the brain and skull has been proved to be incorrect by Aeby, Th. Bischoff, and others. Aeby states the conclusions which, before Lucæ wrote, he had arrived at, after numerous and careful measurements and comparisons, in this way:[3] "The result of all this is to show that on the whole the difference between man and the highest apes is greater than that between the apes themselves, and we therefore do not for an instant hesitate to assert that the human type of cranium is most markedly different from that of the ape; and that the so-called anthropoid apes in every way resemble their natural relatives, and even the lower kinds of mammals, incomparably more than they resemble man. We cannot judge of the skull from one detail, from one point of view,

---

[1] *Anthropogenie*, pp. 478, 483, 487, 489, 697. *Nat. Schöpfungsgeschichte*, pp. 572, 574. *Generelle Morphologie*, ii. p. 153. *Ueber die Entstehung*, etc. p. 61.

[2] Cf. *Archiv für Anthr.* vi. 15, v. 520.   [3] *Die Schädelformen*, pp. 77, 82.

we must consider its whole shape, and this enables us to estimate it rightly, and to compare it with others. But if we compare in this way man and the ape, we see, of course, that they as well as all other vertebrate animals are formed as it were on a common ground-plan, but that on this ground-plan entirely different structures are erected. Their formation actually corresponds very seldom in any single detail, more often it only appears to do so; as a whole they have nothing in common. In the whole series of mammals there is no gap which could be distantly compared with that which separates man from the ape.[1] Even the lowest human skulls are so far removed from the highest ape skulls in every way, and approach so much more nearly to those of their higher relatives, that from a purely morphological point of view it were

[1] On p. 78 Aeby gives a table of the different heights of the cranium. Marten, 35; Gorilla, 82; Hylobates, Pithecus Satyrus, 98; Man, smallest height (Conga), 123—medium height, 146; and he observes, "We see how much the height increases towards the end of the list. Beginning with 35 in the marten, it gradually increases to 98 in the orang, and then suddenly rises to 146 in man. It is an important fact that each of the 63 degrees within which animals vary (35 to 98) corresponds regularly to a special form, and that there is no large gap within these degrees. The series of forms proceeds gradually up to the highest ape, and it is quite unbroken. It is entirely different with man. There is an interval of quite 48 degrees between the average man and the last of the animal forms. If we consider individual characteristics and go downwards to the last link in the chain which only occurs occasionally, there still remains an interval of 25 degrees which is never filled. This is the more remarkable, because on both sides of this interval the dimensions vary considerably. Huxley says that the gorilla is nearer to man than to the lowest of his own relatives. This assertion evidently by no means corresponds to the facts, because we find that the distance between the gorilla and the average man is 64, and that even from the lowest man it is 41 degrees, so that the gorilla is really much farther from man than even from the marten, and is as far from the latter as from the lion. The chain of development breaks off suddenly with the highest ape, and begins again much farther on with man."

better to give up the disagreeable expression of resemblance to monkeys. The ostentation with which this expression is used is the less justifiable because it does not correspond to the real state of the case, and can only engender erroneous impressions. Even the superficial likeness is not so great as has often been asserted. If we attach so much importance to this, we certainly must not look for it among the so-called manlike apes; we must rather look to the gibbon or the small American monkeys. At any rate their skulls bear the greatest resemblance to the human skull, although in many other ways they do not stand so high." Giebel speaks in the same strain. "Our comparisons lead us to the conclusion that nowhere in all the series of mammals is there such an enormous gap, with reference to the morphology of the skull, as that which separates the skulls of men from those of apes."[1]

Aeby also discusses the assertion that the difference between man and the ape is less apparent in youth than in the adult condition. He lays stress on the fact that this assertion rests principally on the comparison between young apes and grown men;[2] a comparison between

---

[1] "Eine antidarwinistische Vergleichung der Menschen und Orang-schädel," *Zts. für die ges. Naturwiss.* 28th vol. (1866) p. 401; cf. Huber, *Die Lehre Darwins*, p. 133.

[2] "Earlier anatomists who have written on the structure of the simiæ, founded all their observations on orangs of immature age; hence their remarks on the facial angle, teeth, and the relative proportions of the cranium and face are erroneous when applied to the adult animal, and have led, as Mr. Owen has clearly proved, to an opinion that the transition from mankind to the simiæ is much more gradual than it really is. It is well known that in the immature and undeveloped state, anatomical relations are in many instances nearer than they appear when the entire being is perfected and prepared for all the functions for which nature has destined it."—Prichard, *Researches*, etc. i. 286. "The resemblance between young apes and human children is much greater than that between old

the skulls of men and apes of the same age, which he himself has made, shows that no doubt there is a slight likeness between the types in youth, but that it is not nearly enough to overthrow the assertion that there is a sharp distinction between the human and apish skulls. They are really entirely different, even in the first stage, and at all times the gap between man and the ape is incomparably greater than that between the ape and the other animals."[1]

With regard to the development of the brain, Th. Bischoff gives us the following as the result of his observations. "The brains of man, of the orang, chimpanzee, and gorilla are nearly related, in spite of the great differences between them. But if we compare in succession the human brain with that of an orang, the brain of the latter with that of a chimpanzee, and so on through a hylobates, semnopithecus, etc. . . . we shall nowhere find a larger, or nearly so large a gulf, in the brain development of two of the series, as we find between the brains of man and the orang or chimpanzee. The gulf which separates the convolutions of a man's brain from the convolutions in the brain of an orang or a chimpanzee, cannot be bridged over by pointing to the gulf which separates the orang or chimpanzee from the lemur. The latter is filled up by the different intermediate kinds of apes; the stages with which to fill up the former have still to be found."[2] Professor

---

apes and grown up, fully developed men. But with every month and year which passes the skull of even the most manlike ape becomes less like that of man."—Virchow, *Menschen und Affenschädel*, p. 22. See above, p. 135.

[1] Pp. 83, 87; cf. Lucæ, *Archiv für Anthr.* vi. 30, 33, v. 518.

[2] *Die Grosshirnwendungen*, p. 102.

Ranke, speaking at a meeting of the German Anthropological Society in Berlin,[1] August 1880, gave an account of the scientific work lately done by Th. v. Bischoff, A. Ecker, and R. Virchow. In the course of his remarks he said, "The popular writings of the present day would almost lead us to suppose that the differences between man and the anthropoid apes are really so slight, that if the latter were committed to the care of a German schoolmaster for a few generations they would develop into men. This view is decidedly controverted by comparative and pathological anatomy, and by the history of development. The savants I have named are distinctly opposed to that popular philosophical tendency in natural science which falsely seeks to intrench itself behind the name of a great English savant. The most eminent biologists are distinctly and openly opposed to the way in which scientific conclusions are now made use of to establish assertions in natural philosophy."

At any rate, the differences between man and the apes are greater than is agreeable to those who would apply the theory of descent to both. Vogt thinks it necessary to ask,[2] "Can we find stages which will bridge over the gulf still existing between the ape and the negro, and which will lead step by step from the manlike ape to the negro, and from him to the white man?" He answers that it is possible, of course, that a species of ape may be found which stands nearer to man than the gorilla; but that it would be folly to rely on the mere

---

[1] The account may be found in the 13th volume of the *Archiv für Anthr.*
[2] *Vorlesungen*, i. p. 244.

possibility of such an event. It is still more unlikely that a race of men will be found who are nearer the apes than are the negroes; the world seems to have been too thoroughly examined in this respect to leave room for such a "hope." There is only one stage which he thinks he has found, the so-called microcephali, men who from their youth upwards are idiots, and whose outward appearance, according to Vogt, gives a distinctly apelike impression. He thinks that microcephalism is a state "which in all its essential characteristics leads us back to the stock from which the race of men was developed; to the common ancient stock of the primatæ, from which both we and the apes have sprung." But if it is possible that, by a check in his development and formation, man should be brought nearer to the ape, and "sink down to the ape," we cannot deny, he says, that it is possible that similarly the ape by a continuation of development may be brought nearer to man.[1] It is admitted that Vogt wrote all his treatises about microcephalism without ever examining the brain of a microcephalous idiot; he only made use of pictures and moulds of the skull.[2] Since then several microcephalous idiots have been thoroughly examined, the matter was discussed at the meeting of the Anthropological Society at Stuttgard in 1872,[3] and has also been treated in several books and pamphlets by Aeby,

---

[1] *Vorlesungen*, i. p. 346. Vogt has treated the matter more in detail in French, in "Mémoires sur les microcéphales ou hommes-singes;" in German, in "Ueber die Mikrocephalen oder Affen-Menschen," in the *Archiv für Anthr.* ii. 129. Also shortly in his essay, "Menschen, Affen-Menschen, Affen und Prof. Th. Bischoff in München," in Moleschott's *Untersuchungen zur Naturlehre des Menschen und der Thiere*, x. 493, Giessen 1868.

[2] *Archiv für Anthr.* v. 496, 499.   [3] *Archiv für Anthr.* v. 496.

Luschka, Ecker, Virchow, Bischoff, and others,[1] and it may now be considered as proved that microcephalism is simply a pathological phenomenon belonging to disease, which not even an evolutionist can use to prove man's descent from the ape.

Speaking at the meeting of the Anthropological Society at Constance in 1877, Krollmann said: "It was formerly suggested that the microcephalous idiots might be a reversion of the human race to a long extinct ancestor, a reversion to the ape. This view may now be considered as having been completely refuted." Virchow also gave an account of a microcephalous girl whom he had carefully observed. He said: "Psychologically the child does not in the least resemble an ape. All the positive powers and qualities of the ape are wanting, there is nothing of the psychology of the ape, the psychology is simply that of an incomplete little child. Every feature is human; the child is a human being of low organization, and in no way differs from the human type."[2]

According to the account given by A. de Quatrefages of the progress of anthropology in France,[3] the eminent French physiologist Gratiolet speaks just in the same way about microcephalism as the German savants I have mentioned. According to this account the doctrine of man's relationship to the ape finds much less support among French anthropologists than it does in Germany. "Anthropologists," says Quatrefages,

---

[1] Aeby, *Die Schädelformen*, p. 87. *Archiv für Anthr.* vi. 263, vii. 1. Virchow, *Menschen und Affenschädel*, p. 27. Peschel, *Volkerkunde*, p. 67.

[2] *Correspondenz-blatt der deutschen Gesellschaft für Anthropologie*, No. 9, Sept. 1877, pp. 131, 135.

[3] *Rapport*, p. 247.

" who are partly disagreed on many other points, are at one on this point and have arrived at the same conclusions, namely, that nothing warrants the assertion that the brain of the ape is a human brain arrested in its development, and that the latter is a more fully developed ape's brain (Gratiolet); that an examination of the organism in general, and of the extremities in particular, shows us that combined with a common ground-plan there exist differences of form and structure which are incompatible with the idea of a common descent for man and the ape (Gratiolet, Alix); that apes do not approach by perfection to man, and the human type does not approach by degradation to the ape (Bert); that there exists no possible bridge between man and the ape, unless we turn the laws of development upside down (Pruner Bey)," and so on.

Therefore, to recapitulate what we have said, even supposing the theory of descent to be true, its extension to man remains arbitrary, because man differs more markedly from the highest apes than do any two kinds of animals which stand next to one another; and because there are no intermediate forms which can bridge over the gulf between man and the ape, it having been proved that microcephalous idiots are not this intermediate form. Only one thing is still possible; such intermediate forms may have existed, and have died out like other species, or forms of organic beings. Have we then any proofs that apes more man-like than the gorilla, or men more ape-like than the negro, have existed? Huxley has discussed this question most exhaustively in the third part of the book I have mentioned, and he, certainly an unprejudiced witness, ends his discussion with the confession that the question must be answered in the negative, and that we must rest content with the hope that perhaps, "in still older strata, the fossilized bones of an ape more anthropoid, or a man more pithecoid, than any yet known, await the researches of some unborn palæontologist."[1]

Theologians yet unborn may deal with these. The human skulls which have been found up to the present time, and which are supposed to be of great antiquity, do not differ from the skulls of the present day. Against the assertion that "the earliest of the human skulls which have been found show a bestial conformation,"[2] or that "the surest and most important conclusion which has been attained to by investigation into prehistoric times is, that the oldest human remains show signs of a low organization, in part lower than that of the savages of the present day,"[3] we may set Virchow's statement, that "It is just the oldest skulls which show no signs of a lower race."[4] Vogt, speaking of a skull found in the cave of Furfooz, says that we are struck by the tremendous prognathism which is shown in the upper jaw; but he goes on to add, "The teeth are more ape-like than I have ever seen them in any skull; but even among strictly straight-toothed peoples we find single examples of such positions, which are in their case abnormal."[5] Virchow

---

[1] *Evidences*, p. 159. Strauss also relies on this "slender hope." In *Der alte und der neue Glaube*, p. 193, he says it is "extremely probable" that in future ages "we may possibly find fossil men at a much lower stage of development, much nearer to their animal origin."

[2] Strauss, *Der alte und der neue Glaube*, p. 193.

[3] Schaafhausen in the *Archiv für Anthr.* viii. 249.

[4] *Die Urbevölkerung Europa's*, Berlin 1874, p. 46. Cf. Aeby, *Die Schädelformen*, p. 89. Nadaillac, *L'ancienneté de l'homme*, p. 189.

[5] *Archiv für Anthr.* i. 34.

says of the same skull, that its prognathism is no greater than that of many Flemish skulls in the present day, and if we were to conclude from it that the race to which it belonged was an inferior race, the same conclusion must be applied to the Flemings.[1] Several strangely shaped under jaws have been found in France, and people have endeavoured to use them as proofs of the existence of a special race of men standing nearer to the apes.[2] Of this Aeby says, "We cannot think that this conclusion has the slightest weight, when we consider the endless number of variations which, as every anatomist knows, are found even now in this bone, the under jaw. In my opinion it is very rash to make an under jaw the type of a peculiar race, because some parts have some peculiarities, or because its teeth are somewhat unusually formed. If weight is to be attached to such details as these, we may well ask that the limits of the existing structure should first be a little more studied."[3]

The skulls which have been most talked about, and which according to the opinion of many are the oldest known, are two which were found respectively at Engis on the Maas, and in the Neanderthal between Dusseldorf and Elberfeld. As regards the first Huxley says, "I confess I can find no character in the remains of that cranium which if it were a recent skull would give any trustworthy clue as to the race to which it might appertain. Its contours and measurements agree very well with those of some Australian skulls

---

[1] *Archiv für Anthr.* vi. 115.
[2] Ausland, 1866, p. 791. Le Hon, *L'homme fossile*, p. 41.
[3] *Die Schädelformen*, p. 89.

which I have examined; ... on the other hand, its measurements agree equally well with those of some European skulls. And assuredly there is no mark of degradation about any part of its structure. It is in fact a fair average human skull, which might have belonged to a philosopher, or might have contained the thoughtless brains of a savage."[1] Aeby, Lucæ, and Virchow also say that this skull has no peculiarities which do not exist now-a-days.[2]

The so-called Neanderthal skull was found, together with some other human bones, in 1856, in a cave with the remains of extinct animals. Professor Fuhlrott of Elberfeld was the first to make it known, and since then many treatises have been written about it.[3] Only the upper parts of the skull, situated above the roof of the orbits, have been preserved. The cranium is of unusual size, and of elliptical form. Its most striking peculiarity consists in the unusual development of the frontal sinuses, owing to which the superciliary ridges which coalesce completely in the centre are rendered so prominent that the frontal bone exhibits a considerable hollow or depression behind them. The forehead is narrow and low, whereas the middle and hinder portions of the cranial arch are well developed. The importance of the discovery of this skull has been much exaggerated by some. Schaafhausen was inclined to see in the

---

[1] *Evidences*, p. 156.
[2] *Archiv für Anthr.* vi. 14. A. von Frantzius, *Die vierte allg. Versammlung der deutschen Gesellschaft für Anthropologie*, Brunswick 1874, p. 48.
[3] C. Fuhlrott, *Der fossile Mensch aus dem Neanderthal, und sein Verhältniss zum Alter des Menschengeschlechts*, Duisburg 1865. *Archiv für Anthr.* viii. 66.

Neanderthal skull the "type of the man of the Tertiary period;"[1] the Englishman King wished to draw from it conclusions as to the earlier existence of a special race of men, essentially different from the present race, and this race he proposed to call Homo Neanderthalensis.[2] Lyell, however, observes, "As to the remarkable Neanderthal skeleton, it is at present too isolated and exceptional, and its age too uncertain, to warrant us in relying on its abnormal and ape-like characters as bearing on the question whether the farther back we trace man into the past, the more we shall find him approach in bodily conformation to those species of the anthropoid quadrumana which are most akin to him in structure."[3] And Huxley says even more decidedly, "In no sense then can the Neanderthal bones be regarded as the remains of a human being intermediate between man and apes. At most they demonstrate the existence of a man whose skull may be said to revert somewhat towards the pithecoid type."[4] Since then several eminent anatomists and anthropologists have expressed their opinions about the Neanderthal skull. Aeby, Virchow, Hyrtl, Lucæ all say that it is undoubtedly a pathological skull, and ought therefore to be no more considered in the question of the skull formation of the earliest men than a microcephalous skull is considered in the question of the present formation.[5]

---

[1] *Archiv für Anthr.* v. 118.   [2] Ausland, 1863, p. 1056.
[3] *Antiquity of Man*, p. 419.   [4] *Evidences*, p. 157.
[5] Aeby, *Die Schädelformen*, p. 89. Virchow, *Die Urbevölkerung Europa's*, p. 46. Cf. Frantzius, *Die 4 allg. Vers.* etc. p. 48. Lucæ in the *Archiv für Anthr.* vi. 14. J. W. Spengel, *Archiv für Anthr.* viii. 49,

Neither in the past then do we find any intermediate forms which are calculated to bridge over the gulf between man and the ape, and we are justified in saying that even if according to the theory of descent it were shown to be likely that several nearly connected species of animals had a common stock, this conclusion would not properly be applied to a common descent of men and apes; because even if we only consider the bodily conditions, they are separated from one another by a wider gulf than are the higher apes from the lower, or than are any two different species of animals which can be called nearly related, and this gulf is filled up by no intermediate forms.

"Even in the oldest times," says Aeby, "no forms of human skulls have been found which are not in existence now-a-days. Any believer in the truth of the theory of descent may no doubt consistently apply it to men, but he must not hope to be able to adduce one single fact in support of his hypothesis from the history of mankind, so far as we can trace it at present. As far back as we can go, we find man in his present shape. The only likeness between man and the pithecoid type exists in the caricatures which have been made by several authors, with a complete contempt for truth by exaggerating single features."[1]

Considering these results of anthropological inquiry, it is astonishing that two contemporary French theologians should have brought forward the old pre-

denies the pathological character of the Neanderthal skull, but he describes several "neanderthaloid" skulls which are now in existence, especially some from the islands of the Zuyder Zee.

[1] *Die Schädelformen*, p 90.

Adamite hypothesis, and should have supposed that the oldest human remains found by geologists are not those of men of our race. Fabre d'Envieu thinks that these discoveries point to the fact of the existence on the earth, before the creation of man which is described in the Hexæmeron, of "races of men, or some other reasonable animals," who had died out before the creation of our common ancestor.[1] H. de Valroger rather more cautiously suggests that a kind of animal may possibly have existed in the Tertiary period as "a forerunner of man," which more nearly resembled the human type than do the gorilla, chimpanzee, and orang, but which nevertheless was incapable of the intellectual, moral, and religious development of which all races of our species are capable.[2] At any rate, these could not have been men, nor could they have been reasonable animals.

[1] *Les origines*, etc. pp. 329, 454, 478.
[2] *Les précurseurs de l'homme à l'époque tertiaire*, *Correspondant*, t. 93, p. 456. These theologians follow Boucher de Perthes, who, speaking of the race of men who made the implements found by him at Amiens (see Lect. 35), says: "Ces hommes n'ont plus leurs héritiers sur la terre; nous n'en sommes point les fils; le chaos les separe de la création actuelle."

XXIX.

MAN AND BEAST—*Conclusion.*

It is admitted by theologians, as I have mentioned in my discussion on the theory of descent, that possibly organic life may have begun with simple forms, and have developed gradually into its later multiplicity—only that this did not take place entirely through influences and forces working by chance, as is assumed in the Darwinian theory, but because, as Michelis expresses it, the Creator chose the method of developing the organic form genetically as the way of attaining to the perfect organization, which in man was united to intellectual development.[1] In connection with this some[2] even think that the Biblical teaching will admit of our believing that the creation of man did not take place by the forming of dead matter into a living being, to which all the qualities and attributes of man were given simultaneously, but by the process of adding to the highest and most man-like existing creatures the distinguishing characteristics of human nature. This of course would involve not only a higher development of the faculties which are common to both man and

---

[1] See above, p. 115.
[2] See Warington, *Week of Creation*, p. 124; also Frohschammer, *Das Christenthum*, etc. p. 185; and St. George Mivart, *On the Genesis of Species*, London 1871, p. 277; cf. *Contemporary Review*, vol. xix. (January 1872) p. 185; *Dublin Review*, N. S. vol. xviii. (No. 35, January 1872) p. 198.

beast, but also the gift of new faculties of a higher order—that is to say, a new creative impulse was necessary for the creation of man.

It is quite clear that this view is even more entirely opposed to Hæckel's *Anthropogenie* than to the Bible. But I do not think that such a view at all agrees with the teaching of the Biblical record, although the latter must not be interpreted literally;[1] nor do I believe that it is sufficiently borne out by scientific facts. Let us look at these facts rather more closely.

You will have perhaps observed that in the special discussions in my last lecture, I spoke of Huxley, Vogt, and Hæckel, but not of Darwin, although he is not only in a certain sense their leader, but has also discussed the question of man's descent most exhaustively. In this I do Darwin no wrong. He says himself that in that portion of his book which treats of the descent of man, he adduces hardly any new facts. He then refers to the authors I have named, and, strange to say, he mentions with them people like Büchner and Rolle. Darwin even says, speaking of Hæckel, that his own book on the Descent of Man would probably not have been finished if Hæckel's *History of Creation* had appeared before it, and that he agrees with the latter in almost everything.[2] I have only found one point which Darwin discusses more fully than any other writer, and that is the manner in which our supposed ancestors developed by means of natural and sexual selection into men.

" The early progenitors of man," says Darwin,[3] " were no doubt once covered with hair, both sexes having

[1] See above, vol. i. p. 149.　　[2] *Descent of Man*, i. 4.　　[3] *Ibid.* i. 206.

beards; their ears were pointed and capable of movement; and their bodies were provided with a tail having the proper muscles. . . . The foot . . . was then prehensile, and our progenitors no doubt were arboreal in their habits, frequenting some warm, forest-clad land." Darwin is thinking of Central Africa. "The males were provided with great canine teeth which served them as formidable weapons." You see that this type must be a good deal altered before it can become the human type. And all these alterations have taken place quite gradually in the way that I have shown by the example of animals in explaining the Darwinian theory. Here also, in the development of the beings which have just been described into men, we find on the one hand natural, on the other sexual selection. Small peculiarities appeared in single individuals, which gave them some advantage in the struggle for existence. The individuals so favoured were preserved, while the less favoured ones died out, and the former passed on their favourable qualities to their descendants, in whom these qualities were gradually fixed and increased. This is natural selection. Side by side with this went sexual selection. Certain individuals, possessing certain advantages, paired and reproduced themselves, whereas the individuals not so favoured did not succeed in doing this, or did so more seldom; and as individuals of one sex which possessed special qualities paired with individuals of the other sex also possessed of those qualities, throughout a long series of generations they became gradually hereditary in their descendants.

Let me now try to understand how the type I have

described above can have altered to the human type according to these laws. For instance, let us take the quality of the skin. Our progenitors were thickly covered with hair, as the apes are now; how did it come about that the hair was gradually reduced to what it is now? Natural selection will not help us here, for, as Wallace says,[1] the soft, bare, sensitive skin of man, who does not possess the hairy covering which is common to all apes, is clearly of no advantage in the struggle for existence. Even savages feel the want of such a covering, especially on the back, where with animals the hair is thickest, and they strive to get over it by hanging skins, etc., round them. This hairy covering of the body was therefore not harmful or useless to our progenitors, but rather useful; therefore its gradual complete disappearance cannot be explained by natural selection, by which only advantageous alterations can be preserved, increased, and fixed.

Darwin himself expressly admits this, and he relies upon sexual selection to explain the loss of the hair. The strongest, most powerful men or males among our ancestors, he thinks, were in a position to choose the most attractive women or females. Now we always find that a woman has a less hairy body than a man. It is therefore probable that among our half human ancestors the females first began to lose their hair. This partial loss of hair must have been considered ornamental by the ape-like progenitors of man, as Darwin expresses it, that is, the less hairy females were considered more beutiful than the hairier ones, and were therefore preferred by the males. The descendants of these less

[1] Cf. Huber, *Die Lehre Darwins*, p. 209.

hairy females must have had still less hair, and if this rule was observed throughout a few hundred generations the hair would have gradually decreased.[1] To this Wallace rightly objects, that "as Mr. Darwin says, each race admires its own characteristics carried to a moderate extreme. Hairy races would therefore admire abundant hairiness, just as bearded races now admire fine beards, and any admiration of deficient hairiness would probably be as rare and abnormal as the admiration for partial baldness or scanty hair in women would be among ourselves. Any individual fancy for such an abnormal peculiarity as deficient hair in a hair-covered animal would produce no effect; and that any such fancy should become general with our semi-human ancestors, and so produce universal nakedness, does not seem at all probable when we have no evidence of such a result of sexual selection elsewhere in the whole animal kingdom; it is true that in that early state the struggle for existence would have been severe, and only the best endowed would have survived; but unless we suppose a universal or simultaneous fancy among all the most vigorous and therefore probably the most hairy men for what would be then an unnatural character —deficiency of hair in women, and that this fancy should have persisted in all its force for a long series of generations, it is not easy to see how this severe struggle for existence and survival of the fittest would in any way aid sexual selection in abolishing the hairy covering. On the contrary, it seems more likely that it would entirely prevent it. We can hardly, therefore, impute much influence to sexual selection in the case of

[1] *Descent of Man.* ii. 377.

man, even as regards less important characteristics than the loss of hair, because it requires the very same tastes to persist in the majority of the race during a period of long and unknown duration. All analogy teaches us that there would be no such identity of taste in successive generations; and this seems a fatal objection to the belief that any fixed and definite characteristics could have been produced in man by sexual selection."[1]

It is the same with other transformations. If the members of that "ape-like herd," to use Strauss' expression,[2] from which we are descended were, as he says, "tree animals," and if their feet were prehensile, it was of no advantage to them in the struggle for existence that they gradually became more fitted for walking, and to the same degree more unfitted for climbing. Our foot is admirably suited to our present wants and habits now that we walk in an upright position and are no longer tree animals, and the prehensile foot is equally suited to the wants of the ape. But an intermediate form, a transitional foot, which was neither prehensile and suited for climbing, nor a human foot fitted for walking, could not have been more perfect or of advantage in the struggle for existence. An ape whose foot was not suited for climbing must have played a melancholy part among his companions, and the fact that he was intended to be the ancestor of a posterity who would be able to walk upright after a hundred generations, could have been of little comfort to him. It is very easy to depict on paper the intermediate forms through which the pre-

---

[1] See *Academy*, March 15, 1871, p. 180.
[2] *Der alte und der neue Glaube*, p. 199.

hensile foot of the ape has gradually perfected into the human foot. Each successive form in this series is a step in advance of the preceding, and in this series the foot becomes more perfect the farther it gets from the point of departure, the prehensile foot, and the nearer it approaches to the goal, the human foot. But is each of these intermediate forms more advantageous to the individual who is said to have possessed it than the preceding form in the series? On the contrary, the middle form, which differs from a prehensile foot just as much as from a human foot, is practically the worst, because it is as little fitted for climbing and seizing as for walking; each preceding form is more advantageous to the ape, each succeeding form more advantageous for man. We have therefore for practical use, and this is the one thing to be thought of in the struggle for existence, not a continuously ascending series of steps, but a series in which the practical usefulness of the members first gradually diminishes, and then when it has reached the lowest point gradually increases. This is quite unnatural, and does not in the least harmonize with the Darwinian system.[1]

Wallace draws our attention to another point. The volume or the size of the brain generally speaking stands in direct relationship to the intellectual development. The larger brain of man must therefore, according to Darwin, have developed gradually from the smaller brain of the ape. But the brains of the lowest savages and, so far as can be ascertained from the skulls that have been preserved, the brains of the so-called pre-

[1] Cf. the humourous description in *Moses und die Materialisten*, by Graw, Brunswick 1872, p. 43.

historic races of men, are as regards volume very little below the brains of the highest men, and very much above the brains of the higher animals.

According to Wallace, sections of the skulls show that the capacity of the skull of the lowest savages is always as much as five-sixths of the capacity of that of the highest races of men, whereas that of the gorilla is hardly one-third of that of man. How can we explain the fact that the brain of the lowest man has grown from one-third to five-sixths? Darwinians do not place the Australian negroes and other low races of men very high above the animals as regards their intellectual wants and the exercise of their intellectual faculties; therefore a brain not much larger than that of a gorilla would suffice for them. At any rate natural selection would not have given them a brain superior to their requirements, and yet they possess a brain which as far as volume is concerned is essentially superior to their requirements, and is very little below the brain of a philosopher. This also cannot be explained by the Darwinian theory.

This last observation of Wallace's leads us to another point of view, from which we must look at the "Pithecoid theory." The brain and the faculty of the mind are no doubt unmistakeably connected, but the faculty of the mind is not necessarily the more perfect because the brain is bigger or more developed, and still less does the psychical power depend entirely on the bodily organization.[1] An English savant justly says, "Nobody disputes that there is the strongest analogy and resemblance between the structural organization of the

[1] J. B. Meyer, *Philos. Zeitfragen*, p. 170.

human body and the structural organization of the higher mammalia. The senses and many of the organs of man are the same in kind, though not in degree, as those of the lower animals; and where there is a difference it is often in favour of the brute creation. The eye of the vulture, the scent of the hound, the limbs of the horse, are far more powerful than the corresponding human organs. But this dispute which agitates the comparative anatomists of the present day, and makes them alternately offensive to each other and ridiculous to everybody else, has no practical bearing at all on the question of the proper origin and nature of mankind; for the real distinctive characteristics of man begin just where these resemblances of structural organization leave off. This is the barrier which is absolutely insurmountable by the advocates of the theory of development, because the differences between the animals and man are not differences of degree, but differences of kind."[1]

There is no doubt that, however great the likeness between the bodily form of the gorilla and that of man may be thought to be, no reasonable and unprejudiced observer can deny that so far as the spiritual life is concerned, the difference between them is very great, much greater than we should have expected considering the bodily resemblance. This shows that man's spiritual life has nothing whatever to do with the bodily form, especially with the conformation of the brain; for otherwise we could not comprehend why a similar spiritual life is not found in the ape, why he does not stand much nearer to man, in this respect at least, than

[1] *Edinburgh Review*, April 1863, p. 566.

the dog for instance, whose bodily organization altogether, and whose skull and brain in particular, are much more different from man's, and yet who is not always inferior to the ape in "intelligence," if we may use the word. We must therefore suppose that something exists in man which does not exist in the animal, even in the gorilla, and as man and the gorilla are too nearly alike in body to allow the presence of this something in man, and its absence in the gorilla to be explained by the difference in their bodily conformation, we must suppose that the quality which makes man man, and distinguishes him essentially from the animal, is of a spiritual nature.[1]

I cannot discuss this subject here in all its bearings ; I must confine myself to a few of the main points, and will specially consider what has been brought forward in favour of the statement connected with the pithecoid theory — that in psychical matters also the difference between man and the animals is one of degree and not of essence, and that therefore the human soul may have been formed in a natural manner, by gradual perfecting from the animal soul.

Among the philosophers who have occupied themselves in modern times with the so-called animal soul, Frohschammer is one of those who place the psychical element in the animal at its highest. At the same time, he says unhesitatingly that the difference between the animal and man is one of quality and essence, not only of degree ; not such as could be caused entirely by the richer, more complex organization of the human body.[2] We cannot of course, he adds, directly observe and

---

[1] Cf. *Natur und Offenbarung*, ix. 477. [2] *Das Christenthum*, p. 162.

compare human souls and animal souls; we can only observe their workings and manifestations, and must draw our conclusions as to their causes and their nature from these observations. The question is, therefore, whether we find any assured facts which lead us to conclude that there is a decided, unchangeable, unsurmountable difference between the animal and the human soul. This will enable us to decide whether the difference is one of essence or of degree. "But," continues Frohschammer, "human life and human history furnish us with facts which at least give us perfect certainty that as a matter of fact there is between the psychical life and actions of man and those of the animal a very decided difference; yes, even a gulf which is practically impassable, so far as our experience goes. These facts are both well known and general, and on account of them the common sense of man believes in the essential difference between animal and human souls. One of the facts which strikes us first is this, that man has a language, that is, he is able to form connected series of tones, sounds, words (or other signs), in order by this means to express and impart his inward condition, feelings, thoughts, his experiences, and his opinions. Another fact which strikes us immediately, is that mankind has a historical consciousness, a consciousness of itself, its destinies, actions, and tasks, in which the whole animal world, and all kinds of animals, are deficient. In connection with this is the fact that each separate man is able to set himself a high inward either spiritual or ethical task, apart from the simply physical task of preserving life, whereas animals simply know nothing about such a task, and make the preservation and the comfort of their physical existence the object of their actions. Besides the consciousness of a moral law, men are distinguished also by the feeling and idea of justice, and by the common system of law and the order of society, which are founded on this. Another quality which distinguishes man is the idea of God, and religious belief and worship, of which animals are entirely incapable. Lastly, man is the only creature who is capable of understanding the arts and sciences, while animals cannot accomplish any abstract thought or theory, or any practice founded on them."

I must refer you to the works of Frohschammer and other philosophers[1] for further discussions on this point. As regards speech, the supporters of the pithecoid theory will only acknowledge a difference of degree, not of essence, between animals and men in this matter. Darwin mentions the case of an ape in Paraguay who, when he is excited, utters at least six different sounds, which excite similar emotions in other apes; and also the still more remarkable fact "that the dog, since being domesticated, has learnt to bark in at least four or five distinct tones. . . . We have the bark of eagerness, as in the chase; that of anger; the yelping or howling bark of despair, as when shut up; that of joy, as when starting on a walk with his master; and the very distinct one of demand or supplication, as when wishing for a door or a window to be opened." Darwin further says that only *articulate* language is peculiar to man, but he adds that "it is not the mere power of articulation that distinguishes man from other

---

[1] Waitz, *Anthropologie*, i. 308. J. B. Meyer, *Philos. Zeitfragen*, p. 170. Huber, *Zur Kritik*, etc. p. 50.

animals, for, as every one knows, parrots can talk; but it is his large power of connecting definite sounds with definite ideas; and this obviously depends on the development of the mental faculties."[1]

It is true that many animals can be taught to articulate words, but this is not speech, for the animals do not connect any ideas with these words. But the tones which the animals produce of themselves are not only not articulate, but are not speech at all, because by these sounds they only express emotions of pleasure or pain, as man himself also does instinctively, but they do not express ideas or thoughts, which man can do under certain circumstances—as in the case of the deaf and dumb for instance—even without articulate speech. We can distinguish, 1st, sounds which, although neither articulate nor rational, are yet the expression of a *verbum mentale;* 2nd, sounds which are articulate but not rational; 3rd, sounds which are rational but not articulate; 4th, sounds which are both rational and articulate; 5th, movements which do not express thought; 6th, movements which do express thought. The sounds made by apes and dogs, of which Darwin speaks, belong to the first category; the words spoken by parrots to the second; to the third belong sounds by which a man can express either his assent or his objections to a speech to which he is listening; the fourth category is speech, as it is found amongst all, even the lowest men; and the movements described in the sixth category are substitutes for speech where this is physically impos-

---

[1] *Descent of Man,* i. 54. Cf. Strauss, *Der alte und der neue Glaube,* p. 199.

sible.[1] "Animals do not speak," says Frohschammer rightly, "because they are mentally incapable of speech, that is, because they are not really able to *think*. Man's power of thought is the cause of his power of speech, not, as has been asserted, his power of speech the cause of his power of thought; although, of course, the power of thought is stimulated and developed by speech. For this reason a being incapable of thought can *never* be taught really to speak, although, parrot-like, it may imitate words; on the other hand, a being possessing real power of thought, if it fulfils even to a slight degree the primary conditions of the development of its spiritual powers, will form for itself some signs by which it can impart thought, even though, like the deaf and dumb, it cannot hear a human sound."[2] There is a correct thought in the fact that the Greeks have only one word, λόγος, for reason and speech, and call the animals ἄλογα ζῶα, *mutum pecus;* and, as Max Müller says, speech is the Rubicon which no animal will ever dare to cross.

It is too bad that, in the face of all this, Hæckel should literally say in his *Generelle Morphologie*,[3] that "birds, parrots, with highly differentiated gullets and tongues, etc., can learn speech—that is, the power of making articulate sounds—just as perfectly as man.". The fact that parrots can only learn a few words, and therefore cannot learn speech "as perfectly as man," is only one part of the folly of this observation. Who

[1] *Quarterly Review*, vol. cxxxvii. (July 1874) p. 43. (The article is probably by St. George Mivart.)
[2] *Das Christenthum*, p. 165. Cf. J. B. Meyer, *Philos. Zeitfragen*, p. 160. Huber, *Zur Kritik*, etc. p. 50. H. Wedewer, *Die neue Sprachwissenschaft und der Urstand der Menschheit*, Freiburg 1867, pp. 7, 41.
[3] ii. 430.

would call the power of articulating words which parrots acquire by training real speech? "The most important step," Hæckel goes on to say, "in the development of real men from real apes, was the differentiation of the gullet, which resulted in the development of speech, and by this means produced the power of plain communication and historical tradition." It would be an interesting task for a historian to collect the historical traditions of their race from the parrots, who, as Hæckel assures us, can learn our language just as perfectly as a Frenchman can learn German.

I must do Hæckel the justice to say that in his *History of Creation*[1] he does not bring forward with quite so much assurance this argument for similarity between man and brutes drawn from the parrots. But he has not omitted to add an equally ingenious argument, and he says, "Very many wild tribes can count no further than 10 or 20, whereas some very clever dogs have been made to count up to 40, and even beyond 60. And yet the faculty of appreciating number is the beginning of mathematics;" so that, I suppose, Hæckel means to imply that dogs will probably be able at some time or other to accomplish fractions and the rule of three. In the latest edition of the *History of Creation*, Hæckel repeats the following naïve assertion, "If, as is usually done, we divide the different emotions of the soul into three principal groups,—sensation, will, and thought,—we shall find in regard to every one of them that the most highly developed birds and mammals are on a level with the lowest human beings, or even decidedly surpass them.

[1] P. 597.

The will is as distinctly and strongly developed in higher animals as in men of character. . . . The affections of the higher animals are not less tender and warm than those of man. The fidelity and devotion of the dog, the maternal love of the lioness, the conjugal love and connubial fidelity of doves and love-birds are proverbial, and might serve as examples to many men. . . . Lastly, with regard to thought, . . . this much may with certainty be inferred, . . . that the processes of thinking here follow the same laws as in ourselves. . . . In all cases, as in man, it is the path of induction and deduction which leads to the formation of conclusions." [1]

In the *Generelle Morphologie* Hæckel points to the fact that "the beginnings and sometimes the more perfect stages of all matters of government and society are found amongst animals, often even in animals far removed from men, as, *e.g.*, among the insects, the ants;" for which reason he recommends to statesmen, teachers of political economy, and above all to historians, the study of comparative zoology, if they

[1] P. 653. In the *Gen. Morphologie*, ii. 435, Hæckel states all this even more plainly, and adds, "There are men who are even lower than the higher animals, because of the imperfect development of their reason. This holds good not only of the lower races of men, but also of many individuals of the highest races, even of those in whom one would suppose that the mass of acquired knowledge had sharpened the powers of thought. In this respect some of the numerous assertions made by opponents of the theory of descent are specially interesting; they show to a perfectly astounding degree a want of natural, clear, decided form and connection of thought, which certainly places them amongst the more reasonable dogs, horses, and elephants. As these animals are generally not warped by the mountains of dogmas and prejudices which pervert the thoughts of most men from their youth up, we often find that their judgments are more correct and natural than those of so-called 'savants.'"

would attain to a true and scientific understanding of the corresponding human institutions.

Hæckel even seems quite to disregard the fact, which in this matter is fatal to the pithecoid theory, that our nearest relatives, the apes, are as regards speech very much behind parrots and ravens; and as regards "the institutions of government and society," clearly far behind ants and bees; whereas according to the pithecoid theory, they should approach man as much in these points as in bodily organization.

The arguments brought forward by K. Vogt in support of the theory that the difference between man and the animals with regard to spiritual things is one of degree and not of essence, are so unspeakably absurd, that in justice to him we must suppose that he does not believe them himself. What can we think of Vogt's assertion, that the cuffs which the old bears give the younger ones show distinctly that animals are not devoid of the ideas of parental authority and filial obedience, that is, of the "fundamental ideas of human and Christian morality." Or to his concluding from the fact that even the most courageous dog will show senseless fear in the presence of strange appearances of which his nose can give him no warning, that the dog is evidently afraid of ghosts; and then proceeding to see in this "fear of the supernatural, of the unknown," the germ of religious ideas "which are found developed in a high degree in our intelligent domestic animals the dog and the horse, and which men only develops farther, and forms into a system of faith."[1]

I need scarcely say that we find similar statements

[1] *Vorlesungen*, i. 294. Cf. J. B. Meyer, *Philos. Zeitfragen*, p. 393.

in the works of Büchner[1] and men like him. But even Darwin hardly rises above Vogt and Hæckel in this matter. "Animals," he says, "manifestly feel emulation. They love approbation or praise; and a dog carrying a basket for his master exhibits in a high degree self-complacency and pride. There can, I think, be no doubt that a dog feels shame, as distinct from fear, and something very like modesty when begging too often for food. A great dog scorns the snarling of a little dog, and this may be called magnanimity. . . . Monkeys certainly dislike being laughed at; and they sometimes invent imaginary offences. . . . The idea of property is common to every dog with a bone, and to most or all birds with their nests. . . . No one supposes that one of the lower animals reflects whence he comes or whither he goes,—what is death or what is life, and so forth. But can we feel sure that an old dog with an excellent memory and some power of imagination, as shown by his dreams, never reflects on his past pleasures in the chase? and this would be a form of self-consciousness. . . . It is often difficult to judge whether animals have any feeling for each other's sufferings. Who can say what cows feel when they surround and stare intently on a dying or dead companion? . . . I agree with Agassiz that dogs possess something very like a conscience. They certainly possess some power of self-command, and this does not appear to be wholly the result of fear. . . . A dog will refrain from stealing food in the absence of his master. . . . What a strong feeling of inward satisfaction must impel a bird,

[1] *Sechs Vorlesungen*, etc. p. 187.

so full of activity, to brood day after day over her eggs," etc. etc.[1]

Many of the observations on which Darwin and others rest their description of the spiritual life of animals have been made not by themselves, or by other capable inquirers, but belong to the category of animal stories, which as far as authenticity is concerned may be ranked with hunting stories. Those observations which are really trustworthy partly only show us what human training can do with animals, and partly assume quite another aspect, if we do not humanize the animal; that is, if we do not call the actions of animals, which outwardly have a certain likeness to human actions, by names taken from human actions, and thus disregard the difference between the instinct of the animal and the conscious, free action of the man. With reference to this there is this very important fact, which Darwin himself lays stress on, namely, that man has to learn his skill by practice, whereas the beaver builds his canal, and the bird his nest, quite, or very nearly as well, the first time he tries it as when he is old;[2] and also that animals make no progress in this respect, on the contrary they build their nests and catch their prey just as they did hundreds of years ago; that even the tamed and trained animals if left to themselves go back to their former state, and that the dog's son does not learn from his father the tricks which the latter was taught.[3]

If on the one hand, in order to bring man and the

---

[1] *Descent of Man*, i. pp. 42, 52, 62, 76, 78, 79.
[2] *Ibid.* 1.
[3] Huber, *Zur Kritik*, p. 50.

animals as nearly together as possible with reference even to their spiritual qualities, the "spiritual life" of the animals is idealized, on the other hand the description given of the spiritual life of the lowest races of man is as unfavourable as possible. Here also we do not find the cool criticism and impartiality which is necessary. If the conditions of "savage" races are thoroughly and scientifically examined, many things appear to be different from what the supporters of man's connection with the apes would wish. O. Peschel, after numerous separate investigations, says, "Even those races which after the first superficial examination were placed far below our own stage of civilisation, have, on more intimate knowledge, been placed much nearer civilised races."[1] And an English savant points out that the two writers who have worked in England most diligently on this subject, Sir John Lubbock and Edward Burnet Taylor, have collected the best evidence against the pithecoid theory. He adds, "But if we are under no slight obligations to these writers for their patient, candid, and laborious toil, how much greater must be the obligation due to that author who has so profoundly influenced them, and whose suggestive writings have produced so great an effect on nineteenth century biology : a deep debt of gratitude will indeed one day be due to Mr. Darwin, —one difficult to estimate. This sentiment, however, will be mainly due to him for his having in fact become the occasion of the *reductio ad absurdum* of that system which he set out to maintain—namely, the origin of man by natural selection, and the suffi-

[1] *Volkerkunde*, p. 139. Waitz, *Anthropologie*, i. 312, 315, 325.

ciency of mechancial causes to account for the harmony, variety, beauty, and sweetness of that teeming world of life, of which man is the actual and, we believe, ordained observer, historian, and master. But the study of savage life has taught us much. Our poor obscurely-thinking, roughly-speaking, childishly-acting, impulsive cousin of the wilds, the *Homo sylvaticus*, is not a useless tenant of his woods and plains, his rocks and rivers. His humble testimony is of the highest value in supporting the claims of his most civilised brothers to a higher than a merely brutal orgin. The religion of Abraham and Chrysostom, the intellect of Aristotle and Newton, the art of Raphael, of Shakespeare, of Mozart ... are different *in kind* from complex entanglements of merely animal instincts and sensible impressions; and this becomes more certain to us when we find the very same moral, intellectual, and artistic nature (though disguised, obscured, and often profoundly misunderstood) present even in the rude, uncultured soul of the lowest of our race, the poor savage—*Homo sylvaticus*."[1]

To speak frankly, it has only been with some repugnance that I have discussed the theory of our relationship to the ape in detail. It is certainly depressing to find that such a question can come up for discussion in the middle of the nineteenth century, that, to use the words of the Psalmist, "Man that is in honour and understandeth not, is like the beasts that perish."[2] But as things stand, I could not avoid such a discussion. These theories are brought forward in the popular and superficial books and pamphlets

[1] *Quarterly Review*, vol. cxxxvii. (July 1874) p. 77. [2] Ps. xlix. 20.

on scientific subjects from which the so-called educated people learn their wisdom,[1] and the poor readers are persuaded, very often to their great dismay, that they are dealing with the results of most careful, conscientious, and exhaustive observations and investigations. They believe that natural science, which is admitted to be an accurate science, resting simply on observation and induction, which is known to be pursued in our time with a thoroughness which was not even dreamt of formerly, and which has consequently already reached the greatest results,—they believe that this science necessarily leads to these conclusions, and that the reader must therefore either ignore science, or give up the old belief that God on the sixth day of the Hexæmeron first finished the creation of the animals, including the apes, and then made man in His image.

There is no way by which we can answer such misconceptions and save the honour both of the Bible and of science, except by showing what science really has discovered and can discover; what is the result of sober conscientious investigation, and what, on the other hand, belongs to the realm of airy hypothesis and fantastic speculation, which may no doubt delight our imagination, but which the sober understanding will only despise,—speculations which a student will only mingle with his scientific conclusions if his fancy runs away with his understanding, or if he mixes up his philosophical or theological views with his scientific opinions. Neither of these is very likely to happen to the leaders in science, whether they believe in the

[1] Cf. *e.g. Morgenblatt*, 1862, 1 Heft.

Bible or not. But the peculiar element of the great mass of amateurs and those who have a smattering of science, is a mere hodge-podge of the true and the untrue, of certain and uncertain scientific statements, of rash hypotheses and philosophical and theological opinions. And the same must be said of authors who like Vogt and Hæckel propagate their atheistic opinions with the zeal of missionaries, and, as has been justly said of Hæckel, use scientific facts only as mortar for the stones supplied by fancy or by philosophizing unbelief.[1]

Earnest men of science protest quite as strongly as could any theologian against such a misuse of science. Thus Aeby adds to the statements I have quoted above:[2] "It is very pleasant to read how the three anthropomorphous apes attained to human form; how the wild ancestors of our race stood tribe against tribe, kind against kind; how gradually, through increasing civilisation, they recognised that they were brothers, intermingled, intercrossed, removed the original differences by hybrid forms, and so were slowly but surely brought to the final unity. But we look in vain for any foundation on fact for all this. We know the human type as a solitary island, from which no bridge leads to the neighbouring land of the mammals. And at present there is no scientific document, but only the speculations of the human spirit, to tell us whether it was torn off from that land ages ago, or whether it rose independently from the ocean of Creation." Oscar Fraas speaks still more strongly. "The idea that the human race came from one of these kinds of apes is the most insane ever conceived by man

[1] See above, p. 113.   [2] See above, p. 150.   *Die Schädelformen*, p. 90.

about the history of man, worthy to be preserved in a new edition of the *History of Human Folly;* besides, there is no pretence that this absurd idea is founded on fact. We may therefore calmly leave the gorilla in the tropical swamps of Lower Guinea,[1] the only place on this planet where he is found. The proof of man's relationship to this monster has still to be discovered.[2]"

A. de Quatrefages speaks in the same strain.[3] "The idea that the apes are our ancestors has caused great sensation, because it has been defended in the name of philosophy and controverted in the name of theology, and has therefore been connected with the controversies which have only too often drawn savants across the bounds of a province they ought never to have left. We do not pretend to be either theologians or philosophers, we are purely men of science, and therefore care only for scientific truth. In the name of this truth I must acknowledge that natural science knows nothing as yet about the origin of man; but in the name of the same truth I can assert that neither a gorilla, nor an orang-outang, nor a chimpanzee, nor a sea-cow, nor a fish, nor any other animal, was our ancestor."

A necessary result of the theory of man's descent from the animals is the view, which is widely held at present, that man was originally in a barbarous condition, similar to that which we find now amongst the so-called savage races; and also the assertion that "the scientific traces of former races" contradict the Biblical statement, according to which the first men created by God were at any rate, as regards their bodily and

---

[1] German: Gabon-gina, *i.e.* the basin of the Gaboon river in Lower Guinea.
[2] *Vor der Sündfluth*, p. 399.   [3] *Hist. de l'homme*, iii. 50.

spiritual condition, more perfect than the present savages.[1] If, then, the earliest human remains which have been found in different countries—and besides the skulls I have mentioned, implements, weapons, etc. have been found of which I will speak later—do in reality point to a lower stage of civilisation, this proves nothing as to the condition of the first men. Although savage races still exist, yet long before them civilised men have existed in other countries, and therefore the existence of tribes in an earlier stage of progress in the European countries in which their traces have been found does not prevent our assuming that in other countries peoples with a higher culture existed contemporaneously with them; and that their ancestors, in the lands from which they had wandered into Europe, stood on a higher stage of culture, but in their isolation they were not able to maintain it.

The description of the development of human culture as described by several modern anthropologists, rests on an arbitrary construction. I have mentioned before that Hæckel and others have arranged the species of animals which exist now or have existed, in an order which begins with the most imperfect, and proceeds to more and more perfect forms; and that they then go on to assert that the more imperfect forms were historically and genealogically the first, and that the natural system of zoology shows us likewise the history of the development of the animal kingdom. Just in the same way the anthropologists I have mentioned arrange the different stages of human culture which

[1] Frohschammer, *Das Christenthum*, p. 185. Strauss, *Der alte und der neue Glaube*, p. 226.

can be discovered among present and past races, in a series which begins with the most barbarous savages and culminates in European civilisation, and they then assert that this artificial systematic order shows us the historic succession of the stages of culture, that the most imperfect and the first in the systematic order was also chronologically the first, etc. Both constructions are equally arbitrary; in both the very thing which is to be proved is treated as proved or self-evident. No doubt, on the whole, a general progress in culture can be historically proved; but in many single cases there have been retrograde steps. Compare, for instance, the Egyptians under the Pharaohs and the Ptolemies, with their descendants. And it is well known that many tribes who have been shut off from the world of culture have sunk to barbarism; and when once a tribe has, like the existing so-called savage tribes, sunk to barbarism, it does not usually return to a higher stage of civilisation unless an external impulse be given by contact with more highly civilised peoples. History contradicts the theory of a gradual development of *all* mankind from primitive barbarism—the theory of the Savagists, as its supporters have been called in England; history shows us now a degeneration and now a progress of the separate portions of mankind, but so far as historical recollection goes back we always find some peoples who have a culture surpassing that of our present savages.[1] The only historical records we have of the first period of the human race are those of the Bible; these, as I have said, are not controverted

[1] Hettinger, *Apologie*, ii. 1, p. 313. Zöckler, *Geschichte der Beziehungen*, ii. 744.

by anthropology, and the legends of other peoples confirm them, for a golden age is the extreme boundary of all national histories.

In conclusion, I will mention one curious way in which some Darwinians have applied the theory of the struggle for existence to man. "The supremacy," says Hæckel, "which, thanks to natural selection, the white races have attained over other races of men in the struggle for existence will no doubt increase more and more, so that only a few races will be able to prolong the struggle for existence with white men for any length of time. Already the Papuans, the Hottentots, the Australian negroes, the Malays or Polynesians, and the Red Indians are decreasing year by year, and give way more and more rapidly to the white intruders."[1] The facts which have been collected by several investigators, most of which are to be found in a book on this subject by Gerland,[2] show that there is no reason for supposing that these races have a mysterious natural tendency to disappear; the excesses which exist among them, infanticide, etc., the wars of tribes with one another, the pernicious physical and moral influence exercised upon them by many of the so-called civilised races, sufficiently explain the dying out of those races; they must be possessed of a truly marvellous power of resistance to be able to withstand all these harmful influences.

In the next lecture I shall begin the discussion of the unity of the human race. To-day I will only make one remark on this subject, which is connected

---

[1] *Entstehung*, etc. p. 74. Cf. *Nat. Schöpfungsgeschichte*, p. 618.
[2] Gerland, *Ueber das Aussterben der Naturvölker*, Leipzig 1868. Cf. Th. Waitz, *Anthropologie*, i. 158. Quatrefages, *Rapport*, p. 356. Rauch, *Die Einheit des Menschengeschlechts*, p. 258.

with the theory of descent, and its application to man. Some theologians have supposed that the propagation of Darwin's theory would have at least one good result, in that it would silence the doubts as to the possibility of the common descent of the different races of men. No doubt if apes and men are of one race, negroes and Caucasians may be related. Lyell, Wallace, Huxley, and others admit this unhesitatingly; Huxley even says that he believes there is nothing to prove that mankind is descended from more than one pair.[1] Others, however, maintain that although according to Darwin's theory the *possibility* of the common descent of mankind must be admitted, there is nothing to prevent our assuming that in different lands,—perhaps in the far south of Asia, where the orang is found, and in Africa, where the gorilla lives,—quite independently of one another, but under almost similar natural conditions, animal life developed from imperfect forms into the ape and the man.[2] Under these circumstances we cannot be surprised if men like Vogt, who are never more consistent than in their love for everything that is not in harmony " with the thousand year old lawbook of the old Jews,"[3] maintain in one breath the possibility of our descent from the quadrupeds, and

---

[1] Lyell, *The Antiquity of Man.* Huxley, *On our Knowledge*, etc., p. 117.
[2] *Archiv für Anthr.* iii. 264. Hæckel, *Nat. Schöpfungsgeschichte*, pp. 590, 598, 621. He thinks that the race of "speechless primæval man" (Alali or Pithecanthropi) sprang from an extinct species of Anthropoidæ; but that as all human languages cannot be derived from one common language, these divided into several races, who all formed their own primæval language, and that in this way different kinds of "real men, Homines," originated independently of one another. The present men are descended from at least two of these species.
[3] *Vorlesungen*, i. p. 6.

the impossibility of the descent of both negroes and Europeans from one pair. "There are people," says Th. H. Martin, "who appeal consecutively to two contradictory statements, which are both false, but which will both serve their object. One of these statements exaggerates the mutability of species, and enables them to assert, in opposition to the Bible, that if only we go far enough back, we shall undoubtedly find human ancestors who were not men, but monkeys, that the apes also must have had animals of the lower kinds as ancestors, and so on to the lowest rung in the ladder of living beings. The other statement, on the other hand, exaggerates the immutability of races, and enables them to assert, in opposition to the Bible, that men of different races do not belong to the same species, and cannot therefore be brothers and be descended from the same ancestors, however far back one may go. It seems as if one would have to choose between these contradictory exaggerations. But no; there are people who instead of choosing between them assume both. They will not have negroes for their brothers, but they will have apes for their ancestors, not from brotherly hatred to the negroes, not from filial affection for the apes, nor from love for science, with which such arbitrary and contradictory assertions would ill harmonize, but in order twice to give the lie to the Bible, once in the name of the unlimited mutability of species, and once in the name of the absolute immutability of races,—as if we did not know that the differences of race are less durable than the difference of species."[1]

[1] *Les Sciences*, p. 104. See also Pfaff, *Die neuesten Forschungen*, p. 108.

XXX.

THE UNITY OF THE HUMAN RACE.

THE descent of all men from one pair is certainly asserted by Holy Scripture, and is also necessarily assumed in the Christian doctrine of original sin. But in the Old Testament not only is Adam said to be the ancestor of the whole human race, but Noah is also said to be the ancestor of all the peoples now existing. For Genesis says that all the then living men, with the exception of Noah and his family, were destroyed by the Deluge, and that the different lands were repeopled by the descendants of the three sons of Noah.[1] Genesis tells us nothing of how the different races of men were formed. The so-called "generations" (Gen. x.) give us a series of peoples, who are descended from Shem, Ham, and Japhet; but the series does not pretend to be complete,—only those peoples whom the Israelites in the time of Moses knew of are expressly mentioned,—neither does the division into the descendants of Shem, Ham, and Japhet claim to coincide with the anthropological division of races.[2] It is quite wrong to say, as Frohschammer does,[3] that the account given in the ninth chapter of Genesis of

---

[1] Gen. vi. 16, vii. 21, x. 32.
[2] Kurtz, *Geschichte des Alten Bundes*, i. 29.
[3] *Das Christenthum*, p. 216.

the words spoken by Noah after the shameful deed of Ham, gives us a Biblical statement about the formation of races. He thinks that "from a Biblical point of view, only two races exist; the Ethiopian (descendants of Ham) and perhaps the Caucasian; since the descendants of Shem and Japhet must evidently, from a scientific point of view, be included in this race; but that the formation of the first race was caused by a miracle, for in consequence of the divine curse incurred by Ham, his descendants, according to Genesis, were not only punished by being condemned to slavery, labour, and suffering, but also by the degradation and deterioration of the inner and outer, physical and intellectual nature; that is, by a compulsory natural incapacity to equal the descendants of the other two sons of Noah." This is just as bad as the old mistake of saying that Noah's curse justified slavery. It is worth while for me to show its falsity by a correct explanation of the passage in question, before I proceed to my real subject, especially as commentators sometimes interpret it wrongly.[1]

[1] Cornelius à Lapide on Wisd. xii. 11 : Hæc maledictio etiamnum durat; unde videmus Æthiopes et Mauros, quos vulgo nigros vocant, qui ex Cham prognati sunt, magna ex parte esse mancipia esseque obtusioris ingenii et vilioris præ ceteris servis conditionis. Cornelius explains Gen. ix. 25 correctly. Keil, commenting on Gen. ix. 25, says : "In the sin of Ham is foreshadowed the blot on all his race. It was characterized by sexual sin, and the curse which Noah pronounced on this sin still rests on the descendants of Ham. The Canaanites were partly destroyed and partly condemned to the lowest slavery by the Israelites ; the Phœnicians, with the Carthagenians and Egyptians, were subdued by the Persians, Macedonians, and Romans, and the other tribes descended from Ham either shared the same fate, or, burdened with the sin of their ancestor, are still groaning, as for instance the negroes and other African tribes, in the most oppressive slavery." Lord Arundell of Wardour (*Tradition, principally with Reference to Mythology and the Law of Nations*, London 1872) even thinks that after Noah's curse Canaan became suddenly black, and thus was the ancestor of a "new, unnatural, and ugly race." Cf. *Dublin Review*, new series, vol. xix. (Oct. 1872) p. 438.

In Gen. ix. 25 Noah says: "Cursed be Canaan; a servant of servants shall he be unto his brethren." Here therefore Ham is not cursed, but his son Canaan. But according to the "generations" (Gen. x. 15 seq.), the latter is the ancestor of the Phœnicians and of the pre-Israelite inhabitants of Palestine, *not* of the negroes; and the Ethiopians, the Egyptians, Philistines, etc., are included among Ham's *other* descendants in the generations. Frohschammer therefore arbitrarily inserts into the Bible a connection between the physical and intellectual degradation of the negroes and the curse pronounced by Noah on the Canaanites. The right interpretation of the passage is as follows.

The words of Noah are given in Genesis, not apparently as a wish, but as a prophecy, and it is a prophecy about the destiny of the *descendants* of his three sons. The reward which is given to Shem and Japhet consists essentially in this: that their father, being supernaturally enlightened, reveals to them a brilliant page in the future history of the races that are to spring from them; the descendants of Shem will be specially the people of Jehovah, that is, the recipients of revelation; the descendants of Japhet will extend widely, and will receive a share of the blessing given first of all to the descendants of Shem.[1] Ham's punishment is that to him a dark spot in the history of his race is revealed; the Canaanites who will descend from him will be enslaved by the descendants of Shem and Japhet. It is not the whole

[1] Gen. ix. 26, 27: "Blessed be the Lord God of Shem; and Canaan shall be his servant. God shall enlarge Japhet, and he shall dwell in the tents of Shem, and Canaan shall be his servant."

future of the descendants of Shem, Ham, and Japhet which is here foretold and connected with the moral behaviour of the three ancestors, but only a few portions of it. The history of the descendants of Shem and Japhet has many dark spots, and the history of the descendants of Ham has bright periods, but the supernaturally enlightened eye of the seer perceives neither of these; God has only revealed to him that portion of the future which is comforting for two of the ancestors and humiliating for the third; and therefore we ought not to say that the future destiny of the descendants of Shem, Ham, and Japhet is put forward as a reward and as a punishment for the conduct of Noah's three sons, but rather that to each is revealed, as punishment or as reward, according to their personal conduct, *some* part of the future of their descendants. To one is given as a reward a glimpse of a bright spot, to the third a glimpse of a dark spot in the history of his race. God, who sees the future, beheld the whole course of that history, but to Noah, as to the prophets in later times, He only revealed that portion which it was good for them to know.

Noah says nothing of the descendants of Ham as a whole. He only foretells the future of one of the peoples into which Ham's descendants will branch, the Canaanites. Neither prosperity nor adversity is foretold of the other descendants of Ham, and it is noteworthy that there is not a word about the degradation of the negroes. It is only said that the descendants of Ham would be subjugated by the descendants of Shem and Japhet, and this was fulfilled in the subjugation of the Canaanite inhabitants of Palestine by the Israelites, and in the subjugation of the Canaanite Phœnicians at Tyre and Carthage by the Greeks and Romans. The descendants of Canaan are here rightly mentioned, because the sin of Ham, shameless immorality, was especially rampant among them, as we know from the accounts given in the Bible of Sodom and Gomorrha, and the narratives of ancient writers about the immorality of the Phœnicians and Carthaginians. The fall of these descendants of Ham, and their subjection to peoples descended from Shem and Japhet, is the only thing revealed to Noah concerning the destiny of the family of Ham; and it was very natural that Moses should mention this old prophecy in Genesis, for when he wrote it his people had already been commanded by God to take possession of Palestine, and to destroy the Canaanite inhabitants as a punishment for the abominations they had committed; and thus partly to carry out the judgment which had been predicted by Noah. As I have said, it had been foretold to the other two brothers that the prosperity of the future would first be realized in the children of Shem, and by them it would be communicated to the numerous descendants of Japhet. Nothing is said of the descendants of Ham in reference to this point, for, as a punishment for his fault, only a dark page of the future history of his race is to be revealed to Ham. The next divine prophecy which can be applied to the sons of Ham teaches us that they are not to be shut out from the welfare of the future : "In thy seed," it is said to Abraham, "all people of the earth shall be blessed,"— *all* people, that is, the descendants of Ham not excepted.

The Bible therefore teaches us nothing about the origin of the different races of men, and the only Biblical statement which we have to defend in the face of natural science, is the assertion that all men are descended from one pair, all the peoples now existing from the sons of Noah. We may, however, put the question to natural science in this form. Are the different races of men now existing, different species in the sense above mentioned,[1] or only varieties of the same species? If the first is the case, it is impossible that all men can have sprung from one pair; if the latter, it is not proved that all men have really sprung from one pair, but only that they may have done so. For we have supposed in the case of the animals, that many individuals of the same species were originally created; therefore, even if it were proved that all men belonged to one species, we might yet suppose that several pairs of the same species had been the ancestors of mankind. Whether this is the case, or whether all men are descended from one pair, is not a question for natural science. We have therefore only to ask science if it can prove that men form several species; if it cannot do this, it is impossible that science and theology can contradict one another on the question of the unity of the human race, for in this case science can make no objection to the doctrine of the descent of all men from one pair.

Burmeister no doubt says, "The whole doctrine appears in so unfavourable a light to the unprejudiced inquirer whose eyes are purified by science, that he may safely assume that no calm observer would even

[1] See above, p. 33.

have dreamed of tracing back all mankind to one pair, if the Mosaic history of creation had not asserted it. In order to uphold the authority of Holy Scripture, even in matters utterly alien from its whole character, several inquirers, who are for the most part hardly sufficiently acquainted with the results of natural science, have taken upon themselves to defend the Old Testament myth, and have supported a scientific theory founded on it, which on nearer examination proves to be untenable."[1] But it is evidently incorrect to say that those who defend the theory of the unity of mankind are "for the most part insufficiently acquainted with the results of natural science."

Burmeister himself says that Prichard's *Researches into the Physical History of Mankind* is the principal work on this subject, from which we may surely conclude that this writer is sufficiently acquainted with the results of natural science. In spite of this, he defends the theory of the unity of the human race. If there is one scientific man of our century who need not be defended against the charge of insufficient acquaintance with the results of natural science, it is Alexander von Humboldt. It would be very unjust to accuse him of being prejudiced in favour of the Bible; he expressly praises modern science because, on the Continent at least, it has at last thrown off "Semitic influences."[2] But Humboldt declares himself decidedly in favour of the theory of the unity of mankind.[3] He appeals to the late Johannes Müller as concurring with him in this, and calls him the greatest anatomist

---

[1] *Geschichte der Schöpfung.* 7th ed. p. 620.
[2] *Kosmos*, i. 284. [3] *Ibid.* i. 379.

of our time ; praise which, so far as I know, has been disputed by none of his fellows. The Englishman, Owen, is held, not only in his own country, to be one of the greatest authorities on comparative anatomy ; he speaks in just the same way. Among the elder men of science, no one has investigated our question so diligently as Blumenbach ; and his observations have led him to the same result. One of the most eminent anthropologists in France at the present day is Armand de Quatrefages. I know no more decided monogenist. The most exhaustive work in modern German literature on this subject is the *Anthropologie der Naturvolker*, by Th. Waitz; the possibility of the descent of all men from one pair is expressly asserted in it, although the author himself—for reasons which will be discussed later—thinks it improbable that there was only one ancestral pair. Among the savants who believe in the unity of the human race I will mention Linnæus, Buffon, Cuvier, J. G. St. Hilaire, Steffens, Schubert, Rudolph and Andreas Wagner, K. E. von Baer, H. von Meyer, Burdach, Wilbrand, Flourens, Hugh Miller, Sir John Herschel,[1] Lyell, Huxley.[2] Are these for the most part men who are "insufficiently acquainted with the results of natural science," and does Burmeister claim such sufficient knowledge for himself, Oken, Carus, Karl Vogt, Agassiz,[3] Giebel, etc., alone ? And if we admit that a few monogenists—

[1] Cf. Ausland, 1863, p. 1048.
[2] Cf. H. Lüken, *Die Einheit*, etc. Zöckler, "Die einheitl. Abstammung," etc., in the *Jahrbuch für Deutsche Theologie*, viii. 51. *Natur und Off.* ii. 49, iii. 398, iv. 65.
[3] He originally believed in the unity of mankind ; he now thinks that whole nations were created at once. See *Jahrbuch für Deutsche Theologie*, vi. 711. Waitz, *Anthropol.* i. 218.

certainly it is not the case with most of those above mentioned—have been influenced by their respect for the Bible, are all polygenists free from the suspicion of having been influenced in their inquiries by the wish to come to a conclusion that contradicts the Bible? And has it not been said by more than one inquirer, that the desire to justify slavery has clouded the sight of American polygenists?[1]

At any rate the position which the Bible, with its doctrine of the unity of mankind, takes up against science, as it is represented by the most eminent men

[1] "In setting up the theory that the human race consists of several species, was the positive knowledge which we possess of the species and races of animals, and especially of the mammals and domestic animals, properly attended to and weighed? or did the theory originate in the feeling that the negro, and especially the negro slave, differs from the European,—the *Homo Japeticus* of Bory de St. Vincent,—and appears ugly to him; or even in the wish to think of the negro as without the claims and rights of the European? Earnest and able men have adduced zoological reasons against this theory, and yet it does not die out easily, because zoological reasons do not affect all the persons who think that they are entitled to express an opinion on such matters. Is not the theory that the human race consists of different species necessary to the consciences of the Anglo-Americans, however little it may be confirmed by natural history? The aborigines have been driven back with inhuman severity, the African races have been selfishly enslaved. It was only natural that men should say, 'We need recognise no duty towards these men, for they are of another and inferior race.' I do not mean in any way to accuse Morton, Nott, Gliddon, and others of having disputed this theory simply in order to get credit for it. But I appeal to the experience of all countries and times; when one people is acting unjustly towards another, does not the former invariably believe that the oppressed nation is very bad and incapable, and does it not repeat this belief emphatically and often? It is not very easy to escape from the influence of a general belief of this kind unless we are decidedly opposed to it."—K. E. von Baer, see *Bericht über die Zusammenkunft einiger Anthropologen*, pp. 17, 24. "If the assertions of all American writers ought to be received with caution, this is specially the case with those assertions which seek to justify negro slavery on scientific grounds."—Perty, *Grundzüge*, etc. p. 423. Also Tiedemann, *Das Hirn*, etc. p. 67. Waitz, i. 105. Vogt, *Köhlerglaube*, p. 84. De Quatrefages, *L'unité*, p. x.; *Rapport*, p. 97.

of the present day, is not so unfavourable as Burmeister wishes to make out. On the contrary, we may say unhesitatingly that in this respect also the Bible contradicts no scientific conclusion; for if the impossibility of the descent of all mankind from one pair is not held to be a scientific conclusion by Humboldt and the other writers I have mentioned, for the present at least we need not consider it as such.

Nevertheless we will look more closely at the state of the question. If by species we understand the aggregate of all the individuals who are able to produce among themselves an absolutely fertile progeny, there is no doubt that the question whether mankind is a species must be answered in the affirmative. "The races of mankind," says Johannes Müller, are forms of one single species, which can pair productively, and can reproduce themselves by generation. They are not species of a genus, were they such their hybrids would be sterile amongst themselves.[1] The experiences on this point are so numerous and various, that there can be no doubt about it.[2] We find therefore amongst men the conditions which are considered in the animal world to be the most distinct signs of species.

Let us go on to some other points in which all, even the most different races of men, resemble one another. These are—the anatomical form of the body, the liability to sickness, limit of age, normal temperature of the body, average rate of pulse, length of pregnancy, periodicity of some of the functions. Such similarity is never found in

---

[1] *Handbuch der Physiologie*, ii. 773.
[2] Cf. Prichard, i. 185 seq., and specially Baer, *Op. cit.* p. 17 seq. Waitz, *Anthropol.* i. 195. Peschel, *Volkerkunde*, p. 9. Quatrefages, *Rapport*, p. 439.

the animal world in the case of the different species of a genus, but only in the case of varieties of a species.[1]

In the matter of size also, as Burmeister observes,[2] there is no essential difference. "The northern nations are no doubt smaller on the whole than those of the temperate zones, but there are no real nations of dwarfs. Five feet, a height which is not exceeded by many individuals in Europe, is the minimum, below which a whole nation does not easily fall; while, on the other hand, six feet is the maximum height, which whole nations rarely exceed, although everywhere there are individuals taller than this. The height of the Patagonians stands hardly in the ratio of 3 to 2 to that of the Eskimos, while amongst the different varieties of the dog we find the ratio of 1 to 12, and amongst the varieties of the tame bull, 1 to 6.[3]

The most striking differences between the different races of men lie in the colour of the skin, the character of the hair, and the form of the skull and the pelvis.

[1] Delitzsch, *Genesis*, p. 241. Cf. Prichard, i. 151 seq. Perty, *Grundzüge*, p. 19. Waitz, *Anthropol.* i. 124. Quatrefages, *Rapport*, p. 343. Rauch, *Die Einheit*, p. 50.

[2] *Geschichte der Schöpfung.* p. 506, 7th ed. p. 622. Cf. Strücker, *Ueber Zwerg und Riesenvolker.* See *Im neuen Reich*, 1879, ii. 153.

[3] Peschel, *Volkerkunde*, p. 82 : "The average height of man according to the data now before me is 1·60 of a metre ; but this average has been obtained from many very different single instances. If all men were arranged according to their height, we should have a series whose separate members would differ only 1–100th of a millimetre. But in this series men of the same race would not always be together. Not all Patagonians are almost 2, nor all Bushmen 1·18 metres high (Peschel's highest measurements are, *op. cit.* p. 84 : Patagonians 1·80, Polynesians 1·93, the lowest of the Bushmen 1·30 metres). Many of the Cuirassiers and Imperial Guards would be among the first, and the Lapps in Northern Europe and Andaman Islanders in the Gulf of Bengal would be among the last. We find nothing like this in any kind of animal which includes many species; the races of domestic animals would furnish the only analogy to it. Quatrefages, *Hist. de L'homme*, iv. p. 20 ; *Rapport*, p. 280.

The different races have been grouped according to colour and form of skull.[1] Blumenbach, who on this subject is the most eminent of the older savants (1752–1840), divides them into five races, which he calls the Caucasian, Mongolian, Ethiopian, American, and Malay. The most striking characteristic of these five races is the colour of the skin; the Caucasians are white, the Mongols yellow, the Ethiopians black, the Americans a coppery red, and the Malays brown. And yet Peschel says, " If we had other more marked characteristics for distinguishing races, no one would venture to call the colour of the skin such, for it varies both in shade and in colour, not only in every tribe, but often in the individuals of a single tribe."[2]

As to the hair, its colour varies so much that it can hardly be considered as distinguishing the races; the character of the hair is more important, and some modern anthropologists have laid great stress on this. We can distinguish a smooth or straight, a curly or wavy, a frizzy or a tufted growth of the hair. And the form of the transverse section of the single hairs differs; it is sometimes round, sometimes elliptical. If the largest diameter of the transverse section of the hair is 100, the smallest diameter sinks from 95 in the South Americans to 34 in the Papuans in New Guinea. The tendency to curliness and to frizziness increases with the increased flatness of the hair, with which greater fineness is also usually connected. Generally speaking the Americans and Mongols have round straight hair, the Europeans and Semitic races

[1] Cf. Waitz, *Anthropologie*, i. 260. Zöckler, *Op. cit.* p. 53.
[2] *Volkerkunde*, p. 93.

curly, and the negroes and Australians frizzy hair; the tufted growth of hair, in which the hairs are collected into separate tufts, is found amongst the Papuans, the Hottentots, the Bushmen, and a few other African tribes. But here also we find gradual transitions which make a sharp separation of the races impossible. We find also important differences in the growth of the beard and of the hair on other parts of the body; but these are not distinct and invariable enough to make them a distinguishing mark of race, at any rate it is not right to say, as Hæckel does,[1] that after speech the nature of the growth of the hair may be made the basis of classification of the human race.

Blumenbach in his classification has laid special stress on the form of the skull. Before his time the Dutchman Peter Camper (†1789) had made an ingenious rule for this, which depends on the so-called facial angle.[2] In order to get this you look at the skull from the side, and first draw a line from the opening of the ear to the base of the nose, then a second line from the most prominent part of the brow to the outer edge of the upper jawbone where the roots of the teeth are: the angle at which these two lines intersect each other is the facial angle. The minimum of the facial angle, which only unhealthy forms, such as cretins, do not reach, is, according to Burmeister, 75 degrees.[3] At 70 degrees, according to others at much fewer, the ape type begins, and henceforth the angle diminishes through all possible degrees amongst the mammals.

---

[1] *Nat. Schöpfungsgeschichte*, p. 602. Peschel, *Volkerkunde*, p. 96.
[2] Prichard, i. 279. Wiseman, *On the Connection*, etc. i. 168.
[3] *Geschichte der Schöpfung*, p. 510 (7th ed. 627).

In regularly formed human skulls the facial angle varies according to usual calculations between 72 and 85 degrees; the larger it is the nobler and finer is the shape of the skull all through. In Greek statues in which we admire the ideal of the human form, the facial angle is 90 degrees, just as if the old masters had wished to express by this means the highest spiritual perfection of their gods and heroes. An increase above 90 degrees becomes ugly, and the healthy human head assumes the form of one with water on the brain. Blumenbach said that the facial angle was an inadequate characteristic in the classification of races, and modern anthropologists have either quite given up this criterion or essentially modified it, and have also proved that the figures usually given for the facial angle are incorrect.[1]

Blumenbach distinguishes three principal forms of the skull. The oval skull is broadest at the top of the forehead, it has a spherical crown, the back of the head is arched towards the top, the forehead is high and straight, the cheek-bones small, the jaw small and straight, the chin small. In the square-faced or pyramidal skull the contour of the face is on the whole round, the forehead broad and narrow, the cheek-bones prominent, the chin broad and straight, the crown of the head rather flat, the back of the head flat, and the greatest diameter of the skull is at the level of the

---

[1] Aeby, *Die Schädelformen*, p. 81. H. v. Ihering, "Ueber das Wesen der Prognathie," *Archiv für Anthropologie*, v. 379. According to Aeby the facial angle in the Pithecus Satyrus and Gorilla is 39, in the Hylobates 54, in the Cebus 60. In man he gives it as 68–80. In none of the Europeans examined by him did the facial angle reach to 80 degrees (in a Swede it was 71, in a Turk, Dane, Jew, Dutchman, Lapp 75, in a Russian and a Cossack 76, in an Australian 77, in a Hindoo and a Greek 78, in a Bugi 80), and yet this is often given as the minimum for Europeans.

cheek-bones or the ear. The elongated skull has a small face, the greatest diameter of which is through the cheek-bones, a small narrow receding forehead, a projecting jaw, a receding chin, a narrow, almost angular crown, and the back of the head projecting.[1] According to Blumenbach, the first form charcterizes the Caucasian races, the second the Mongolian, the third the Ethiopians. He thinks that in this respect the Americans and Malays are varieties holding a middle position between the Caucasian race on the one hand, and the Mongolian and Ethiopian on the other.

In this classification of skulls, stress is laid on the shape of the face and the inclination of the forehead. A later anthropologist, the Swede Anders Retzius, thought it expedient to lay more stress on the actual cranium.[2] He says that the diversity in the outward shape of skulls is produced principally by the development of one of the three lobes of the cerebrum. The length of the skull at the back, and its narrow shape, which characterize the negro races, depend partly on the smaller size of the cerebrum, partly on the striking smallness of its middle lobe. This is very large in pyramidal (Mongolian) skulls; on the other hand, the posterior lobe, which in the negroes is the most developed, is extremely small. In the oval (Caucasian) skulls the anterior lobe of the cerebrum predominates, and by this means the forehead is more rounded, and a general development of the brain takes place, which causes the anterior lobe to project farther than is the

---

[1] Burmeister, *Geschichte der Schöpfung*, p. 509 (7th ed. p. 626).
[2] Cf. Burmeister, p. 510 (p. 627). A. Wagner, *Gesch. der Urwelt*, ii. 32. *Ausland*, 1866, p. 686. Vogt, *Vorlesungen*, i. 57.

case with the pyramidal skulls. Retzius bases his division of nations into long-skulled and short-skulled (Dolichokephali and Brachykephali), on the size of the posterior lobe; he includes in the first the elongated and oval (Ethiopian and Caucasian races), and in the second the pyramidal (Mongolian race). He divides both classes again according to the position of the jaw, with which the inclination of the forehead harmonizes, into straight-jawed and slanting-jawed nations (orthognathous and prognathous). In this way he gets four principal types. To the long-skulled races with straight-jaws belong the Celtic, Germanic, Romance, and Hindoo races; to the round-skulled races with straight jaws, the Slavs, Lapps, Persians, Turks, Polynesians, etc.; to the round-skulled with slanting jaws, the Tartars, Mongols, Malays, and several West American tribes; to the long-skulled races with slanting jaws, the Australian, Chinese, Japanese, Negroes, Eskimos, and most East American tribes.

You will observe — and this is not unimportant — that these different groups do not correspond. The differences between the different tribes would be much more remarkable if the same races which differed in colour differed also in form of the skull, and if, according to the classification of Blumenbach and that of Retzius, the same races could be joined and the same separated. But this is not the case. Blumenbach's classification, according to the form of the skull, gives no separate place to the Americans and Malays. In his system the Germanic and Slavic peoples belong to one group, as they do also in point of colour. In Retzius' system they belong to different groups. On the other hand, Retzius includes Negroes, Australians, and Greenlanders in one group, whereas Blumenbach divides them. Each principle of classification therefore, if we hold to it alone, leads us to combinations and divisions which according to the other principle of classification are unnatural. We may therefore conclude from this that there is not so clear a line of demarcation between the races of mankind as there is between species of animals which, though they resemble one another, are yet different.

If we group the races of mankind according to the shape of the skull, we must except not only the pathological abnormal instances which occasionally occur, but also those which we occasionally find in whole races, which are produced not naturally, but artificially. In many races, for instance, there is a custom of pressing or binding up the skull directly after the birth of the child, so as to give it a shape which approaches to that considered as the ideal of a beautiful skull in those tribes, some trying to flatten the skull as much as possible, others to make it as high as possible. This practice exists principally amongst American races, but it occurs in other countries, and it was found sometimes in ancient times, as old writers tell us. Savants still dispute whether such artificial shaping of the skull if it is carried out throughout a series of generations may not become hereditary.[1]

The measurement and classification of skulls has been carried out very vigorously and carefully in late years by anthropologists. But unfortunately craniologists have not yet decided on any certain process of

[1] A. Wagner, ii. 39. Burmeister, *Geschichte der Schöpfung*, p. 514 (631). *Archiv für Anthropologie*, ii. 21.

measurement,[1] and therefore skulls are classed by them very differently. Instead of Retzius' classification, Aeby divides skulls into broad and narrow, Eurykephalous and Stenokephalous;[2] Hermann Welcker into narrow or long skulls (Dolichokephalous), straight skulls (Orthokephalous),—which are called middle skulls (Mesokephalous) by Broca and others,—and broad or short skulls (Brachykephalous), and he bases this division on the relation of the diameter in length to the diameter in breadth at one given place in the skull. If the first is taken as 100, the "index of breadth," as the percentage of the diameter of breadth is called, varies between 58 and 98, or if we leave out exceptional cases, between 67 and 85. If the index of breadth sinks below 74, the skulls are called Dolichokephalous; if it rises above 78, Brachykephalous; skulls with an index of breadth of 74–78 are called Orthokephalous or Mesokephalous. The index of height, as the measure of the height of the skull given in percentage of the diameter of length is called, varies between 70 and 82, and by it we distinguish between high and flat skulls, Hypsikephalous and Platykephalous. As a rule the narrower skulls are higher, and the broader, flatter.[3] In the same way, in recent times the human brain has been carefully measured and weighed, and the facial angle has been measured more accurately than by Camper;

---

[1] Cf. H. v. Ihering, *Die 5, allgemeine Versammlung der Deutschen Gesellschaft für Anthropologie*, etc., Dresden 1874, Brunswick 1875, p. 68. *Archiv für Anthropol.* i. 90, 250.

[2] *Die Schädelformen*, p. 28.

[3] Peschel, *Volkerkunde*, p. 55. *Archiv für Anthr.* i. 127. Pfaff, *Schöpfungsgeschichte*, p. 715.

Welcker enumerates prognathous, orthognathous (mesognathous) and opisthognathous skulls, and it has been found that generally speaking prognathism occurs in narrow skulls, whereas the middle and broad skulls are mostly mesognathous, and sometimes opisthognathous.[1]

Considering the accuracy which modern anthropologists hold to be necessary in these measurements, many more skulls, from more countries than has hitherto been possible, must be measured before any certain conclusions can be arrived at. But even the measurements which have been made hitherto show that great variations exist within single tribes, and hence it seems very unlikely that we shall be able to found a distinct classification of races on the basis of the different skull formations. The index of breadth in the Malays, for instance, varies between 73 and 82. The Negro skulls are universally narrow and high; the index of breadth falls as low as 68, and the index of height rises to 69; but still Negro skulls occur in which the index of breadth is 77, and Slavic and German skulls whose index of breadth is less than 73. Prognathism occurs principally among the lower races; but Welcker reckons the Eskimos and Hottentots amongst the mesognathous races, and cases of prognathism among the English and French are not unknown.

The pelvis, the circle of strong wide bones at the lower end of the hollow of the stomach, is also differently formed; four principal forms have been distinguished: the oval, round, square and wedge shaped; or three if the oval and round forms are united.[2] This point,

---

[1] Peschel, *Volkerkunde*, p. 77.
[2] M. J. Weber, *Die Lehre von dem Ur-und Rassenformen der Schädel*

however, is of minor importance to our object, as the differences in this respect are less evident and constant than in the case of the skulls.

Lastly, speech is considered; some anthropologists, as *e.g.* the Englishman Latham, make use of the differences of speech as the main principle of classification, and treat the differences in bodily shape as of secondary importance. I shall return to this point; but other anthropologists are evidently not wrong in saying that in a natural history of the varieties of mankind the differences in the bodily formation of man must be first attended to. Language is at any rate a much more unstable element than the bodily type. It can be transmitted from our race to another, quite different in bodily formation and in descent.

Our next task therefore will be to examine what weight must be attached, first to the differences in the shape of the skull and in the colour of the skin, and then to the differences in language, in face of the similarity which we find among all men. The characteristics which are common to all mankind, and among them specially the power that all races have of crossbreeding, prove at any rate that the races of men are not different species of a genus, but varieties of a species.[1]

und Becken des Menschen, Düsseldorf 1830. Prichard, i. 377. A. Wagner, ii. 96. Peschel, *Volkerkunde,* p. 80.

[1] " If the colour of the Negro were of such importance, that because of it Negroes and Europeans must be pronounced by natural science to be two different species of the human race, all the parts of the body would differ in them just as generally as does the colour, and this is not the case. We do no doubt find slight differences between every limb of the Negro and of the European, but they are differences of degree and not of kind as would be the case if the two bodies belonged to different species. Look at the differences between the horse and the donkey, or the ox and

Two things are, however, still possible. (1) The different races of men have common ancestors, either one pair or several similar pairs. The differences in colour, shape of the skull, etc., have developed in the descendants of these ancestors. (2) Each race had special ancestors, who resembled each other in the points in which men resemble each other now, and differed in the points in which men differ from one another now.

According to the first assumption, the many intermediate stages in the forms of the skull and in the colour of the skin show us how a great part of mankind has gradually deviated from the primitive type. If the first ancestors were Caucasians, the Negroes would be farthest removed from them, and be connected with them by the countless intermediate types which have more or less of the pure Caucasian and the pure Negro type. On the other hand, according to the second assumption, the Negroes would be just as near to their own ancestors, the black Adam and the black Eve, as the Caucasians to theirs ; the races who do not purely

the buffalo ; not only is the colour and quality of the hair, and the size different, but every single bone, every single muscle is different also ; a difference which is so thorough that a practised eye can tell at once whether a single bone belongs to a horse or a donkey, an ox or a buffalo. Of course there are differences between the skulls of Negroes and of Europeans; but they are not of the same kind as those between the skulls of a horse and a donkey ; and any one who has tried to trace out the way in which the bones of animals belonging to any genus differ, will know that these differences are always more apparent and greater than the dissimilarities between the most different peoples of the earth. A common bond unites and runs through the human race, its presence always betrays humanity, and the intelligent observer can never be in doubt as to whether he has to do with a single species or only with the genus man, under which are included 100 species. This is at present still a scientific fact."—Burmeister, *Geol. Bilder*, i. 69.

represent either type, would he considered as degenerate, or as mongrels, in whom the original differences had been obliterated.

It is not necessary for our object that we should prove the second theory to be quite untenable and the first alone correct, considered in the light of comparative anthropology. It is quite sufficient if we can prove scientifically that the first theory is tenable, that the descent of the different existing races of men from the same or similar ancestors is possible, and that the origin of the present differences may be explained without the assumption of different ancestors. If this proof can be given,—and this I shall try to do in my next lecture,—it cannot be asserted that the doctrine of the unity of mankind contradicts scientific anthropology.

XXXI.

THE UNITY OF THE HUMAN RACE—*Continued.*

As I mentioned in my last lecture, the classifications of the different races according to their supposed relationship will never coincide, if either the shape of the skull or the colour of the hair be exclusively considered. In the division of mankind into five races which at present obtains, and which Blumenbach first introduced, the physical and geographical conditions are considered in such a way that no one single factor becomes of importance. I will now give a short sketch of the five races, based on Burmeister's description, which varies from the ordinary classification by including the Malays in the Caucasian race, and thus not making them a separate race; while the aboriginal inhabitants of Australia are counted as a fifth race, and are not included in the Ethiopian race. I hope you will not overlook the frequency with which Burmeister, who opposes the theory of the unity of mankind, is obliged to mention differences in the same races, and resemblances between different races, —a clear proof that the different race types are not sharply defined, but connected by many intermediate stages.

1. The American races resemble one another much more than do the races which extend throughout all

the zones in other parts of the earth. It has almost become a proverb, says Morton, one of the men who knows most about the American races, that he who has seen one Indian tribe has seen all; to such an extent do the individuals of this race resemble one another, in spite of the large geographical extent and the extremely different climates of their land.[1] In all there is seen the same long straight hair, the cinnamon coloured skin, the gloomy brow, the dull sleepy eye, the full tightly set lips, and the projecting but wide nose, to which characteristics we may add the projecting though rounded cheek-bones, the scanty beards of the men, the stature, rather broad at the shoulders, but lean and not very vigorous, and the comparatively small hands and feet. The form of the skull varies much. Although perhaps originally it everywhere approached nearest to the pyramidal type, yet the skulls of the Americans nowhere have the purely Mongolian shape, leaning rather towards special forms, sometimes oval, sometimes even elongated. These natural differences are much intensified by the artificial deformities which are caused by binding up or pressing the heads of new-born children, in the most widely different nations both in North and South America. The colour of the skin is reddish, according to Morton's description a cinnamon brown. This colour has not been produced by the custom which prevails in many tribes of painting the skin, but nature has been aided by art. No one who knows the manifold shades of colour in the Eastern races will wonder that the red

---

[1] Cf. "Prince Maximilian zu Wied," in the *Verhandlungen des naturhist. Vereins*, Bonn 1863, xx. Corr. p. 54. Peschel, *Volkerkunde*, p. 430.

colour is not equally deep in all the nations. Indeed the differences of colour in Americans are very much less than in the Eastern nations. Americans are never black like Negroes, nor white like Europeans, they vary between a darker or lighter shade of cinnamon brown, which sometimes shades into copper colour, and sometimes more into red. Strange to say, the deepest shades are found in the northern and southern tribes, especially in the Californians and Patagonians, while the middle tribes, living almost under the Equator, are the lightest. Morton separates the Eskimos from the American races, and connects them with the Mongolian. Burmeister takes the same view, by reason of the large head, which is long at the back and flat at the forehead, the great breadth and flatness of the face, the small black eyes, the small round mouth, the tendency to fatness, which the Americans are entirely without, and the whiter skin.

2. The Mongolian race is connected with the American through the Eskimos. Its special characteristics are, a decidedly pyramidal form of skull, a broad flat face with a low forehead, small slanting eyes, high projecting cheek-bones, a powerful, rather projecting broad jaw, a scanty beard, and black straight hair like the Americans; a low, full stature inclined to corpulency, and a yellowish skin, sometimes inclining to brown and sometimes to white. The inhabitants of Middle and Eastern Asia, and probably the North polar tribes, belong to the Mongolian race. It is divided into several different groups, among which the Mongols proper, with the Kalmucks and Buriates of Central Asia, stand out as the most decided type of the race. The

Chinese approach the Malay race in their bodily formation. The Japanese come next to the Chinese, and through them the Mongolian type is transferred to the inhabitants of the Aleutian and Kurile Islands, and from them it stretches on to the Eskimos, who form the transition to the American races. On the continent of Asia the Mongol tribes of the Kamtschadales, Tungusians, and Samoiedes spread as far as Europe, where they join the Tschudis and Lapps. The latter are by some included amongst the Mongol peoples, whereas Burmeister classes them amongst the Tartar Caucasian peoples, although he admits that a near relation exists between them and the neighbouring Mongol tribes.

3. The Caucasian race has an oval form of skull, usually a high rounded forehead, the back of the head round, large open eyes, straight teeth, a straight chin, a thick beard, and soft, smooth, or curly hair. The colour is more uncertain. In the purest Caucasian types, indeed, we find a reddish white skin, but very few nations preserve it; in the southern nations of the Caucasian race, especially in the places where it approaches the negro races, the colour of the skin is brown, and is even sometimes so dark that it resembles that of some nations of the negro race. The colour of the hair and eyes harmonize generally speaking with that of the skin. Purely white Caucasians have mostly fair or reddish hair and blue eyes; in the more darkly coloured peoples we find brown hair, black hair with brown eyes, and lastly black eyes also. At this stage the resemblance to the (Malay) Southern Islands, or to certain Ethiopian nations, is unmistakeable.

The Caucasian race comprises the population of Europe, that of Africa on the coast of the Mediterranean, and that of Asia to the Eastern Highlands of Mongolia. Burmeister thinks that it is impossible to divide the Caucasian race according to colour or any other bodily characteristic, because of the great variations; he divides the West Caucasians according to speech into Indogerman, Semitic, and Berber races. The latter only exist in the scanty remnant of the Kabyles and Kopts; they attained their highest prosperity formerly in the old Egyptians. Their colour was darker than that of most of the Semitic and Indogermanic races, it was brown, even coppery, it seems to have somewhat resembled the colouring of the Hottentots; according to Herodotus their black hair was crisp, whereas examination of the mummies shows us straight hair. To these Western Caucasian tribes, Burmeister adds as Eastern portions of the Caucasian type, two tribes, which also have an oval form of skull: the Malays and the Scythians. The first are brown in colour, sometimes lighter than the Berbers, sometimes just as dark. Their bodies are gracefully formed, but generally not very large, roundish skulls, black straight hair, small eyes, noses broad at the base, and tolerably thick lips. These qualities cause them to resemble several Mongolian tribes, especially the Chinese. Blumenbach and others, as I have said, class the Malays as a separate race, but they make it include more peoples than does Burmeister. The latter divides the Malays into two such families, the Western and the Eastern. He calls the former the true Malays, and numbers among them the inhabitants of the Malacca peninsula, Sumatra,

Java, Borneo, the Phillippines and the Moluccas. The Eastern sub-family of the Malays comprises the inhabitants of New Zealand, and the farther Australian groups of islands. The inhabitants of the latter are more symmetrically formed, they are slenderer, stronger, and in particular more muscular, also browner than the Malay peoples.

The last tribe which Burmeister includes in the Cancasian race is the Scythian. In a few tribes of this people, the Turkomans and Turks, the human body is of a very perfect type, really rivalling the ideals of Greek perfection. But most of the people resemble in part Mongolian, in part Slav forms. To these belong in the east the Jakuts, in the west the Lapps and Finns,—the former are by some included amongst the Mongols,—in the centre the Tartars, Kirghiz, and Usbeks. A branch of the Scythian people, the Magyars, has pushed through the Slav races as far as Hungary.

4. Just as the last-mentioned Caucasian peoples bear a distinct relation to the Mongols, the nations of the Ethiopian race join on to the Caucasian Berbers through their likeness to them in bodily form and language. The general qualities of this fourth race are most completely developed in the negroes: black colour, woolly crisp hair, a narrow forehead, a short nose broad at the base, a projecting jaw, lips which are rather projecting and flat than thick, long arms with small hands, shorter legs with small calves and flat feet. To this race belong all the African peoples south of the Sahara. They are divided into three large families, the Negroes, Kaffirs, and Hottentots, also the Papuans on the Island groups north of New Holland. The actual Negroes are

divided into numerous peoples with an elongated form of skull, but with a skin sometimes brown, sometimes deep black. The Kaffirs situated in Central Africa beyond the Equator, and on the east coast farther south up to Port Natal, are vigorous and of high stature; their colour is not nut brown, but rather bronze brown or black, and they have a large nose with a high bridge, and a higher forehead than the negroes. There is something rather noble and European in their physiognomy. The Hottentots in Southern Africa have a light copper coloured skin, their bodies are smaller and more weakly built, they have remarkably small hands and feet, narrow, rather crooked eyes, and rounder skulls. In this they resemble the Mongolians. The Papuans, or Australian negroes, resemble the real negroes very nearly, but have longer, thicker hair, which is, however, woolly and crisp, and their skulls are round, not elongated, although they have preserved the projecting jaw of the true negroes. The forehead is higher than with the true negroes, and resembles the Kaffir type.

5. Whereas Blumenbach and others count the Malays as the fifth race, Burmeister makes out that the aboriginal inhabitants of Australia are the fifth race. They have the deep black skin, the small elongated form of skull, the projecting jaw, the thick lips, and the flat nose of the negro; but they are distinguished from the latter by their coarse, smooth, or slightly curly hair, which is not very long, and *never* woolly; and also by having remarkably large stomachs and remarkably slender limbs. These peoples, says Burmeister, remind us of the ape, the caricature of man. The physical and moral degradation of most of the tribes, their wanderings

in the forests, their cannibalism, and the artificial deformities which they like, go far towards making this resemblance greater. The Australians are classed by others, together with the Papuans mentioned above, as one family of the Ethiopian race; and Burmeister's description has been shown by further investigations to have been very much exaggerated.[1]

Among other classifications I will only mention O. Peschel's. He distinguishes seven races; the first includes the Australians (New Hollanders), mentioned last by Burmeister; the second the Australian and Asiatic Papuans; the third race, which he calls the "Mongol-like peoples," includes the Malay tribes, the South-Eastern Asiatics (the inhabitants of Further India, Tibetians, and Chinese), the Coreans and Japanese, the Mongol tribes in the north of the Old World, the Behring tribes (Eskimos), and the American aborigines. The Drawida, or aborigines of Hindostan, are the fourth race, the fifth the Hottentots and Bushmen, the sixth the negroes. The seventh, the "midland" race, corresponds generally to the Caucasian.

The great difference which exists between the classifications of different anthropologists shows plainly enough that a sharp separation of the races is not possible. "If it were easy," says Peschel, "to define the boundaries between the different races, anthropologists would not differ so much as they do now; when one thinks that mankind should be divided into two, and another into a hundred and fifty varieties, races, or families."[2] Even if we put aside these ex-

---

[1] *Corr.-blatt der deutschen Gesellschaft für Anthropol.* Sept. 1881, p. 85.
[2] *Volkerkunde*, p. 14.

tremes, we find that Cuvier and Th. Waitz enumerate three races, Blumenbach and Burmeister five, Prichard and Peschel seven, Agassiz eight, Friedrich Müller and Hæckel twelve, Morton twenty-two. Burmeister, as we have seen, adds the Malays, whom Blumenbach makes a separate race, to the Caucasians; Peschel adds them to the Mongols; and the latter says of the Americans, that it were in vain to seek, even from these writers who say that they are a separate race, for any common characteristics which distinguish them from the Asiatic Mongols."[1]

Peschel further lays stress on the fact that no single characteristic is the special property of any race of men; but that, on the contrary, all the races merge into one another by imperceptible degrees. "The usual method of classifying the different races," he adds, "is very misleading; for men do not notice the frequency with which certain characteristics occur, but they seek out of many individuals that one which differs most from the individuals of other races, and make him the type."[2]

A German, a Patagonian, a Kalmuck, and a negro no doubt differ from one another very much, but there are so many intermediate stages between them, that the transition from each separate tribe to the one next to it is not very abrupt. If you put the darkest and the lightest blue you can find next to each other you have contrasting colours; but if all the shades of blue are put together in proper order, the contrast will vanish, and the transition from the lightest to the darkest shades will become so gradual as to be unnoticed. In the sketch which I gave of Burmeister's

[1] *Volkerkunde*, p. 431. [2] *Ibid.* p. 14.

system I alluded to these intermediate stages between the separate races; they are not absent in any single group, and we have seen that the transition type is so strongly marked in several tribes that anthropologists cannot agree whether they belong to one race or another. "The Finns," says Waitz, "are a link between the Caucasian and the Mongolian races, and the Hindoos have often been considered to be a link between the Caucasian and the Malay race. The Tschuktschis and Yoriakes, the Eskimos and some other tribes of Western America, the form of whose skull resembles that of the Mongols, come between the Asiatics and Americans, and the Eskimos themselves, who on the Atlantic are easily distinguishable, and sharply separated from the American Indians, gradually merge into the latter on the coast of the Pacific."[1]

"So long as extremes in diversity of colour and configuration were alone considered," says Humboldt, "and the first liveliness of sensible impression was yielded to, there might have been a disposition to consider races, not as mere varieties, but as originally different kinds of men. The permanency of certain types, even amidst the most inimical operation of external, especially climatic influences, appeared to favour such an assumption, short though the time be through which historical information has come down to us. . . . The greater number of the contrasts which in former times were believed to have been discovered, have been disposed of by the industrious work of Tiedemann, on the Brain of the Negro and European, and by the anatomical inquiries of Vrolik and of Weber, on the Form of the Pelvis.

[1] *Anthropologie*, i. 241.

If we look generally at the dark-skinned African nations, on which Prichard's admirable work has thrown so much light, and compare them with the races of the South Indian and West Australian Archipelagos, with the Papuans and Alfourous, we see clearly that a black skin, woolly hair, and negro-like features are by no means always conjoined. . . . The old classification of Blumenbach's into five races may be followed, or we may assume with Prichard that seven races exist: still no very distinct or natural principle of classification is recognisable in such arrangements. The extremes of configuration and colour are distinguished, without notice being taken of the tribes which cannot be included in either class."[1]

As regards the different forms of skull, Aeby says: "The fact that there is no interruption in the series of normal forms, because the extremes are connected by countless intermediate forms, and further, that each normal form is only the imaginary centre of a series of individual organisms, which often equal the main series in detail, is of great importance. This continuity in the forms of skull is the more remarkable, because it is in harmony with all the other circumstances of mankind. If we break the organic connection of the extremes, they are no doubt sharply separated, and if any one, as is often the case, contrasts the negro and the European, it is easy to make splendid school pictures in most vivid colours of the different races of mankind. But then they are school pictures, and their outlines are remorselessly obliterated by the reality."[2]

[1] *Cosmos*, i. 379.   [2] *Die Schädelformen*, p. 57.

In conclusion it will suffice if we mention in detail the intermediate forms of the two races whose types are farthest removed from one another, the Caucasian and the Ethiopian.[1] In the southern nations of the Caucasian race, says Burmeister, the colour of the skin is brown, sometimes so dark as to resemble certain nations of the negro race, and as regards the colouring of the hair and the eyes also, the likeness to certain Ethiopian peoples is unmistakeable. The Berbers of Nubia in the upper valley of the Nile show this transition most plainly. They have a good figure, an oval face, a hooked nose, like the Caucasians; the lips are thick but not puffed out, the hair crisp and curly but not woolly as with the negroes; the colour is bronze, something between the ebony black of the true negro and the olive shade of the Egyptians. The inhabitants of the Nuba in Kordofan are even more like the negroes; their colour is not quite so dark, but it is coppery; their features have something negro-like in them, but they are more regular; the nose is smaller than that of the Europeans, but it is less flat than that of the negroes; the lips are not so thick and the cheek-bones not so projecting; the hair is woolly with some, but with most it resembles that of the Europeans, only it is thicker and always curly. A few of the Bedouin tribes between the Nile and the Red Sea are dark brown, and in some cases almost black; the hair is black and curly although not woolly: the whole form of body is more like Europeans than negroes.

All these nations are included in the Caucasian race. In the Ethiopian negroes the intensity of colour varies

[1] Cf. Waitz, *Anthropologie*, i. 234.

according to the peoples and individuals, very few have a deep black skin. Flat noses, thick lips, and projecting jaws are the rule no doubt, but there are frequent exceptions, and we often find European physiognomies in the middle of the African type. Sometimes this may proceed from an intermixture with Europeans; but much more often this is out of the question, and these instances must be examples of original transitional forms to the Caucasian race. Some tribes are deep black, but their physiognomies are not at all negro-like, their features being rather European or Indian. The woolly hair is the most constant characteristic of the negro race, but among the Fellahs, for example, it is frequently not found. The Kaffirs have the dark colour and woolly hair in common with the negroes, but in their features and bodily shape they differ from them, and show a surprising likeness to Europeans, although geographically they are farther from the Caucasian than from the negro race. The Hottentots resemble the negroes in having woolly hair, flat noses, and thick lips, but they differ from them in having a yellow coloured skin, projecting cheek-bones and narrow eyes; and in this respect and in the form of their skull they resemble the Chinese, that is, the Mongolian type.

"There is, perhaps, not one tribe," says Prichard, "in which all the characters ascribed to the negro are found in the highest degree, and in general they are distributed to different races in all manners of ways, and combined in each instance with more or fewer of the characters belonging to the European or the Asiatic."[1]

"The alleged persistency of the negro type," says Waitz,

[1] *Researches*, etc. ii. 340.

is almost entirely imaginary; this type is in reality confined to comparatively few peoples, and we find with the negro many other types which may partly be considered as transitions to European forms, and partly are simply variations and modifications of the negro type itself."[1]

"If the different races all had a separate origin," says K. E. v. Baer,[2] "we should expect to find that their characteristics were especially marked in certain regions, or, as races may change their abode very considerably, at least in certain peoples. Now it is well known that the prognathous face is most conspicuous in the negroes of Guinea, and specially on the Slave Coast, where the European colonies in America principally obtained their slaves. But not very far from them we find tribes said by all who have seen them to be much handsomer. The Joloffs, *e.g.*, have higher foreheads, their jaws project very little, their teeth are straight, and they are well formed, but they are quite black. Their neighbours, the Mandingoes, have much more the characteristics which we are accustomed to consider as typical of the negroes, projecting jaws, flat noses, flat foreheads, but they are less black in colour. It would be desirable to have measurements of the bodies and skulls of both tribes, in order to be able to judge more thoroughly whether the other characteristics which distinguish negroes from Europeans are divided amongst them. What we know, even already, does not seem to me to favour the separate origin of negroes, for I should expect to find all the characteristics in which they differ

---

[1] *Anthropologie*, i. 239.
[2] *Bericht über die Zusammenkunft einiger Anthropologen*, p. 68.

from Europeans united. I am of the same opinion when I examine the original home of the Mongol races. The skull seems to me to be broadest in the middle of Asia, amongst the actual Mongolian peoples. The broad and flat *face* is much more widely distributed. This characteristic is very conspicuous in the Tunguses, who have decidedly longer skulls. In the Eskimo the skull is quite long, and the face remains broad. Which people represents the type?"

As I have said, these numerous intermediate forms make it seem probable that the different races have a common origin, however little Europeans and negroes, in whom the type of their race is most completely developed, may resemble one another. It is specially worthy of remark that the principal criterions of race, the form of the skull and the colour of the skin, do not, as we have seen, coincide in several cases; that if we look only to the form of the skull, many tribes would appear to belong to one race, and if we look only to the colour of the skin to another.

Further, we must guard against the error of supposing that all the characteristic peculiarities of a race, or even of a tribe, a certain form of skull for instance, are equally strongly marked in all the individuals. It has been often asserted that peculiarities which had been observed, as I mentioned before, in single individuals only, were characteristic of a tribe. Retzius says that the Slavs belong to the decidedly round skulled peoples, because he found this form existing in the few Slav heads which he could examine. Baer, who was able to examine many more Russian skulls, found that this form existed in a few Little Russian heads, but not in others which were put down as Russian, without any more definite specification of their place of birth.[1] The same savant became persuaded, after visiting a collection containing a great many negro skulls, that the differences in this race, of which modern travellers speak so much, had been very inadequately observed, and that the form of skull of certain tribes in Guinea had been erroneously considered to represent the whole negro race.[2]

To this we must add the fact that what is the rule in one race is found at least exceptionally in other races; and that "there appear to exist everywhere on the earth, individuals who in external characteristics differ considerably from their race, and show the type of a strange race, although the assumption of an intermixture with that race is inadmissible."[3] Red hair generally occurs only in the Caucasian race; but we find red haired individuals in every race, even among the negroes. In the same way we find amongst ourselves people whose hair resembles the black woolly hair of the negroes; others, the colour of whose skin is unusually dark, and a still greater number whose faces are shaped like those of the negroes or Mongols. Amongst the negroes we find oval, amongst Europeans elongated skulls; indeed we may say that in every race we find forms of skulls which are foreign to it.[4]

[1] *Bericht*, etc. p. 4.
[2] *Das.* p. 6. Tiedemann, *Das Hirn des Negers*, p. 49.
[3] Waitz, *Anthropologie*, i. 243.
[4] Waitz, *Anthropol.* i. 251. "Peculiarities of race are not absolute; the tendency to variation often produces them in single cases in other races, and climatic influences also tend to produce them. We find the woolly, curly hair almost as strongly marked amongst Europeans as amongst negroes. Their special form of face and skull also sometimes occurs

As regards language, which I have hitherto left out in my discussions, I think, that on Kaulen's authority,[1] I may say that what follows is the result of the studies in comparative philology, which especially in recent years have been carried on with great success. The hundreds of different languages which are known to exist at present do not form so many independent genetically different systems, but simply represent varieties of higher units, the groups of languages; these again are differentiations of a small number of principal languages, which are called root languages. It is admitted that the separate tribes who speak languages belonging to one root were originally only one nation, and that the growth of lower forms of language (families, languages, dialects, etc.) was the result of the gradual division of this nation.[2] As the course of philology hitherto has increased the extent, but diminished the number of the co-ordinate groups, we are justified in expecting that further investigation will prove even those root languages, which at present are disconnected, to be historical species of one *summum genus* of language. It has

amongst Europeans, and according to Weber, besides the predominating oval form of skull, the long square shaped form of skull is also sometimes found amongst the latter, showing a sporadic tendency towards the negro and Mongol type. Vrolik has thrown a good deal of light on the differences in the pelvis of the separate races; it often differs very much from the European type, and especially amongst negroes and Bushmen; but here also we find variations from the race type. Weber's investigations show that in the different races examples of a form of pelvis with an oval, round, square, and wedge-shaped entrance are found."—J. Müller, *Physiologie*, ii. 773.

[1] *Die Sprachverwirrung zu Babel*, Mainz 1861. Cf. Max Müller, *Lectures on the Science of Language*. Wedewer, *Die neuere Sprachwissenschaft und der Urstand der Menscheit*, Freiburg 1867, p. 43.

[2] Kaulen, *Op. cit.* p. 16.

been already shown that some root languages, such as the Indo-Germanic and the Semitic, have a common origin.[1]

But even before a general conclusion has been attained, the fact that nations who agree in the root language are identical in origin, affords weighty support to the theory of the original unity of the human race. For if physiological differences can exist between nations speaking the same root language (supposing that they have preserved their own language), it follows that such differences can appear in one and the same race. Now we find, for instance, that within the Indo-Germanic nations physiological differences, such as those between the almost black Hindoos and the white Germans, do exist; and as here there can be no question of any change of language, the existence of physiological differences between men cannot prove that their genetical unity is impossible. In the same way the Arabic language is divided between members of the Caucasian and the Ethiopian races.[2]

We obtain a similar proof if we examine the nature of the differences existing between languages. These, in so far as they make a language independent, are simply formal, and do not rest on physiological, but on

---

[1] Kaulen, *Op. cit.* p. 21. "We are justified in hoping that at a time not far distant it will be shown to be probable, if not certain, that all the languages of the earth are connected with one another."—Wedewer, *Op. cit.* p. 55.

[2] Kaulen, *Op. cit.* p. 202. On examining a large collection of Russian skulls, Baer found (see *Bericht*, etc. p. 4) "that the skull form of one people, that is, the average form which was obtained after examining a number of individuals, may differ very much from the skull form of another people, who are supposed from their language to be related."

psychological and historical grounds. But philology cannot yet use this truth so as to distinguish between the common properties and the differences of *families* of languages; still less can it judge of the relation of the *root* languages, and the races which must be assigned to them. Philology therefore at any rate cannot prove that the different languages must be traced back to several originally and entirely different beginnings, and that they have not their first historical origin in a common language; nor that the differentiation of language may not have taken place in the manner described by the Bible in the wonderful account of the confusion of languages at Babel.[1]

[1] Kaulen, *Op. cit.* p. 26 seq., 65 seq.

XXXII.

THE UNITY OF THE HUMAN RACE—*Conclusion.*

THE theory of the specific unity of mankind is borne out by the fact that all races of men are able to intermix and are fertile; that they have the same anatomical structure, the same length of life, and other points in common, which I have enumerated before, and as to which I have observed that in the animal world such similarity is only found among individuals and varieties of one species, but never among the species of one genus. We must add to this the similarity of the spiritual powers and characteristics, for however great may be the intellectual, moral, and social differences between the different peoples,[1] there can be no doubt that they all possess the same spiritual powers and characteristics. We find differences of degree in the spiritual qualities possessed by members of a nation, and even of a family, just as much as in those possessed by members of different races; but in spite of all the differences of degree, we find everywhere among men the same spiritual capacity, reason, memory, self-consciousness, conscience, power of speech, etc.; and experience teaches us that the apparent differences are produced by habit and education, and specially by external influences. Negroes who grow up under

---

[1] Burmeister, *Geol. Bilder*, ii. 138.

external influences similar to those of Europeans may attain to the same spiritual development; and Europeans who grow up amongst savage tribes will not surpass the culture of their surroundings.[1]

The specific unity of mankind may therefore be considered as certainly proved. But this does not prove that the whole race has descended from one pair. It would still be possible that all men now living might be descended from several pairs of ancestors, who resembled one another in all the physical and spiritual characteristics which we find now are common to all mankind; but who differed from one another in those points in which the several races of men differ from each other now. The question therefore is, Can it be scientifically proved that we must assume a plurality of ancestors? Cannot the differences which we find coexisting with the resemblances between men

[1] Waitz, *Anthropol.* i. 304 seq., comes to the conclusion that the difference in the culture of the separate races depends much more on the difference in their condition of life and destinies and other causes, than on their original spiritual capacity. Of course the latter cause may have had some effect. This assumption is possible, but it cannot be proved; the course of our inquiry shows that it is more probable that culture, and want of culture, if once it exists, is generally preserved equally easily by all the peoples of the earth; but that when a people once attains to a high stage of development, its progress is made much easier, because it transmits to its descendants a greater capacity for culture, in consequence of that to which it has itself attained. The individual assimilates the culture or want of culture which he finds prevailing amongst the people to which he belongs. And yet at the higher stages of culture, the single individuals are they who bring about the great progress of the State in religion, in art, and in science. Persons so spiritually eminent and endowed with genius are not wanting even in the most barbarous peoples,—there is no specific difference between peoples in this respect,—but in these latter, as a rule, they have either no influence, or only a very slight influence which leads to no result, p. 475. Cf. *Einige Bemerkungen über die Seelenfähigkeiten der Neger*, by Tiedemann; *Das Hirn des Negers*, etc. p. 64. Perty, *Grundzüge*, etc. p. 424. Rauch, *Die Einheit*, etc. p. 237.

be explained without the assumption of several ancestors?

As regards the physical qualities of men, these differences are principally those differences in colour and in the form of skull, on which rests the division of men into races. The contrasts which we find in these points lose a good deal of their weight, as we have seen, by reason of the numerous intermediate forms which exist. Men cannot be divided into races so that the special characteristics of a race are all found amongst all the individuals belonging to that race, and amongst these alone; on the contrary, we have seen that the races are not sharply divided from one another, that transitions from one to the other occur, and that we find individuals and whole tribes who possess some of the special characteristics of one race and some of another. No doubt some people think they can explain the existence of these transition forms by assuming that they have been produced by the intermixture of the race types, which were originally distinct from one another. But we must ask whether this hypothesis is the only one by which the phenomenon now before us can be explained; and whether the differences of race as they now appear can be explained by other causes in such a manner that the idea of original unity can be preserved. In order to answer this question we must glance at the method in which varieties and races are formed in other organic beings, animals and plants.

"The species of animals and plants," says Joh. Müller, "alter as they spread themselves over the surface of the earth; these changes take place within the limits of the kind and species; but they reproduce themselves as types of the variations of the species throughout the generations of organic beings. The present races of animals have sprung from the conjunction of many different conditions, both internal and external, which sometimes cannot be distinguished, and the most remarkable forms in these races are found in those animals which are capable of the most extended distribution over the earth."[1] I have on a former occasion spoken in detail about the mutability of species, and the origin of varieties and races; and I have already pointed out that in this respect the observations made and instigated by Darwin have produced a result favourable to the theory of the unity of mankind.[2] And although we must remember that these alterations take place within the limits prescribed to the kinds and species, we must not suppose that the power of alteration is very limited, at any rate not so limited as many zoologists and botanists have assumed. The fact on which Müller lays stress, that the limits of mutability in one species are wider than in another, and widest of all in those animals which are capable of spreading themselves most extensively over the earth, is worthy of notice. And here we must observe further, that variations among wild kinds of plants and animals are less frequent and important than they are among species of organic beings whom man takes under his care. In the natural, wild condition, most plants and animals are confined to certain limits. The greatest variations are found among our ordinary domestic animals and plants, which from time immemorial have belonged to

[1] *Physiologie*, ii. 768, 772.
[2] See above, p. 66.

the household of man.¹ The varieties into which the species of dogs, cattle, sheep, and goats, and the species of vegetables and fruit have diverged, are much more numerous and different than is the case with man. But if we find that the most remarkable power of variation exists in those kinds of organisms which are capable of the widest extension on the earth, we may, according to this analogy, expect to find that the limits wherein variation is possible in man are very wide. For, as Peschel says, "the spot on earth is still to be found which cannot be inhabited or at least visited by some tribe."² "It is undeniable," says Waitz, "that the same races of men can live successively in very different climates, and that they have in some cases done so, but this is the case with very few animals; further, that the whole mode of life and all the outward conditions to which the same tribe is subjected may alter in the most complete manner, and often do so alter, but not so with animals; lastly, that the same race can go through very different stages of spiritual culture, and does go through them, but not so the animals. Therefore, as the circumstances and conditions under which man can exist are so much wider than those under which any one species of animal can exist, we see that there is no want of correspondence with the laws of nature, if the variability of his outward form is less limited than that of animals."³

We must, no doubt, suppose that men spread themselves over the different lands of the earth gradually and very slowly, so that the climatic differences were never marked. But if we assume this, the process of

---

[1] Prichard, *Researches*, i. 339. [2] *Volkerkunde*, p. 21. [3] *Anthropologie*, i. 213.

acclimatization is quite conceivable. Peschel says, "If the transitions to other climates take place gradually and at long intervals, there is no doubt that the same race of men may people every zone of the earth. For no one denies that the Hindoo of high caste, whether his home is in Bengal, in Madras, or in Scinde, or any other hot climate, is of Arian descent, just as much as the northern inhabitants of Iceland; and that the unknown ancestors of both must have inhabited a common home. All ethnologists are agreed that the aborigines of America, with, at most, the exception of the Eskimos, form one race, and this one race succeeds in adapting itself to all the climatic conditions, from the Arctic circle to the Equator, and again to the 50th degree of latitude. We find Chinese in Maimatschin on the Siberian frontier, where the mean temperature is below freezing-point, and the thermometer falls to −40 degrees Reaumür in winter; and also on the island of Singapore, which is almost under the Equator."[1]

The observations which have been made as to the origin and inheritance of bodily qualities, serve in some measure to show us how the differences between the separate races and peoples may have been formed during this gradual distribution of men over the earth.

It has been ascertained that these characteristics when once, from whatever cause, established, often become hereditary, even when they are very remarkable and almost unnatural; as, *e.g.*, six fingers on the hand, six toes on the foot, horny growths on the skin, etc.[2]

---

[1] *Volkerkunde*, p. 21. Quatrefages, *Rapport*, etc. p. 206.
[2] Prichard, *Op. cit.* i. 347. Waitz, *Anthropologie*, i. 90. "Gratio Kelleia, the Maltese, who was born with six fingers on each hand, and the like number of toes to each of his feet, married when he was twenty-

Such cases as these make it at least appear conceivable, that if a bodily peculiarity has once originated, it may become lasting, if throughout several generations those individuals who possess it intermarry with one another only, and if the conditions which may influence it are favourable to its preservation.[1] At any rate, as Waitz says, they show us a way in which the origin of different races is possible.

two years of age, and as I suppose there were no six-fingered ladies in Malta, he married an ordinary five-fingered person. The result of that marriage was four children; the first, who was christened Salvator, had six fingers and six toes, like his father; the second was George, who had five fingers and toes, but one of them was deformed, showing a tendency to variation; the third was André, he had five fingers and five toes quite perfect; the fourth was a girl, Marie, she had five fingers and five toes, but the thumbs were deformed, showing a tendency towards the sixth. These children . . . all married, and of course it happened that they all married five-fingered and five-toed persons. Now, let us see what were the results. Salvator had four children, they were two boys, a girl, and another boy; the first two boys and the girl were six-fingered and six-toed, like their grandfather; the fourth boy had only five fingers and five toes. George had two girls with six fingers and six toes; one girl with six fingers and five toes on the right side, and with five fingers and five toes on the left, and one boy with five fingers and five toes. The third, André, had many children, whose hands and feet were all regularly developed. Marie four, a boy with six toes, the others normal. Reaumür narrates this case only as far as the third generation. Had the cousins intermarried, a six-fingered variety of the human race might have been set up."—Huxley, *On our Knowledge*, p. 95 seq. Darwin, *The Variation of Plants and Animals under Domestication*, ii. 4 seq.

[1] "The oftener like pairs with like without any foreign intermixture, the longer will the type to which the breeding individuals belong be preserved. If we take a brood of parents as nearly alike as possible, and if their progeny pair together again, and this interbreeding continues within the family, we shall get a breed, a race, whose members will preserve the type of the original ancestors, whatever the individual peculiarities may be. Sometimes when the form-giving type is once fixed through a series of generations in the members of a family, even the intermixture of a foreign element will not suffice to eradicate it, and the intruding element will be absorbed by the old ancestral one. This no doubt explains the fact that in many royal houses the type of the family is preserved in an astonishing manner, in spite of alliances with other houses, as is the case with the Bourbons, and also with several German royal houses."—Müller, *Physiologie*, ii. 770.

An English traveller[1] describes a family in Hauran, on the eastern shore of the Jordan, in which, although the parents were white, and had no negro among their ancestors, the children were black. Here the external conditions were favourable to the preservation of this peculiarity; for the Arabian population of this region is distinguished by having a darker skin, a flatter face, and crisper hair than any other tribe of their race. It is said also that the opposite sometimes takes place, and that white children are born amongst the negro tribes, and that the tendency to such exceptions is inherited.[2]

No doubt in this respect climate and other external conditions have an influence. Even Burmeister admits that climate and the sun have a certain influence on the colour of the skin. "It is said that individuals of the African race do become paler in the temperate zones, if they have lived for several generations under the influence of more slanting sun's rays, although they never become as white as Europeans. On the other hand, white nations become darker under a tropical sun, but they do not become black in Africa, or red in America; their darker colour is of a peculiar shade, easily distinguishable, it is simply an intensification of the original national colour. It is for this reason that in the same nation the noble and rich classes seem to be lighter coloured than the poorer classes; for the former expose themselves less to the sun, and shelter themselves artificially from its rays,

[1] Cf. Wiseman, *On the Connection between Science and Revealed Religion*, p. 195.
[2] Prichard, i. 368.

whereas the poor man is always exposed to them without shelter, and feels their whole effect. In nations where differences of class do not exist, the effects thus produced by them on the outward appearance disappear, and all the individuals of the Papuan race are equally dark, just as all the individuals of the Botokudi are equally reddish brown; in Mexicans and Peruvians, however, shades of colour were formerly and are still distinguished, similar to those which an attentive observer may notice any day amongst ourselves in Europe. They are the consequences of a descent from the better class of families or of the mode of life, like so many of the differences which result from a higher spiritual development.[1]

Observations by the microscope have taught us the following facts about the situation of the colouring matter. The human skin consists of two layers, the outer skin (epidermis) and the under skin (cutis). The former is divided into the cuticle (stratum corneum) and the stratum mucosum or rete malpighii. The cutis and the cuticle are alike in all races, the differences only appear in the cells of the stratum mucosum, which are filled with a granular colouring matter. According as these colour cells are confined to the bottom of the stratum muscosum, or become thicker, and in some few cases even stretch up into the cuticle, is the colour of the skin lighter or darker. Certain parts of the body are more darkly coloured in every man, as the warts; freckles, moles, and stains in different parts of the body are produced by the

[1] *Geschichte der Schöpfung*, p. 507 (634). Cf. Waitz, *Anthropologie*, i. 51, 55.

same cause as the colour of the Negro ; cases have been observed in which the whole skin in Europeans becomes quite dark, although only temporarily.[1] There exists therefore a disposition to a darker colouring, and we may consequently believe it to be possible that in the youth of the human race, and under the influence of climatic conditions, this tendency was developed and became permanent in the races which at the present time are not white.[2]

Climatic and other local conditions seem to have a certain influence on the formation of the skulls. A series of observations, quoted by Baer,[3] seem to prove that tribes who live on the sea-coast, or in plains, have flatter skulls ; hillmen, on the other hand, higher, more rounded skulls. But at any rate, just as the climate affects the colour of the skin, the mode of life and the spiritual development must have a great effect on the general bodily condition of man, especially on the form of the skull and face. Prichard quotes the following example.[4] Two hundred years ago, a great multitude of the native Irish were driven from the counties of Antrim and Down to the sea-coast, where they have been almost ever since in unusually miserable circumstances. The consequence has been that they are still distinguished by very degraded features, being remarkable for "open projecting mouths, with prominent teeth and exposed gums; their advancing cheek-bones and depressed noses bear barbarism on their

---

[1] Peschel, *Volkerkunde*, p. 91. Burmeister, *Geol. Bilder*, ii. 134.
[2] A. Wagner, *Gesch. der Urwelt*, ii. 180, 254. Rauch, *Einheit*, etc. p. 82.
[3] *Bericht*, etc. p. 9.
[4] Prichard, *Researches*, ii. 349.

very front." "They are five feet two on an average, pot-bellied, bow-legged, and abortively featured." The low stature and an abnormal thinness of the limbs is everywhere the outward sign of low and barbarous conditions of life. This is seen especially in the Bushmen and the aborigines of Terra del Fuego and Australia.[1]

Baer[2] found in the Tartar races evident signs of the influence of the mode of life, and especially of the food, on the skulls and shapes of the face. "The Tartars of Kasan have by no means broad faces and high cheek-bones, their faces are narrow, sometimes long, with large projecting and often hooked noses. Their skulls are of the medium form, in which none of the dimensions preponderate over the others. I found that the Tartars on the Kur river were still handsomer, for they were without a certain vulgarity which I observed in the Volga Tartars. Why is it that other Tartars who live in the Volga Ural steppes not far from the Kasan Tartars, and who speak the same language, have broad faces, broader and less projecting noses, and altogether a much rougher appearance? Like Prichard, I find the cause in the different mode of life; for I would observe especially that this is no case of different peoples, collected together under one name by the ethnologist, but of one people which looks on itself as the same. The Tartars of Kasan and of the Kur, like their neighbours in the Trans-caucasian provinces, are old inhabitants, live in regular houses, which among the Kasan Tartars at any rate are kept

---

[1] Waitz, *Anthropologie*, i. 63. Cf. Vogt, *Vorlesungen*, ii. 229.
[2] *Bericht*, etc. p. 10.

clean, and follow agriculture and gardening besides cattle trade; the cereals, especially wheat and rice, form a considerable portion of their food. The Tartars of the steppes are nomads; they have therefore moveable kibitkas, live only on animal food, and their confined dwellings give little opportunity for cleanliness. If we go farther east, and examine tribes who speak a language belonging to the Turkish Tartar family, although some of them go by different names, we find that the face gets broader and the cheek-bones more prominent. The prominence of the cheek-bones, which is usually found with breadth of skull if the food is distinctly animal, reminds us of the fact that carnivorous animals are distinguished from graminivorous animals by prominent cheek-bones, and suggests the possibility that we may see in this the influence of food on the variations of the human race. I am inclined to admit this possibility, for I find that in all the tribes which live solely on animal food, the cheek-bones are more prominent than in those which, like the Hindoos and the Indo-Germanic peoples, eat a great deal of vegetable food." [1]

I do not quote these observations in order to infer from them that the origin of the differences in the human races may be explained by the influences of climate, mode of life, and other outward conditions; but, first of all, in order to show that these influences may be productive of great changes in mankind. And even if the races of mankind are now fixed, so that these influences do not produce such an effect as they must once have produced if they formed the different

[1] Cf. Vogt, *Vorlesungen*, i. 33.

races of mankind, this is the case also with several races of animals. It cannot be said to be incredible that ages ago the variations of which a species was capable were developed, were reproduced, and then remained fixed, that in the early ages such processes of differentiation took place, and stopped when they had attained to their natural limits.

Cardinal Wiseman gives a very fine analogy to this. He says: " In the child, the circulation of the blood, the absorbing and digestive operations, all the functions of life, are the same as in man, with variations only as to the degree of activity; they commence with being, and are regular through its duration. But in its earlier stages there is, besides, a plastic virtue at work within us, traceable to no law of necessity, having no clear dependence on the general course of the ordinary vital powers, which gives growth and solidity to the limbs, characteristic shape to the features, gradual development and strength to the muscles; then to all appearance sinks into inertness and ceases to act, till age seems once more to call the extraordinary laws into activity, to efface the impression, undo the work of their earlier operations. And, in like manner, we must allow that in the world's infancy, besides the regular ordinances of constant and daily course, causes necessary to produce great and permanent effects may have had a power now no longer wanted, and consequently no longer exercised; that there was a tendency to stamp more marked features on the earth and its inhabitants, to produce countries as well as their vegetation, races as much as individuals." [1] It is not unscientific to assume

[1] *On the Connection,* etc. i. 238, 239.

that impressions which were to be characteristic and lasting were formerly more easily imparted, and more indelibly fixed, even if, as Müller says, we cannot completely explain in detail the causes of the formation of race. Baer says, "It seems to me that we may perfectly assume that in the first series of generations the type was more variable, and therefore could be more powerfully affected by the influences of nature." So that the changes in the human type which we still see caused by the transition to different climatic or other conditions, would only be faint repetitions of a great process of differentiation in primitive times.[1]

These remarks are not intended to prove that we must assume on physiological grounds that the different races of mankind have sprung from one primitive race, but only that there is a physiological explanation of this, and therefore that it is possible. As I have before observed, this is all we want, for we may now say that the Biblical doctrine of the unity of mankind does not contradict any certain physiological conclusion; on the contrary, the facts that all human races resemble each other in many important particulars, and that without exception they are able to intermix fruitfully, are distinctly in favour of the specific unity of mankind, and the differences in the races do not prove that they are independent. "There is no reason for assuming," says Baer,[2] "that the different peoples originally come forth different from the hand of nature. On the contrary, there is reason for supposing that they have *become* different through the different influences of climate, food, and social conditions."

[1] Cf. *Jahrbuch für Deutsche Theologie*, vi. 710.   [2] *Studien*, p. 35.

One more argument in favour of the unity of mankind may be mentioned; it is taken by A. de Quatrefages [1] from the geographical distribution of Animals and Plants. No one kind of organic beings—not reckoning the transplanting artificially produced by man—extends over every part of the earth: each kind has originally a limited habitat. Man alone is now cosmopolitan. If, therefore, he does not form an exception to the rule which holds good of all organic beings,—and this would be an arbitrary assumption,—he also must have an original habitat—a "centre of creation" from which he has gradually peopled all lands. But further, the natural habitat of a species is always more limited the more highly it is developed; no species, for instance, of the apes, the most highly developed mammals, is common to both the Old and the New World; and of the anthropoid apes, which are the highest, the chimpanzee and gorilla are only found in the western parts of tropical Africa, the gibbon in India and in some of the islands in the Malay Archipelago, the orang only in Borneo or Sumatra. Therefore, if we follow out the analogy, we must conclude that men also had originally a single very limited habitat. Quatrefages concludes a long discussion on this matter with these words: "As man is a specially privileged being in respect of his bodily organization, he must have appeared first in a single centre of creation, and have been its characteristic and special inhabitant; and this centre cannot have been of greater extent than that in which we now find the gorilla, the orang, and the chimpanzee. This is a conclusion which must be acknowledged by all who

[1] *Rapport*, p. 163.

do not wish to make man a quite exceptional being."
If this argument is right, it proves, not indeed directly
that all men are descended from one pair, but only that
man first appeared in one single not very extended
region, and that all men therefore probably have the
same bodily constitution. But if this is admitted, there
is nothing to prevent the assumption of a single pair
of ancestors.[1]

Many investigators have proved in recent years that
it cannot be said to be impossible that the whole earth
was peopled from one centre. Even those who, like
Waitz and Giebel, do not actually believe that mankind did in reality extend from one centre, expressly
acknowledge that it is possible they may have done so.
"Man," says the latter, "even in his primitive condition, had so many favourable opportunities of
wandering from one end of the world to the other, that
we can hardly doubt the possibility of his having
spread themselves all over it from one centre." Waitz
says, "We cannot suppose that the difficulties in the
way of migration afford a valid reason for disbelieving
the theory that mankind originally came from one spot
on the earth.... These difficulties are evidently nowhere greater or even as great as in the South Sea,
and yet there it is abundantly shown, not only that they
are not insuperable, but also that they do not in the
least hinder either immigration from other countries,
or the spreading of the inhabitants from one group of
islands to the other.... The great similarity which
exists in language, customs, tradition, and religion in
Polynesia, from the Sandwich Islands to New Zealand,

[1] *Tagesfragen*, p. 92. Cf. Waitz, *Anthropol.* i. 226.

will not allow us to suppose that these islanders are of different races."[1]

The greatest difficulties lie in the relation between the Americans and the races of the Old World. But an emigration from the Old World into the New might first have taken place at Behring Straits, which are only ten miles wide in the narrowest part.[2] Other tribes might have migrated by the Aleutian Islands.[3] Then again a series of island groups extends from Southern Asia in the direction of South America, which succeed one another very closely for 100 degrees of longitude, although for the remaining 50 degrees there are none. The resemblance of the inhabitants of these islands to one another in bodily structure, language, and habits shows that this chain of islands, as far as the Sandwich Islands, was populated by degrees from Asia. If we might assume that the gap which now exists was originally broken up by intermediate islands, that the islands of this tropical chain are as it were the remaining pillars of a bridge which originally stretched from Asia to America, it would be easy to understand how these tribes penetrated into America.[4] Neither is it incon-

---

[1] *Anthropologie*, i. 225, 226. "The Maui-Myth proves just as conclusively as the common language that the Polynesian races were originally one and the same. It is true that they are now divided, and marvellously scattered in far distant islands, but evidently migrations must have occurred. The Polynesians are probably the most wandering race on earth; they are the gypsies of the sea." Hochstetter, *Neuseeland*, Stuttgard 1863, p. 56. Cf. O. Peschel, *Die Wanderungen der Südsuvolker*, Ausland 1864, p. 361. Rauch, *Die Einheit*, etc. p. 334. Quatrefages, *Les Polynesiens et leurs migrations*, Paris 1866; *Rapport*, p. 192; *Etudes religieuses* (Paris 1867), n. s. xiii. 25.

[2] Peschel, *Volkerkunde*, p. 428.

[3] Rauch, *Die Einheit*, pp. 282, 348.

[4] "The whole shape of the Pacific Ocean, with its countless groups of islands, gives one the idea of a submerged continent, whose highest

ceivable that the inhabitants of these islands, or of the eastern coast of Asia, reached America in ships, perhaps driven there by storms. There are instances in later times of Japanese ships being driven to the Sandwich Islands, to the Northern Sea, and even to the mouth of the river Columbia.[1]

In these ways therefore Mongol and Malay immigrants may have reached America from the East; and it is not impossible that from the West, from Europe, that is, from the seat of the Caucasian race, single emigrations may have taken place. From the tenth century onwards the Northmen reached the east coast of America by Iceland and Greenland; it is not impossible that in ancient times also Europeans were driven on to the shores of America in the same way.[2]

summits still reach above the surface of the sea; and judging from the frequency with which lagoon islands occur, it seems as if the sea-bed were still sinking."—Vogt, *Geologie*, ii. 1005.

[1] A. Wagner, ii. 233. For other examples, see Rauch, *Die Einheit*, etc. p. 343. "Captain Cook found on Otaheite three inhabitants of Wattero, who had been driven in a boat for a distance of 550 nautical miles. In 1696, two boats, which had left Ancorso with thirty persons, reached Samax, one of the Phillippine islands, after having been driven 800 miles by storms. In 1721, two boats, with thirty men, women, and children, went from the island of Faroidex to Guajan, one of the Ladrone or Mariane islands, a distance of 200 miles. Kotzebue made the acquaintance of a certain Kadu in the Radack islands who had come from the island of Ulea, 1500 miles off."—Giebel, *Tagesfragen*, p. 90.

[2] "It is quite possible that in the dim antiquity America may have been peopled from Europe in this way. In a book called *De Mensura terrae*, written by Dicuil, an Irish monk, in 825, we are told that as early as 795, that is, in the time of Charlemagne, Irish monks had gone to Iceland in order to introduce Christianity amongst the inhabitants who had come there from North America; and who, at a later date, withdrew to America again, flying from the heathen Northmen and leaving behind them Irish books, sacring bells, and croziers. In 861, the first Northmen were driven by storms to Iceland, and after Harold Harfager's battle of Stafanger, many migrations thither took place, so that by the end of the ninth century the island was largely populated by Norwegians and Danes, interspersed with a few Swedes and Irish. Between 984-986 the

These observations show that it cannot be proved that the earth could not have been peopled from one centre. Former discussions have shown that it is physiologically possible that all the races of mankind may have originated from one primitive race; that the resemblance of all the races in many important points, and their unlimited power of intermixing fruitfully, are distinctly in favour of the specific unity of mankind, and that the differences do not prove that the races are originally separate. The doctrine of the unity of mankind, *i.e.* that the different races of man are not to be traced back to different ancestors, is therefore one which does not contradict the result of scientific inquiry in the widest sense of the word. Now, if the Bible goes on to teach that mankind is not only descended from similar, but from the same ancestors, that is, from a single pair, that is a statement on which natural science can give no judgment, for it is purely historical. Agassiz draws an analogy from the bees and other of the lower animals who live in swarms, and concludes from this that it is unlikely that men should have sprung from one pair; but Waitz readily admits " that this is a very weak proof." Waitz himself thinks that the assumption of a single primitive pair is improbable, because " we nowhere find that nature acts so carelessly

---

west coast of Greenland was peopled for the first time. In 986, Biarne Herjulfson, driven out of his course on his way from Iceland to Greenland, came to Nantucket, New Scotland, Newfoundland, and the mouth of the Taunton. On hearing his narrative, others at once departed to the distant land, Thorwald Eirekson in 1002 and Thorfinn Karsefne in 1007, from Greenland. According to Dicuil, S. Brandan made a voyage of discovery to America, and remained there from 562-572. According to one legend, the Irish visited the southern part of North America as early as the end of the eighth century."—Giebel, *Tagesfragen*, p. 91.

as to make the appearance and preservation of a species or genus at any time dependent on so slight a thing as the existence of a single human life." But he adds himself that this reason, which seems to him to be "almost the only point on this subject admitting of discussion, only rests on a teleological, not on a physical or physiological observation, and that its importance must not be over-estimated."[1]

More weight must be attached to an objection thus stated by Vogt. "Whoever believes in the Bible must believe in the whole Bible. Whoever believes Adam to be the one father of the human race must admit the same of Noah, who with his three sons remained alone after the Deluge on the earth. But what wonderful productiveness must have been inherent in the three tribes of Shem, Ham, and Japhet to produce, in a period of 500 years at the most, millions of descendants in Egypt alone; while the monuments of Khorsahad, Nineveh, etc., also bear witness to the existence of very large nations who peopled Asia immediately (*i.e.* some centuries) after the Flood. Even mice and rabbits would despair of a similar increase in their descendants in so short a time."[2] In my next lecture I shall consider whether the time which has elapsed since the Deluge is really so short as Vogt here supposes. But even if this were the case it would not afford ground for an

---

[1] *Anthropol.* i. 226. See also J. Grimm's *Ueberlegung; Gesch. der deutschen sprache,* p. 22 (Perty, *Grundzüge,* p. 17). "It is probable that more than one pair was created, if only because the first mother might possibly have given birth to sons or to daughters only, which would have put a stop to all further reproduction ; and also because it would prevent an intermarriage of brothers and sisters, which nature abhors." On this last question see below, p. 245.

[2] *Köhlerglaube,* etc. p. 80.

argument against the descent of mankind from one pair. If between the ages of twenty-five and fifty a human pair were on an average to give birth to six children, the number of men existing 450 years after the Deluge might have been 800 million souls, that is, almost as many as are supposed to exist now. The numbers do not increase in such a ratio now no doubt in any country; they need not have increased in *this* ratio in the earliest times, but they probably increased much faster than they do now. Nor is it incredible that there is now no great general increase in the number of mankind, because the number of inhabitants which the earth is able or intended to support has been reached; but that, on the contrary, so long as this number was not reached, the increase was more rapid and uninterrupted.[1] If we suppose that a yearly increase of only $2\frac{1}{2}$ per cent. took place, and a similar increase takes place even now under favourable conditions in thinly populated countries, 500 years after the Deluge 106 million people might have existed; and if an increase of $3\frac{1}{2}$ per cent. took place, 180 million might have existed. We find instances of a similar rapid increase in modern times. At the end of the last century a few English sailors and a few natives of Tahiti settled on an island in the Pacific. In the year 1800 there were nineteen children, one man, and some women; in 1855, although several had died through unlooked for occurrences, there were 187 persons: this is an increase of more than $3\frac{1}{2}$ per cent.[2] It is said that on an island which

---

[1] A. Wagner, *Gesch. der Urwelt*, ii. 278. Pfaff, *Schöpfungsgeschichte*, p. 661. F. v. Rougemont, *Der Urmensch*, Berlin 1870, p. 15.

[2] *Natur und Offenbarung*, iii. 69.

was first inhabited in 1589 by some shipwrecked English, and was visited in 1667 by a Dutch ship, a population of 12,000 souls was found, all the descendants of four mothers. Acosta in describing the natural history of New Spain 100 years after its discovery, says that even before his time it was not uncommon for people to possess from 70,000 to 100,000 sheep; and yet before the country was discovered by the Spaniards there were no sheep there, and the whole race was descended from those which had been brought by the Spaniards. It is well known also that horses and cattle have only existed in America since its discovery by Columbus; they are now found there in countless numbers in both a tame and a wild condition. Acosta speaks of numerous wild herds of cattle which wandered about the island of Hispaniola, and which afforded sport for the chase; in 1585, 35,000 were exported from this island, and 64,000 from New Spain. From Paraguay and New Spain alone one million ox hides were exported every year at the end of the last century; yet the numerous cattle in these regions are descended from seven cows and one bull which were left there in 1546. If these animals could multiply to such an extent in a comparatively short space of time, in spite of the depredations of men and wild beasts, why should not the human race have multiplied in a like degree, under more favourable conditions and in a longer period?[1]

It cannot therefore be proved that the descent of mankind from one pair is impossible, and here again

[1] Wiseman, *On the Connection between Science and Revealed Religion*, p. 237. A. Wagner, ii. 280.

there is no contradiction between revelation and science. Is it the conviction that his scientific arguments are untenable that induces Vogt to number himself amongst exegetes, and to "extract" from the Bible itself the real reason for the differences between the races of mankind which are distributed over the earth? "After Abel's murder," he says,[1] "the murderer Cain was Adam's only progeny; for Seth and the other sons and daughters mentioned in Genesis were not born at that time. In spite of this we are told Cain took his wife with him in his flight and founded a town, after a mark had been placed on his forehead so that no one should kill him. This sign could only have been meant for man; for the wolf eats the marked sheep." It is very easy to explain this misunderstanding. Genesis only gives us a few fragmentary notices of primitive history, and we find facts placed close together in the narrative which chronologically are a long way apart. Therefore although it is stated in Gen. iv. 17 that "Cain knew his wife; and she conceived and bare Enoch: and he builded a city, and called the name of the city after the name of his son, Enoch," the time of his brother's murder and the flight of Cain, and the time of the foundation of the first city are not given, and may be separated by centuries. Vogt has invented the fact that Cain founded the city at once. The wife of Cain was either one of the daughters of Adam who followed him into banishment,—for Genesis does not say that Adam had at that time no children except Cain,—or one of his sisters who was born after Seth, or one of his nieces. S. Augus-

[1] *Vorlesungen*, ii. 225. Cf. Quenstedt, *Sonst und Zetzt*, p. 254.

tine¹ declared that the marriage with a sister which has been such a stumbling-block to K. Hase, J. Grimm, and others, was inevitable in the first age if mankind is descended from one pair. We must not conclude from Cain's saying when he is flying from the land of Eden (Gen. iv. 14), "Every one that findeth me shall slay me," that he supposed that other countries were also inhabited. He seems rather to refer to the vengeance which he fears if his father's family should spread. But if he fears to be recognised as the murderer outside Eden, that shows that there was only one human family, the family of Adam, and that no other existed which was not connected with it.²

[1] *Civ. Dei*, xv. 16. [2] Delitzsch, *Genesis*, p. 169.

XXXIII.

THE DURATION OF LIFE IN THE FIRST AGE. OLD TESTAMENT CHRONOLOGY.

The statements in Genesis about the duration of human life in the earliest age gave rise to discussion even in the time of the Fathers. "The days of our age are threescore years and ten; and if by reason of strength they be fourscore years, yet is their strength labour and sorrow,"[1] says Moses in his psalm. But in the table of generations from Adam to Noah, which he gives in the fifth chapter of Genesis, we find very few who do not exceed 900 years. Methuselah died at the age of 969. Noah attained to an age of 950 years. The duration of life diminished in the post-diluvian epoch; in the table of generations in the eleventh chapter we find that Shem is said to be 600 years old, the three persons next to him less than 500, the others less than 200. The age of the three Israelite patriarchs was only 175, 180, and 147 years respectively. S. Augustine[2] mentions a theory according to which the years by which the age of the antediluvian men was calculated were only 36 days long, that is, only one-tenth of ours: this theory also suggests that the length of the year varied with the different nations, being six months with the Acarnanians, three with the Arcadians, four, or perhaps only one, with the Egyptians. But S. Augustine refutes

---

[1] Ps. xc. 10.   [2] *Civ. Dei*, xv. 12; cf. Lact. *Inst.* ii. 12.

it by pointing out that according to the Hebrew text, whose figures, as we shall see, are here at any rate more trustworthy than those of the old Greek translation which differ from them, Seth had a son when he was 105, and Canaan when he was 71; and if we were to adopt the above computation, they would be only ten and seven respectively.

In recent times a Danish scholar has tried to show that the duration of life in the patriarchs was the same as the present, by assuming that the years were shorter. But for this hypothesis he is compelled to alter a series of figures which is rather hazardous, and, as after Noah the duration of life in Genesis gets less and less, also to assume that the years first mean a period of one month, then two, four, and six, and from the time of Moses onwards twelve months, all of which is still more questionable.[1] There is no hint in Genesis that the author calls different periods of time a "year" in different portions of his work. On the contrary, the chronological statements in the narrative of the Deluge show, as S. Augustine has said, that in the earliest times years and months mean the same as they do in the later—whether the years were reckoned according to the sun or the moon makes no difference to our point. The Flood began in Noah's 600th year, on the 17th day of the 2nd month; on the 27th day of the 7th month the Ark rested on Ararat; on the 1st day of the 10th month the tops of the mountains appeared; after another period of forty and thrice seven days, on the 1st day of the 601st year the earth was dry.[2]

---

[1] Rask, see A. Wagner, *Geschichte der Urwelt*, i. 310; also Dillmann, *Genesis*, p. 120.   [2] Gen. vii. 11, viii. 4-13.

The author of Genesis has then given us the duration of the patriarchs' lives in years like ours, and we are not justified in altering the figures and in changing the meaning of year. The narrative in Genesis as it lies before us can only be understood to mean that the patriarchs attained a much greater age than is the case now, and that in the antediluvian period that age was ten times as great as the present.

Flavius Josephus [1] pointed out long ago that the historians of other ancient nations, Manetho, Berosus, and others, record the great age of the first men, according to the traditions of their own countries. This tradition exists among many peoples not mentioned by Josephus. But if, as has often been asserted, the statements of the Biblical narrative must be rejected as being physically impossible, these traditions afford its trustworthiness a very weak support. Let us see if this assertion is well founded.

We may say, with Kurtz and others, "The question whether an age of seven, eight, or nine hundred years was possible in the early period of the human race cannot be decided by contemporary physiology, and the physiologist is imprudent, or unscientifically arrogant, if he speaks of impossibility in this respect." [2] The physiologist can only fix the normal length of human life by the help of experience; his observations can only be made in the present time, that is, he can only say that under present conditions men cannot attain to such an age as it is said the patriarchs reached.

---

[1] *Ant.* i. 3. 9; cf. Lüken, *Die Traditionen*, p. 165.
[2] Kurtz, *Geschichte des Alten Bundes*, i. p. 74. Delitzsch, *Genesis*, pp. 183, 542.

Besides, the normal length of life fixed by physiology is sometimes, even now-a-days, far exceeded. There are several sufficiently well authenticated instances of an age of 150 to 200 years in the present time.[1] According to the statements of modern travellers such age is actually not rare among the Arabs of the African desert. But if under exceptionally favourable conditions human life can reach an age twice and thrice as great as that fixed as the normal age by physiology, it cannot be said that man cannot have reached an age ten times as great under some special conditions. Observation of contemporary facts, which is the only ground physiology has to go on, will not justify us either in denying or asserting the former existence of different conditions.

We cannot certainly say what kind of conditions must have existed to enable men to reach so great an age. The external conditions under which man lived in the primitive age were probably different, and man's bodily constitution probably differed from what it is now in those points which could render possible such a prolongation of life. I have already said[2] that before the Deluge the climatic and atmospheric conditions probably differed from those at present existing; the long duration of life in the antediluvian men may be connected with this, even if it were not solely caused by it.

We must therefore be content with saying that man existed in the primeval age, according to God's plan, under such external and internal conditions that he was able to live very much longer than he

---

[1] Prichard, *Researches*, i. p. 125. Rauch, *Die Einheit*, p. 65.
[2] Vol. i. p. 430. Cf. Pianciani, *Cosmogonia*, p. 516.

does now. Holy Scripture does not say why God gave men in the primeval age a so much longer life than now, and it is therefore hardly possible to give a certain and completely exhaustive answer to this question. But we may say, with Delitzsch,[1] "If Lamech, Noah's father, the ninth in the series of the patriarchs, was for fifty-six years a contemporary of Adam, if Noah knew Adam's grandson Enoch, if Noah did not die till Abraham was sixty years old, there is every possible guarantee that tradition must have been preserved unaltered in the chosen race. And the life of the ungodly also lasted for centuries, in order that all the potentialities which sin hides within itself should come to light and be judged. Just as the first age of the Church was to show the power of the Spirit of God, the first age of man was to show the terrible consequences of the revolt from God in all their fulness and might. After the Deluge, the duration of life soon sank to the limit which is usual now, so that in future it should not be possible for sin to grow to such a gigantic height."

But it is necessary to consider whether we have Divine authority for believing that the patriarchs attained to this great age because it is so stated in Genesis. I think not. Not only has Bunsen endeavoured to explain the figures in the fifth chapter by saying that they are cyclical figures, in which the epochs of the antediluvian world are given, and not the ages of the patriarchs;[2] but the Abbé Chevallier has tried to explain the eleventh chapter in just the same

[1] *Genesis*, 3rd ed. p. 222.   [2] *Bibelwerk*, v. 49.

way.¹ The statement that Shem begat Arphaxad two years after the Flood, and that Shem lived after he begat Arphaxad 500 years, means according to him that the family of Arphaxad began two years after the Flood, but remained for 500 years in Shem's family; the family of Shem therefore lasted all this time, till 502 years after the Flood it separated. I do not quote these suggestions because I believe them to be exegetically admissible, but only in order to show you that some Roman Catholic theologians do not think themselves bound by the narrative in Genesis to believe that the patriarchs reached an age of several hundred years. We must remember that the Holy Scriptures are reverenced in the Catholic Church as a record of revelation and not as a historical record, and if we may, I think unhesitatingly, assume that the question of the duration of each patriarch's life is in no way directly and necessarily connected with the religious truths of the Bible, and that from a religious point of view it is quite immaterial whether Shem lived 100 years or 500. We may, therefore, I think, assert without prejudice to the true doctrine of inspiration, that the author of Genesis has in the chapters in question correctly recorded what he found in tradition concerning the ancestors of his people; but that it need not be assumed that this tradition is strictly historical.²

Just as it has been urged that the lifetime of individuals was too long, it has often been asserted that the period which is said by the Old Testament

---

[1] *Annales de Philosophie chrétienne*, 6 série, t. 5 (t. 85, 1873), p. 28.
[2] Vol. i. p. 15.

to have elapsed between the creation of man and the birth of our Lord is too short. As the question of the antiquity of the human race has come very much to the front in recent geological inquiries, I cannot avoid a detailed discussion of the subject; I will begin with a few remarks on the chronology of the Old Testament in general.

With the exception of the Book of Maccabees, the Old Testament, as we know, has no date. It would have been easy to reckon the years from the exodus, or later, from the founding of the monarchy, but this never became the custom with the Old Testament writers, and we are therefore obliged to reconstruct the Old Testament chronology from the separate dates which they give us at intervals. In doing this I make use of the usual reckoning according to the years before the birth of our Lord.

In order to have a certain and undisputed basis to go upon, I will begin with Cyrus. He conquered Babylon in 537, and in the following year, that is 536, he restored the Jews to their own country; we need not notice other versions of this date, as the differences are very slight. The Babylonian rule over the Jews lasted seventy years, therefore it began in 606. This was the third year of the reign of Joachim, king of Judah. We have many chronological data in the Books of Kings for the next preceding centuries, as the length of the reign of each king of Judah or Israel is given. There is some difficulty in reckoning up these separate dates,[1] but I need not enter into this, as it is a question of at most a few decades. We may put

---

[1] T. R. Tiele, *Chronologie des A. T.* p. 58. Bremen, 1859

the building of Solomon's temple in round numbers in the year 1000. It is said in the First Book of Kings vi. 1 that the building of the temple was begun in the year 480 after the exodus; therefore in round numbers the exodus must have occurred about the year 1500. Further, it is said in Ex. xii. 40 that the Israelites remained in Egypt 430 years; therefore Jacob and his sons must have gone down into Egypt about 1900. The length of time which elapsed between the Deluge and the beginning of the sojourn in Egypt may be gathered from Genesis. In the eleventh chapter we find a genealogical and chronological table, which goes from Shem, Noah's son, to Abraham: Arphaxad the son of Shem was born two years after the Deluge; Arphaxad was thirty-five years old when his son Salah was born, who was thirty years old when he begat his son Eber, etc. By adding up these figures we find that Terah, Abraham's father, was born 222 years after the Deluge. Of Terah, Genesis says (chap. xi. 26) that he was seventy years old when he begat Abraham, Nahor, and Haran. Of course the three sons were not begotten in the seventieth year of their father, but only the eldest of them. According to some, this was the one first mentioned, that is, Abraham; according to others, he is named first, not because he is the eldest, but because he is the most important for the history which follows: so that the date of his birth is not given here; but according to Gen. xii. 4 and Acts vii. 1, it is said to have occurred in the 130th year of his father's life.[1] Therefore, according to one computation, Abraham was born 292

---

[1] Cf. Tiele, *Op. cit.* p. 28.

years after the Deluge, according to the other 352. Isaac was born in Abraham's hundredth year, and Jacob in Isaac's sixtieth; the latter was 130 years old when he went down into Egypt; therefore there were between the Deluge and the going down into Egypt either 582 or 642 years, and the Deluge must have occurred between 2500 and 2600 B.C. In the fifth chapter of Genesis we find a similar genealogical and chronological table for the antediluvian age; by adding up the dates, we find that the time was 1651 years, so that the whole period before our Lord must have been about 4200 years.

Now have these chronological statements any authority? In other words, if we believe the Old Testament to be an inspired book, must we also believe that we have Divine authority for the chronology I have just set forth? The chronological statements in the Old Testament certainly do not belong to the things which God has revealed, but to those which the Biblical historians have recorded on the authority of tradition or of older records; and from a religious point of view the question as to the period that elapsed between the Deluge and the time of Abraham or Moses is of no more importance than the question of the age of the patriarchs. But even if we do not accept the theory of inspiration which I have mentioned, and assume that the Spirit of God prevented the Biblical historians from making any, even chronological, errors in using the materials before them, still two things are possible: first, the ordinary interpretation of the Biblical passages which give us the chronology may be incorrect; and secondly, the text may have been corrupted, and it might be possible by another interpretation or by emendations of the text, or by both together, to obtain a different chronology. In all that belongs to what is revealed in Holy Scripture of the *res fidei et morum*, or is closely and necessarily connected with them, we know that the Church's interpretation is right, and that therefore no new interpretation of anything essential is admissible. But in matters only distantly connected with doctrine, such as purely historical, geographical, scientific, and also chronological statements, the Biblical expressions are not always so clear and unmistakeable, and thus they may be, and have been, differently interpreted; therefore as regards these points new interpretations may be considered.[1] Thus formerly the well-known passage in Joshua was understood to mean that the sun moved round the earth; the progress of astronomy has taught us that the words were meant to give us the popular mode of expression, and that rightly interpreted they are perfectly correct, although they were misunderstood by former commentators. Or to take a still later instance: Catholic exegetes are agreed as to the essential doctrinal meaning of all that the evangelists tell us of our Lord's public teaching; but with regard to the *time* that teaching lasted the Gospels are so ambiguous, that some exegetes put it at two years, others at three, others at four; and that recently a scholar has tried to show that we cannot from the Gospels conclusively disprove the assumption of a ministry of one year only.[2] It must therefore

---

[1] Vol. i. pp. 41 and 85.
[2] Prof. J. F. J. Cassel, see *Programm des Seminarium Theodorianum at Paderborn*, 1851. See above, vol. i. p. 364.

be allowed that the Old Testament chronology may be incorrect, as resting on an incorrect apprehension of the correct statements of the Old Testament writers.

As to the text of the Holy Scriptures we must no doubt assume that no corruptions affecting *res fidei et morum* have slipped into the translations which have been authorized by the Church. But for the rest we may safely suppose that the Hebrew, Greek, and Latin text of the Bible is no more free from corruption than is the text of other old writings. In many places it can be proved that our text is not pure, that, for instance, many of the figures have been corrupted.[1] Therefore the statements of figures which have been used for computing the Old Testament chronology may have been corrupted in our present text, and the calculations founded on them may consequently be wrong.

If, therefore, the inspiration of the Biblical writers prevented their making any incorrect chronological statements, we have no warrant that the copyists and translators of these statements reproduced them correctly, and that their interpreters have understood them and combined them rightly. And, with respect to this, the following fact is worthy of note. The Vulgate coincides exactly with the Hebrew text in its rendering of the chronological statements in the Pentateuch; on the other hand, the Greek translation of the Septuagint differs in many figures, and this so considerably that according to its statements the antediluvian period is 600 years, and that between the Deluge and Abraham 700 to 800 longer. In spite of this difference this Greek

---

[1] Reinke, *Beiträge zur Erklärung des Alten Testaments*, i. 1.

translation, and a Latin one emanating from it, were the versions generally acknowledged as authentic in the Church up to the sixth century, and in the Greek Church they are still held to be so. And more, according to the chronological statements in the Vulgate, which is the official translation of the Western Church, the Deluge occurs about 2500, the Creation about 4200 years before the birth of our Lord; on the other hand, the Roman Martyrology says, "In the year after the Creation of the world 5199, after the Deluge 2957, Jesus Christ was born at Bethlehem." These figures are taken from the older Latin translation, which was founded on the Greek translation of the Septuagint; and when S. Jerome's translation was substituted for it in the Church's use, it was considered either unnecessary or undesirable to correct the figures in the Martyrology.[1] The Roman Catholic Church does not therefore inculcate an anxious adherence to the text and the original interpretation of the chronological statements in the Old Testament; we may treat this question purely scientifically, and are justified in making any alterations in the Old Testament chronology which can be supported on scientific grounds.

Many of the Roman Catholic scholars who have discussed this question in modern times have expressed themselves to this effect. "The Bible," says the French Oratorian, H. de Valroger, "gives us the chronological succession of the events it narrates in a manner which

---

[1] Mabillon lays stress on this fact in his treatise on J. Vossius' writings: De aetate mundi non videtur quidquam statuendum, quia latina Ecclesia LXX. interpretum calculum quatuor primis saeculis secuta est, eundemque etiam nunc Romana Ecclesia retinet in Martyrologio suo ad Natalem Domini.

is sufficient for its divine [religious] object. But as the Holy Ghost did not inspire it in order to found or to promote the science of chronology, we should not expect to find any detailed or exact chronology, any complete system of dates given distinctly, methodically connected and invariably adhered to. We expose ourselves to the danger of error if we try to find things in the Bible which it was not in the design of Providence to put there."[1] "Great freedom has always prevailed," says Bishop Meignan, "in the Church's treatment of Biblical chronology. There are more than one hundred and fifty systems, of which none has been absolutely rejected. At the present time, when conscientious scholars believe that facts which have recently come to light may necessitate a great alteration in the chronology of the first ages, it is more important than ever not hurriedly and arbitrarily to limit the liberty of discussion concerning certain dates, which include all the period before Abraham. . . . The word of God has been handed down through the centuries by transcribers who were certainly carefully directed; and it is certain that in the Bible we possess a text which, considering its age, is wonderfully well preserved. And yet God may have permitted the more unimportant portions to suffer from the ravages of time. The marks denoting figures may easily have been altered. The duration of time is a treasure preserved in fragile vessels."[2] The Jesuit A. Bellynck speaks even more decidedly: "The genealogies of our

---

[1] *Revue des questions historiques*, tome vi. (1863) p. 395. *L'âge du monde*, p. 72.

[2] *Le monde*, etc. pp. 166, 358.

sacred books, from which many dates have been derived, contain numerous gaps. We cannot say how many years may be left out in this broken chain. Science may therefore put back the date of the Deluge for as many centuries as it judges necessary."[1]

If we look once more at the materials from which we deduce the Old Testament chronology which I have just sketched, we certainly find that there is scope for many changes. The Septuagint and the Hebrew-Latin text do not agree as to the length of the Israelites' sojourn in Egypt. The latter simply says, " The time during which the Israelites sojourned in Egypt was 430 years." Instead of this we find in the Septuagint, " The time during which the children of Israel, they and their fathers, sojourned in the land of Egypt and in Canaan was 430 years." According to this these 430 years include besides the years of the sojourn in Egypt, the years between Abraham's coming into Palestine and Jacob's going down into Egypt. The latter period comprises 215 years, therefore only 215 years are left for the sojourn in Egypt; consequently just half the period on which I have founded my calculation of Old Testament chronology. As regards the years between the Exodus and the building of the temple, the Greek translation of 1 Kings vi. 1 gives us 440 instead of the 480 years of the Hebrew text; the difference here is therefore unimportant. This figure 480, however, occurs only once in the Old Testament; and if it were not given in 1 Kings vi. 1,

---

[1] *Etudes religieuses*, 4 série, t. i. (1868) p. 578. Cf. H. Colombier, *Durée des cinq premiers âges du monde d'après la Bible, Etudes rel*, 5 série, t. i. (1872) p. 205.

this period would probably, according to other statements, have been supposed to be longer. The sojourn in the wilderness lasted for forty years; the period of Joshua's hegemony, and the time which elapsed up to the beginning of the period of the Judges are not given, but they may be calculated to be about 60 years. After the Judges we may reckon the reigns of the first kings at about 80 years; David reigned 40 years, Solomon 3 before the building of the temple; Saul's reign with Samuel's hegemony may have been about 40 years. The Book of Judges gives us a series of figures for the period of the Judges; it gives us the duration of the different oppressions of the Israelites by foreign tribes, and the duration of the rule of the separate Judges. If we add these figures we find that they amount to about 400 years; so that with the 40+60+80 years which we had before, the whole period between the Exodus and the building of the temple would come to 580 years. The period given in 1 King vi. 1 is 480 years, so that in this passage the alteration of a single figure would restore harmony, and the Old Testament chronology would be increased by a century.

Further, in the genealogical tables of the fifth and the eleventh chapters of Genesis, the Greek and the Samaritan text give different figures from those of the Hebrew, and of the Vulgate which agrees with it.[1] In the eleventh chapter the Greek text has one member more than the other texts, Cainan, who lived 130 years before he begat a son, and accordingly Cainan is mentioned in S. Luke's pedigree of our Lord (Luke iii. 36).[2]

[1] Cf. Delitzsch, *Genesis*, pp. 189, 273.
[2] Cf. *Theol. Lit.-Bl.* 1870, p. 235.

If we add the figures, we find that the antediluvian period, according to the Hebrew-Latin text, is 1656 years; according to the Samaritan, 1307; according to the Greek, 2262; the period between the Deluge and the birth of Terah, Abraham's father, is, according to the Hebrew text, 222; according to the Samaritan, 872; according to the Greek, 1102 years. According to the Septuagint, therefore, the period from the Deluge down to Abraham is about 1000 years longer than it is according to the Hebrew and Latin texts. Looked at from a critical and exegetical point of view, the figures of the Septuagint ought not, I think, to be preferred to those of the Hebrew text; they rather show plainly that they are freaks of the Greek translator.[1] But, for all that, I should not like to vouch for the integrity of the Hebrew text in this chapter. It consists almost entirely of names and dates, and even before the Greek translation was made several names and figures may have fallen out, and the genealogical tables may thus have originally been longer, and have

[1] E. Preuss, *Die Chronologie der Septuaginta*, Berlin 1859, p. 37. Speaking about the variations in the genealogical tables of Genesis found in the Septuagint, he says: "It struck the Alexandrian Fathers as unnatural that the patriarchs should have begotten children at an age which on an average was only the ninth part of their whole existence. It seemed just as absurd as to assert that in their time a boy of nine years old had had a son. They chose an obvious mode of escape from this dilemma. It was not even necessary to change the figures, but only to alter their division. Where the text said that more than 150 years had elapsed before a child was begotten, they left it untouched. If the text gave less, they added 100 years to the time it mentioned, which they then deducted from the period after the conception of the child. Adam begat Seth in his 130th year, from that time to his death 800 years elapsed. Instead of 130 + 800, the Septuagint has 230 + 700." See also S. Augustine, *Civ. Dei*, xv. 13, but he ascribes the alteration to the copyist, not to the translator. Dillmann, *Genesis*, pp. 123, 219, differs on this point.

been shortened by transcribers to the nine or ten names given in our present text. However sure we may be that no errors which could in any way darken revelation and religious truth can have crept into the text of the Holy Scriptures, we may unhesitatingly say with Valroger, "The genealogies of the patriarchs were no doubt originally complete; but it is possible that many transcribers may have shortened them, perhaps unwittingly, perhaps in order to have symmetrical and more easily preserved lists. Other genealogical tables have been shortened in different books of the Old and New Testaments. It is only necessary to read the fifth and eleventh chapters of Genesis to see that the repeated transcription of many monotonous statements could hardly take place without oversights and errors. But it was not necessary for God to work a miracle in order to preserve the exact figures of the patriarchal generations in all the copies of the different texts. These details were, no doubt, not without interest in the time of Moses; but the salvation of the world did not depend on their being preserved. Whole books of Jewish literature, which are quoted in the Old Testament, have been lost. How much more possible was it that a few chronological statements, a few fragments of the patriarchal genealogies, should disappear from the books which have been preserved in the Old Testament, and that this should happen without in any way injuring the moral and religious importance of the history."[1]

And we must observe, that the genealogical tables in

---

[1] *L'âge du monde*, p. 70. *Revue*, i. c. p. 281. See also Bishop Harold Browne in Speaker's *Commentary*, i. 64.

the eleventh chapter of Genesis are the only materials we have for the computation of the time between the Deluge and Abraham. If, therefore, on considering the extension of mankind and the formation of the different races,[1] and also the results of historical and geological inquiry, it appears that 300 years is too short a time, even a theologian with the strictest exegetical principles " need not," to use Delitzsch's words,[2] " with apologetic prejudice struggle against any disparagement of the chronological network of Genesis," —a disparagement based on an assumed corruption of the text, which from a theological point of view is quite immaterial.

But if we may assume that the period between the Flood and Abraham was longer than the figures in the eleventh chapter of the Hebrew text seem to show, it will not be impossible to harmonize the chronology of theologians and historians. For it is admitted by all thoughtful men of science, that the accounts of long periods of time which occur in the histories of many ancient peoples, the Indians, Chinese, Babylonians, etc., rest on fantastic exaggerations, and at any rate cannot be compared to the Biblical record so far as trustworthiness is concerned.[3] The only people of whom scholars acknowledge that its credibly recorded history reaches farther back than is consistent with the traditional Biblical chronology, is the Egyptian nation. But even here we have as yet no certain results, and if modern Egyptologists put the beginning of Egyptian

---

[1] See above, p. 241.   [2] *Genesis*, p. 184. Cf. p. 272.
[3] Wiseman, *On the Connection*, etc. ii. 4. Meignan, *Le monde*, p. 292.

history at about the year 3900 B.C.,[1] this date, at any rate, is much more in harmony with the Biblical chronology than are the 100,000 years for which many assert that, according to geology, man must have existed on the earth.

Let us therefore put aside the question of how many thousands of years the human race has existed on the earth according to the statements in the Bible, or the calculations of Egyptologists, and let us state the question which will be discussed in the next lecture in this form : Has geology proved that the human race has existed for much more than 6000 years?

---

[1] Cf. W. Fell, "Die neuesten Forschungen auf dem Gebiete der altägyptischen Geschichte und Chronologie," in the *Chilianeum* N. F. i. 1869, p. 73.

XXXIV.

THE ANTIQUITY OF THE HUMAN RACE.

GENERALLY speaking, geologists give us only relative and not absolute calculations of time, that is, they decide which is the oldest or most recent of several formations, but not exactly how old each is. For instance, they say that the Carboniferous system is older than the Triassic, and the latter older than the Oolite; but they do not know how many thousands of years each of these formations is older than the succeeding one, or by how many thousand years any of them has preceded the present day. Its chronology therefore is as if in a handbook of history we were only told that Julius Cæsar, Charlemagne, and Napoleon followed one another in the order in which they are named, without any mention of the intervals that occurred between these men, and between them and the present time.[1] If, then, we ask what is the age of man in this relative sense, geologists unanimously answer, he is the most recent creature on the earth; he appeared later than the animals, in one of the latest of the geological periods. This agrees with the narrative in Genesis, according to which the creation of man concluded the work of the six days.[2]

---

[1] B. Cotta, *Geologische Fragen*, p. 228. *Geologie der Gegenwart*, p. 232.
[2] "Sacred history and geological truth both prove that man is a recent creature on the earth."—Leonhard, *Geologie*, i. 282.

Now, geologists naturally wish to complete this apparently incomplete chronology. For this reason they have repeatedly attempted to express their chronology in figures; for instance, to calculate how many thousand years it must have taken to form the separate strata, and how many thousand years have elapsed since their formation. These calculations have as yet, however, produced no certain result; the time is supposed to be some hundred thousands or millions of years, and we are told that these figures are only approximate guesses, and that no one can vouch for their correctness.[1]

At first the attempt to give in figures the duration of the most recent periods, and with them the approximate age of the human race, seemed to promise some success, and geologists have limited themselves to these periods; that is, according to the description given above to the post-pliocene or quaternary, and the recent periods.[2] Geology here comes into contact with history, for the latter in inquiring into the earliest periods of the existence of the human race, must consider not only written documents, but also the traces of man which are found in the strata or on the surface of the earth; such as graves, old monuments and erections, implements, and sometimes even the remains of men, and of the animals with whom they came in contact. That portion of the inquiry into the earliest history of mankind which does not rest on documentary evidence, but on such geological and archæological investigations as I have described, is becoming in these days more and more a special scientific study, and is called

[1] See vol. i. p. 290. [2] *Ibid.* p. 284.

Primæval History, Historical Anthropology, Archæological Geology, Human Palæontology, or Prehistoric Archæology. These investigations have called forth an almost boundless literature, especially since Lyell's book on the *Antiquity of Man* appeared in the year 1863, and they form at the present time one of the favourite occupations of real and amateur men of science and antiquarians.

The fact that these investigations into primæval history have a theological or religious interest has on the one hand tended to promote them, but on the other has had an unfavourable effect, inasmuch as it has affected the prejudices of several investigators. As I have shown in my last lecture, the Bible, as generally understood, states that the age of the human race is only a few thousand years. Now, geologists must wish either to see the Biblical chronology confirmed or disproved by their science, according to their religious position; and although it has been, perhaps fairly, asserted that a few older geologists, such as Deluc and Cuvier, have allowed their geological calculations to be influenced by the Biblical statements, and that it is for this reason that they have calculated the antiquity of the human race at about 6000 years, there can be no doubt that some modern savants have taken pleasure in estimating the antiquity of the human race at many thousands of years, because they knew that they thus came into conflict with the Bible or the teaching of theologians, and with the belief of Christians.

I shall speak in the following lectures of Prehistoric Archæology. To-day I shall confine myself to geological investigations into the age of the human race.

Before geologists can calculate in figures the duration of any one of their periods, they must first of all have verified two things—1st, Some one effect which has been produced in this period by a definite cause; and 2nd, The measure of the effect which this cause produces in a definite time—a year or a century. A tree increases by one ring every year; if it is sawn through, and if the rings can be counted, its age can be exactly ascertained. Geology has not, of course, at its disposal such simple means of calculation, but men, of whom so far as I know Deluc was the first, have tried to obtain geological measures of time.[1]

The modern attempts which have been made to calculate in figures by means of geology the age of the human race, or to speak more accurately, the age of the human relics which have been found, may generally speaking be divided into two groups.

In the first place, human bones, implements, etc., have been found in different places in the earth, covered more or less deeply with loam, peat, river deposits, stalagmites, etc. These human remains, it is said, originally lay on the surface, and the layers have been gradually deposited upon them. If, therefore, we can calculate how long the latter have taken to form and be deposited, we shall know how long ago the bones and implements lay on the surface, and therefore approximately when the men who left these relics lived. But in order to calculate how many centuries were required for the deposit of these layers, we must know two things; first, the thickness of the layers, and secondly, how much is deposited in a century. If we know both,

[1] Wiseman, *Connection*, etc. i. 366.

the age of the objects in question may be ascertained by a very simple calculation. The first may be found out by measurement; for instance, we know that human bones have been found under a layer of peat 30 feet thick and 40 feet below the sediment of the Nile. But the second equally important element in the calculation is, as we shall see, quite uncertain, because we can get no universally valid formula for the growth of peat and stalagmites, for the increase in river deposits. Therefore these geological formations will not do for a measure of time.

In the second place, human bones or implements have been found in places where, at the time of their deposit, the waters of the sea, of a lake, or a river, must have stood; whereas now either they have receded from thence, or the ground has been raised above their level. Thus in Scotland and in Sweden boats have been found sixty feet above the present level of the sea; in Switzerland lake dwellings at some distance from the present shores of the lakes; in the Somme valley in northern France flint implements and human bones, eighty to one hundred feet above the present river bed. The level of the sea, lake, or river has therefore been altered considerably. If we can find out how much time was necessary for such an alteration in the level and in the distribution of water and land, we shall be able to calculate the time at which those men lived who left these things. In order to calculate this, however, we must not only know how great this alteration is, which can be easily ascertained, but also how much of this alteration has taken place in each century. We shall see that the latter cannot be ascertained with certainty, and that therefore we cannot by this means gain such a geological chronometer as I have described.

Many modern geologists who have made calculations in one of these two ways, have made the mistake of taking as the basis of their calculations either the slowest formations whose progress can be traced by observation, or averages taken from very few observations. But as Pfaff, Dawkins, and others have observed,[1] we ought not to trust to averages at all, because a geological change may take place very slowly in one place and at one time, and very quickly at another place and at another time; and it is unscientific to lay exclusive stress on the changes which take place slowly, as is usually done in most geological calculations of the age of the human race, because there can be no doubt that many important geological changes have taken place in a comparatively short time. G. H. v. Schubert[2] showed by several examples many years ago how deceptive are those chronological calculations which are founded on such changes.

When in the reign of the Emperor Francis I. the petrified trunk of a tree was found, the Emperor wished to know how long a trunk of like thickness must lie in the earth before it could be changed into a mass of stone. It occurred to the Viennese savants of that day that the Emperor Trajan had thrown a bridge over the Danube at Belgrade whose supports were still visible in the water. With the permission of the Turkish Court one of these supports was taken out and removed to Vienna. It was found that there was no change in the

---

[1] Pfaff, *Schöpfungsgeschichte*, pp. 111, 126.
[2] *Die Urwelt und die Fixsterne*, Dresden 1822, p. 279.

centre, but that all round the outside it was petrified to the thickness of half an inch, and changed into agate. As it was known that this trunk had been in the Danube for 1700 years, it was easy to calculate that a period of at least 2-300,000 years would have been necessary for the complete petrifaction of trunks such as have been found of from six to eight feet thick. The calculation would be infallibly correct had it not been proved that under some circumstances petrification takes place much more quickly than it did in the case of the supports of the bridge. Petrified logs of wood have been found in America which had evidently been hewn by European axes, and which therefore had gone through the process of petrification in a few centuries. In Westphalia pebbles and flints have been found, for whose formation geologists would suppose that some thousands of years were necessary, were it not for the fact that when they were split open coins were found which bore the stamp and the date of the coins of the Bishops of Munster, and therefore belonged to the sixteenth and seventeenth centuries.[1] A stream of lava, which flowed from Etna in the time of Thucydides, still lies bare and sterile, with hardly a sign of soil or vegetation. Therefore it takes at least 2000 years before a stream of lava can be covered with fertile earth and plants. If, therefore, we

[1] For similar examples, see Molloy, *Geology*, p. 84. In 1832 thousands of silver coins, belonging partly to the thirteenth and fourteenth centuries, were found in the bed of the Dove, in Derbyshire, buried ten feet below the surface in a hard conglomerate. In the beginning of this century a ship was wrecked near Cape Frio, in Brazil; a few months later the dollars and other valuables which were on board on being sought for were found imbedded in hard quartz-like sandstone. In the museum at Montpellier there may be seen a cannon, enclosed in crystalline limestone, which was found near the mouth of the Rhone in the Mediterranean.

find ten such lava streams, one above the other, all covered on the surface with fertile earth, it shows that the volcano must have been active 20,000 years ago. The calculation is very simple, but it is incorrect. Herculaneum was destroyed 1800 years ago, and is already covered with six such alternating layers of lava and fertile earth; and many of the streams of lava which have issued from Vesuvius and Etna within the memory of man are already fitted for cultivation.

Only a few years ago ruins were excavated near Wroxeter which, with the exception of a small bit of wall, were all covered with a thick layer of earth. Judging by the thickness of these layers, geologists would probably have supposed that these ruins were several thousand years old, but for the facts that Roman coins of the fourth century A.D. have been found there, and that we know from history that in the Roman times this was the site of Uriconium. It has been rightly observed in connection with this in England, that in the case of abbeys which were destroyed only 300 years ago, the earth has been already heaped up to a considerable height.[1]

The following facts, quoted by O. Fraas,[2] show us how little suited the formations of tufa and other watery deposits are for chronological calculations. "In the old Greek watering-place Aidepsos, which was world-renowned even in the time of Sulla, the old Roman baths were dug out from under many yards of calcareous tufa; and when the new baths at

---

[1] Ausland, 1864, p. 399.
[2] *Die alten Höhlenbewohner*, Berlin 1873, p. 29.

Baden Baden were made, they found, deep below the surface, skilfully worked baths dating from the Roman time. Here, therefore, the waters have in the course of sixteen to eighteen centuries accidentally deposited a mass of stone on the surface of the earth; while close by there are human remains of the same period, if not earlier, which are hardly covered by the grass.

Karl Vogt admits, without hesitation, that the thickness of the stalagmite deposits which cover the remains of men and extinct animals in the bone caves, gives no evidence as to the time which was necessary for their formation, and therefore is no criterion of the age of those remains. "The deposit varies to a great extent, sometimes in a remarkable degree in the same caves, according to the quantity of trickling water and to the quality and solubility of the lime."[1] "Who would venture to assert certainly," says Schaaffhausen, "that the covering of stalagmite on the bones of the cave bears is more than 2000 years old? And yet these formations in the Kent caves have been supposed to be 210,000 years old. It has been asserted on trustworthy authority that in a tunnel driven through limestone hills, stalactites 4 inches long and $\frac{1}{4}$ inch thick have been formed in the course of nine months."[2]

Nor can the condition of the bones give us any definite information about their age. "In bone caves where the covering of stalagmite was absent," says Vogt,[3] "and where the soil was quite dry, the bones

---

[1] *Vorlesungen*, ii. 8.
[2] *Archiv für Anthropologie*, v. 119. Cf. same, viii. 270.
[3] *Vorlesungen*, ii. 11.

often mouldered away to such an extent that when they were touched they turned to dust; in those cases where the covering of stalagmite exists they are generally in a much better state of preservation." Formerly it was thought that "fossil" bones could be distinguished from recent bones, because the former stick to the tongue and the latter do not. Bones stick to the tongue because they have lost the organic cartilage; but the rapidity with which this takes place depends on various circumstances. Nor do other differences, which have been observed in examining old bones microscopically and chemically, give us any data for ascertaining their age. For if we succeeded in ascertaining what is the process of the gradual decomposition of the bones under certain circumstances and conditions, we could only deduce from it a universal rule for defining their age if we could assume that the conditions and circumstances have always and everywhere been the same. But we cannot assume this, because the contrary is undoubtedly the case.[1]

These observations will show how uncertain are the means geology possesses for ascertaining the antiquity of the human race. The fact that now after a few years many assertions which were made with great confidence at the beginning of these inquiries are acknowledged to be untenable, is an agreeable proof of the real progress of inquiry. It often happens that when a new subject is brought up for discussion, there is a general belief that the discoveries which have been made will warrant our asserting certain things as assured facts; but then with time, not only do the

[1] *Archiv für Anthropologie*, v. 114, viii. 3.

materials which have to be considered increase, but criticism becomes sharper, and consequently much which was formerly believed to be indisputable becomes uncertain, and much is proved on nearer examination to be untenable. It needs, I think, no prophet to foresee that in a few years it will be generally acknowledged that all attempts to calculate directly the antiquity of man by means of geology *cannot* lead to a conclusion at all certain. I shall speak on another occasion more particularly of the indirect means. To-day I will discuss in detail a few calculations of the kind I have described, which are already acknowledged to be untenable by savants, but are still employed by amateurs, simply because they produce the most remarkable results.

1. Leonard Horner made the following calculation. The base of the colossal statue of Ramses II., at Memphis, which, according to Lepsius, was erected in the year 1360 B.C., is now covered with Nile sediment to a height of 9 feet 4 inches; therefore the Nile has deposited a layer $3\frac{1}{2}$ inches thick in a century. Now in sinking wells and in boring in different places, and at different depths, only remains of still existing kinds of animals have been found; and at no less a depth than 39 feet, fragments of an earthen vessel,—still deeper, bricks have been found. According to the calculation given above, it would take thus more than 12,000 years to form the deposit[1] 39 feet in thickness, which covered the fragments. Now, apart from other considerations, the following objection may be made to this calculation. Horner supposes that the deposit

[1] Ebers, *Ægypten und die Bücher Moses*, 1 Bd. Leipzig 1868, p. 21.

of Nile mud on the base of the Ramses statue began when the statue was erected in 1360 B.C. But if this was so, Memphis must have been under water every year when the Nile overflowed, which is hardly conceivable. So long as Memphis was inhabited, it must have been protected from inundation by its position, or by artificial means; the Nile deposits would probably have begun after the town was deserted, that is, about 500 A.D., consequently the layer of 9 feet 4 inches has been formed in 1400 years, and the deposit went on, therefore, at a much greater rate than $3\frac{1}{2}$ inches in a century. I do not, for all this, assert that the deposit of the Nile in general is more than $3\frac{1}{2}$ inches in a century. Other observations seem amply to prove that on an average it has not much exceeded that figure in the last few centuries. Burmeister quotes observations, according to which it amounts to 4 to $4\frac{1}{2}$ inches;[1] and G. Bischof says, "The bed of the Nile and the land of Egypt are rising gradually, but unequally, according to different circumstances, and less and less as the stream approaches the sea. The increase in this perpendicular rise is much smaller in Lower than in Upper Egypt, and in the Delta it is smaller still; according to an approximate calculation the land has risen 9 feet in 1700 years at the first cataract, at Thebes about 7 feet, and at Heliopolis and Cairo about 5 feet 10 inches. At Rosetta and at the mouth of the Nile the increase in the thickness of the deposit is much smaller than in the narrow valley of Central and Upper Egypt; this is caused by the greater extent of the inun-

[1] *Geschichte der Schöpfung*, p. 18.

dations. The land there has not risen perceptibly in 1700 years."[1] Burmeister, however, says that the ground may have risen more at Thebes than where the shores are higher, because the valley of the Nile widens a good deal, and therefore the river is less rapid and deposits a thicker layer of mud; Parthey estimates the deposit of the stream at Thebes at 6 inches in a century. This would give $8\frac{1}{2}$ feet, not 7, in 1700 years.

These data show that the Nile mud is a very uncertain measure of time, because, as Bischof says, it is deposited unequally in different places, "according to different" circumstances. Therefore even if we knew how much is deposited in *one place* in a century, we cannot tell how great the deposit is in another place; and further, even if we knew how great the deposit is in one spot in *one century*, we still do not know whether it may not be either lesser or greater in another century, because the circumstances by which, according to Burmeister, the deposit is affected may have been very different in the same place in different centuries; and it is very possible that, as he says, "the action of the Nile may have altered considerably at various periods of its history."

We shall therefore never succeed in getting an average of the Nile deposit which will hold good for all places and all centuries, and make of the Nile a comparatively trustworthy measure of time, even though we may make many observations with the greatest possible care. But even if we possessed such an average, the calculation which Horner founds on the discovery of the fragments at a depth of 39 feet would still

[1] *Lehrbuch der Geologie*, 1st ed. ii. 1596, 2nd ed. i. 523.

be doubtful. It could only be correct if those fragments had originally lain on the surface of the earth, and if the yearly deposit of the Nile had regularly been accumulated on them. But who is to prove that this was the case, and that the fragments did not originally lie at the bottom of a well, a cleft in the earth, or a former river-bed. And if this were the case, the whole calculation falls to the ground. Lyell himself quotes a saying of Herodotus,[1] according to which in his time certain spots in Egypt from which the Nile water had been excluded for centuries appeared to have sunk, so that one could look down into them from the adjoining ground; and this because the ground all round had been raised by the gradual accumulation of yearly deposits. Now, if the water were once to break into these sunken places, the deposit there would be greater in a few years than in other places in centuries. And what is to prove that the fragments which have been so often mentioned did not lie in these sunken places together with bones of animals and bricks? The pot of which these are the fragments may possibly have been broken in the time of Herodotus, and have been thrown into one of the sunken places which were shown to him, or it may be of much more recent date. At any rate, it is of no use for measuring time.

In the year 1865 Oscar Fraas, when travelling through the Nile valley, examined more minutely the calculation of the age of the deposits there. He says, rightly, that this calculation if correct would be of the utmost importance, and that it always produces a great effect on the uninitiated; wherefore it is quoted

[1] *Antiquity of Man*, p. 41.

by every author who wishes to reckon the antiquity of man by thousands rather than hundreds of years. For this very reason I think I ought to supplement the objections I have been putting together by some extracts from Fraas' narrative. "In the valley of the Nile more than anywhere," he says, "human hands have taken possession of the soil for thousands of years; it has been pierced with canals and wells, so that the natural conditions have long disappeared. From the cataracts downwards the Nile valley is intersected by a system of canals which, profiting by the natural fall of the valley, carry off the water from the Nile, and spread it out over the whole valley during the flood-time. At this time every farmer may, by erecting dams on his land, cause as much mud to be deposited as he wishes. Every landowner can pierce the dams and so lay his land under water if he wishes, and he can also produce a greater or smaller deposit of Nile mud on his fields by raising or lowering the in- and out-flow. Any piece of dry Nile mud will confirm what has been said; in it, layers, varying from the thickness of a card up to one foot, can be distinguished, and if any one will take the trouble to examine the steep and excoriated banks of the river, he can soon convince himself that there can be nothing like regularity in the deposit. In the face of such incontrovertible facts no one ought to attempt, from the deposits in the Nile valley, to draw any conclusions as to their age. Besides, the impression left on the mind of any unprejudiced geologist after examining the soil of the Nile valley is that it consists of two soils,—an original very ancient stratum, probably dating from the Pliocene period, and a secondary stratum, which the Nile water carries away from one place and deposits in another. The latter is the real fertilizing Nile mud, which very probably, however, is not brought from a great distance, *i.e.* from above the cataracts, but is taken from the neighbouring clay of the old Nile valley. The stream tears away every year some of the old soil of the Nile, which is several fathoms deep along the steep banks below the cataracts, and this, melting in the water, makes the whole stream muddy.[1] When the water is low the steep cliffs of the old Nile bed stand from 20 to 30 feet high. They consist of clay, gravel, and sand, they are split up, as is the whole district, and do not look in the least like a recent alluvial deposit, but rather like an ancient probably marine deposit, dating from a period before man appeared on the earth. If the Nile had formed these strata, the different yearly deposits would be visible on the steep sides of its shores; but instead of this we find at most ten or twelve layers of different thickness,—some a few inches, others several feet thick, —which have the character of an ancient stratified formation, and not of a loam or alluvial soil. A voyage up the Nile will show us, if we have observant eyes, how the mud of these old strata is taken from the steep banks and deposited on the plain; and how it is diligently taken away again from the water by man by means of an artificial system of dams and canals. But no reliance can be placed on any of these calculations as to age."[2]

[1] At Girgeh the Nile has torn away a quantity of houses and half a mosque, so that the interior of the Moorish arched-way is left bare, and the fallen granite pillars picturesquely cover the bank.

[2] *Vor der Sündfluth*, p. 470.

Fraas quotes, besides his own observations, the following remarks of Max Eyth's, who, as chief engineer of the Egyptian Crown Prince, Halim Pasha, carefully examined the agricultural conditions of the Nile valley. "There are no certain data as to the extent to which the soil in the Delta is raised, and all chronological calculations founded on the monuments buried in the Nile mud rest on a complete misunderstanding of the conditions. In the first place, in consequence of different currents, the deposit is not quite even, so that one year a slight incline is formed,—perhaps caused by some accidentally planted bushes which keep back the mud,—where the next year a higher flood and stronger current will sweep away both incline and bushes, and leave only a washed away flat. But any calculation becomes specially impossible where the hand of man has interfered,—and this occurs everywhere in the cultivated land,—because the inundation is of much use to farming, and can easily be guided. A Fellah who makes a dam round the lower end of his field can in one year introduce a few thousand years into the cleverest calculation of a European savant."[1]

"Therefore," says Fraas, "we will put aside the many centuries which may be evolved from the Nile mud. Really it is time that this nonsense which is for ever being repeated in the handbooks should be put an end to, and that arguments should no longer be quoted as coming from science, which can serve at most to take in a credulous layman." The fact that this strongly expressed but, after what has been said, very justi-

---

[1] *Aus dem Orient. Geologische Betrachtungen am Nil*, etc., Stuttgard 1867, p. 212.

fiable wish has as yet in no way been fulfilled,[1] may excuse the detail in which I have discussed this subject.

Quite by chance, just at the time when I was reading Lyell's book, I came across the following passage in a geological paper written, without any reference to Lyell's book, by an Englishman living in India, J. Ferguson. He says: "From these data it will be perceived how fallacious any conclusions must be which are drawn from borings into the strata of deltas, and calculations formed from local superficial deposits. I myself have seen the bricks which formed the foundation of a house I had built carried away, and strewed along the bottom of a river at a depth of 30 or 40 feet below the level of the country. Since then the river has passed on, and a new village now stands on the spot where my bungalow stood, but 40 feet above its ruins; and any one who chooses to dig on the spot may find my 'reliquæ' there, and form what theory he likes as to their antiquity or my age."[2] It may of course be said that the action of the Nile is more regular than that of any other river. I know this; but that does not prove that its action could never have been irregular,—in one year, and in one spot, under special circumstances,—and that it has never produced effects similar to those produced by the Indian river, and even that does not probably every ten years go through such alterations as Ferguson describes.[3]

2. Ferguson's paper treats properly of the changes in

---

[1] Cf. Büchner, *Die Stellung des Menschen*, p. 51.

[2] *Quarterly Journal of the Geological Society*, Aug. 1863, p. 327.

[4] V. Baer, see *Studien*, p. 153, shows in detail that all data and calculations founded on the action of the Nile are "entirely illusory."

the Delta of the Ganges. In it he says that long investigations on the spot have persuaded him that the whole Delta of the Ganges and the present form of the Ganges valley are " of very recent origin ; " and that therefore the inundations and other changes must have progressed very fast, at a rapid rate. In the year 3000 B.C. the only habitable part of the plain in the province of Bengal was the part between the Sutlej and the Jumna ; at the time of our Lord's birth towns could have stood only on the southern hills and at the bottom of the Himalayas ; it was only in A.D. 1000 that the Ganges plain was dry enough for a town like Gour, at a distance from the hills, to grow to any size ; in the fourteenth century only did the Delta become inhabitable, and even in the last century large tracts were reclaimed, which up to that time had been only marshes producing reeds. Surely if a professed geologist thinks that his local investigations lead him to such low figures, it is not necessary always to assume that the larger figures often quoted by geologists in similar cases are perfectly and irrefutably correct ; as, for instance, when the age of the Delta of the Mississippi is estimated at 158,400 years.

The plain in which New Orleans is situated is only 9 feet above the sea, and excavations are often made which go far below this level. In these excavations many layers of cypresses, one above the other, have been brought to light. It is supposed that several woods existed there one after another ; that each forest sank after a certain period, whereupon the ground rose again, and was gradually again covered with trees. If this happened ten times, no doubt 158,400 years is a very short time to allow for it. At a depth of 16 feet charred wood and the skeleton of a man have been found (the skull appears to have belonged to one of the indigenous American races), and the skull was found beneath the roots of a cypress, which seems to belong to the fourth layer from the surface. If we take 14,400 years for each of the layers, the skeleton must be 57,600 years old, so that America must have been peopled at least as long ago as this. Vogt[1] gives all these particulars, which he takes from the American Bennet Dowler, and he assures us that the grounds on which this calculation is based are so simple that very little objection can be made to its result; whereas three pages before[2] he declares that up to this time the efforts to find a "chronological measure" of the time during which man has existed on the earth have borne no great fruit. After Lyell[3] and others[4] had expressed doubts as to the correctness of this calculation, the whole subject was thoroughly discussed by Dr. Schmidt,

---

[1] *Vorlesungen*, ii. 108. Woldrich, *Ueberblick*, etc. p. 56. Schleiden, *Das Alter*, etc. p. 15, gives the time as 258,000 years—evidently a slip of the pen or printer's error, perhaps caused by the fact that large figures come so easily to Schleiden when he is estimating the antiquity of man.

[2] *Vorlesungen*, ii. 105.   [3] *The Antiquity of Man*, p. 13.

[4] "While staying at Swinemünde last summer, I observed, 1500 feet from the end of the west pier, the masts of a brig projecting above the waters of the Baltic. The ship had sunk six weeks before, and was already quite buried in the sand of the Oder, so that all efforts to raise her were useless. From time immemorial the river has poured itself into the sea here without forming a sandbank at this spot; but now a sunken obstacle has produced a sandbank 16 feet high. The Oder is only a brook compared to the Mississippi, and the climate and vegetation at its mouth is northern, and not tropical and luxuriant as it is at the mouth of the father of rivers, where the four successive layers of cypress forests at New Orleans made Vogt think that a human skeleton found beneath them was 57,000 years old. It might be difficult for science to disprove the assertion that that skeleton is not more than 5000 years old."—F. Maurer, see Ausland, 1864, p. 915.

a German savant, who lived for some time in America; and he proved that Dowler's facts were partly incorrect, and that his calculations "rested on such uncertain grounds, and were founded on such baseless and often plainly erroneous hypotheses, that they must be banished from the realm of science into that of ungrounded hypotheses and unscientific statements."[1] Besides this, in the narrative of two American engineers, published in Philadelphia in the year 1861, the antiquity of the whole Mississippi Delta is estimated, in direct contradiction to the previous assumptions, at something under 5000 years.[2]

Schmidt also classes Agassiz' calculation, according to which some human remains found in Florida are 10,000 years old, amongst the "unscientific statements;" other discoveries he simply calls humbug.[3]

The experience of a former age shows us that we may well mistrust American discoveries. The "fossil man of Guadeloupe" made a great sensation in his time; this was a skeleton which was found in 1804 in a so-called tertiary limestone stratum on the coast of Guadeloupe, and was supposed to be of very great age. On a closer examination it was found that this limestone stratum was beyond doubt one of the recent formations which are very quickly produced on that tropical coast, and that this skeleton is certainly not old.[4] After this it was said "that there had been found

---

[1] *Archiv für Anthropologie*, v. 165, 167.

[2] Report upon the Physics and Hydraulics of the Mississippi River, by Humphreys and Abbot; see *Revue Catholique*, Louvain 1867, p. 411.

[3] *Archiv für Anthropologie*, v. 166, 155.

[4] See vol. i. p. 272. Quenstedt, *Sonst und Zetzt*, p. 241. Perty, *Anthropologische Vorträge*, p. 248. Fraas, *Vor der Sündfluth*, p. 448.

at St. Louis human footprints, that is, the print left by naked human feet in clayey soil, which then in the course of time became petrified, but preserved the impressions. Here also it was found on a closer examination that these footprints need not have been more than 300 years old, as they were not imprinted in the soft clay, but hewn out of the hard rock. Wandering Indian tribes often hew out such footprints, in order to intimate their presence and the direction of their wanderings to those who follow them."[1]

Let us therefore put aside the American discoveries, and let us turn to the European, which, generally speaking, have been more closely investigated, and are therefore more suitable for "geological proofs." Besides, Vogt observes[2] that we must remember that the discoveries on the Mississippi, like those on the Nile, deal with human remains, "which are of much more recent date" than the human remains which have been found in Europe. If, therefore, we can prove that these European discoveries do not compel us to put the antiquity of man at much more than 6000 years, we need take no heed of the discoveries which have been made outside Europe.

3. In different places on the coasts of Scotland and Sweden implements and boats have been found under the surface of the earth up to 60 feet above the level of the sea. The places were probably originally sea-beds; and it is shown by this and other facts that the sea has either retired in the course of ages, or that the

---

[1] Burmeister, *Gesch. der Schöpfung*, p. 501. J. P. Smith, *Relation*, etc. p. 364.
[2] *Vorlesungen*, ii. 105.

land has risen. How can we calculate the time when these boats lay on the sea-shore, and since which, therefore, the ground of Scotland and Sweden has been raised 60 feet above the level of the sea? This would be possible if we knew how great the rise was in a century. Now with regard to Scotland, Lyell assumes that since the Roman time the ground may have risen 20 feet; therefore this rise would have taken place in 1700 years, and the other 40 feet consequently in 3400 years. But this calculation is founded only on a supposition. Hugh Miller, who also speaks of these discoveries in Scotland,—and we may say in passing, does not in spite of this contradict the Biblical chronology,—thinks that it cannot be proved that the Scotch coast has risen since the Roman time, so that this will give us no means of reckoning the time.[1] And Lyell himself observes that all such estimates must in the present state of science be considered simply as assumptions, because the amount of rise may not have been the same in all centuries; periods of rise alternating with periods of rest, and possibly of fall also. The rise of the coast in Sweden Lyell believes to have been on an average $2\frac{1}{2}$ feet in a century. The rise now is greater in the north of Sweden and in Norway than in the south.[2] At the North Cape it is said to have been 6 feet in the last 400 years, in Spitzbergen more than this according to

[1] *Sketchbook*, p. 21.
[2] *The Antiquity of Man*, p. 64. In Schonen, the most southern province, it is said that the land has been sinking for centuries. Cf. *Archiv für Anthr.* v. 47. Pfaff, *Schöpfungsgeschichte*, pp. 284, 726, shows that the calculations as to the rise of the land in Sweden are quite untrustworthy.

Lamont. But these are probably exceptions, and the statements are not certain. The average rate must not be put higher than 2½ feet. Darwin does not put it higher even for the west coast of S. America, where we have more proof of sudden alterations of level than anywhere else.

But such average calculations are quite inadmissible. Rises and falls of very different extent have been observed in various regions. The three upright pillars of the temple of Serapis at Pozzuoli, in Italy, give us an instructive example of this. Quenstedt says of these :[1] "8 feet up the pillar we find a band of marine shells 8 feet wide, in which many shells in a very well preserved state are still sticking in the holes. These live only on the surface of the sea; therefore the water must have stood at least 18 feet higher than it does at present. Now as the temple could not well have been built under water, two movements must have taken place; the water rose and fell. But this is merely local; the ruins of the temple of Neptune and the Nymphs, which are 3000 to 4000 feet distant, are under water, and here the upheaval did not take place. In 1807 the pavement of the temple was dry; from that time the water rose gradually, so that in 1845 it stood 28 inches high; in 1852 a decrease took place of about 1 inch a year. The Mediterranean countries are full of such phenomena; on the west coast of Crete beds of shells are found 27 feet above the sea, while 40 miles to the east the ruins of Greek towns can be seen under the water." At Basin Bridge, on the English coast, forests and Roman buildings

[1] *Epochen*, p. 827.

have been found 6 feet below the present level of the sea; and at Morlaix, in France, submarine forests, which sank there suddenly in the eighth century. On the coast of Ireland, at Donegal, a fall of 20 feet has taken place in the last 100 years, for trees, and even old furnaces, now stand under water. At some places on the west coast of Greenland the water already stands above the ruins of the buildings which were erected there by the first Danish settlers.[1]

Besides these gradual upheavals and depressions, other sudden upheavals and depressions of considerable extent take place. I add the following example to those already given.[2]

In June 1819 an enormous dam, 11 geographical miles long, 3 broad, and 10 feet high, was formed by an earthquake in the eastern delta of the Indus, on what had been a perfectly level plain; at the same time the town of Sindren, which was one mile off, sank, together with a piece of land, to such an extent that it was covered by water. On the 23rd of January 1855 a tract of land as large as Yorkshire rose from 1 to 9 feet on the south-west coast of the northern part of New Zealand, and the harbour of Port Nicholson rose from 4 to 5 feet. The effects of the earthquake of 1832 in South America were felt for 1200 miles from north to south; the whole coast of Valparaiso was raised at least 3 feet, the whole country, which is half as large as France, showed distinct signs of upheaval. Similar phenomena occurred on February 20, 1835; most of the land was said to have been raised from 4 to 5 feet, but by April it had sunk again 2 to 3 feet.

[1] Pfaff, *Schöpfungsgeschichte*, p. 288.   [2] See vol. i. p. 430.

At Valparaiso the land has risen 10 feet in ninety years, in the Bay of Cacao 6 feet in six years, at Panco about 24 feet in about eighty years. The upheavals on this coast are not limited to isolated spots; the greater portion of the western coast of South America seems to be affected by them, and it is not only these historical upheavals which make this coast so remarkable, but it is said that numerous signs of former upheavals have been found in widely scattered localities. The island of Sicily has also risen considerably in recent times; at some places the coast is 200 feet above the former level.[1]

One of the books[2] from which I have taken these data speaks of a discovery made in Sweden in 1819, during the digging of a canal between the Mäeler lake and the Baltic, which is looked upon as a proof of the sinking and rising of Sweden. Nails, anchors, and pieces of old boats were found between two walls of rock in layers of rubble and sand; and at a depth of 64 feet a wooden hut was discovered. It was inferred therefore that after the building of the hut this part of the land had sunk gradually to a depth of 64 feet below the level of the sea, that it was then covered with the deposits which were cut through in order to construct the canal, and then rose again.[3] There seems, however, to be a simpler explanation: according to old records a canal existed in this place in the eleventh century, which was used for some time and

---

[1] Molloy, *Geology*, p. 282. C. W. E. Fuchs, *Die vulcanischen Erscheinungen der Erde*, Leipzig 1865, p. 442 seq. O. Peschel, *Neue Probleme der vergleichenden Erkunde*, Leipzig 1870, p. 89 seq.

[2] Fuchs, *Op. cit.* p. 455.   [3] Pfaff, *Schöpfungsgeschichte*, p. 28 seq.

then fell into disuse, so that the deposits 64 feet deep which cover it may have been heaped up by the wind and the water. Others say that the hut was destroyed by the downfall of a sand-hill. At any rate it is not thousands of years old.[1]

These facts prove that the upheaval and depression of the ground is a very varying geological phenomenon which cannot be averaged, and that no distinct rule can be laid down about it which will hold good for all countries and all times. For just as now the upheaval and depression goes on in different countries under different conditions at different rates of progression, so it may have gone on more or less slowly in different centuries in the same country. If, then, it has been ascertained by observations made in this century that Sweden is rising at the rate of $2\frac{1}{2}$ or 4 feet in a hundred years, it does not follow that this gradual upheaval was not greater in former centuries; nor that besides this gradual rise, at some periods and in some places, a sudden rise may not have occurred.[2] At any rate no trustworthy measure of time can be obtained by this means, and all calculations about the age of the implements and boats

---

[1] *Archiv für Anthr.* vii. 276. *Corr.-blatt der D. Gesellschaft für Anthr.* 1875, p. 18. "The assertions of the recent *Géologie Archéologique*, in spite of their incomparable assurance, often lead us to suspect that the whole thing is a joke, and intended to mystify antiquaries. What are we to think of the fisherman's hut, with the hearthstone and the bundle of faggots on it, which was found near the Mäeler lake 64 feet deep in the earth, and which had been sinking so slowly and undisturbedly for 80,000 years at the rate of 10 inches a century, that hut, hearthstone, and faggots had, marvellous to say, escaped destruction?" See Lindenschmidt in the *Archiv für Anthr.* i. 53.

[2] Cf. O. Schmidt, *Oesterr. Wochenschrift*, 1863, ii. p. 388. Cotta, *Geol. Bilder*, p. 49. Pfaff, *Die neuesten Forschungen*, p. 71.

found in Scotland and in Sweden, which are based on the rate at which land is rising, are no more than arbitrary assumptions, because the rate of progression is not sufficiently known, and can never be definitely ascertained.

It is interesting to know what Lyell has said on this subject. "As no accurate observations on the rise of the Swedish coast refer to periods more remote than a century and a half from the present time, and as traditional information, and that derived from ancient buildings on the coast, do not enable the antiquary to trace back any monuments of change for more than five or six centuries, we cannot declare whether the rate of the upheaving force is uniform during very long periods. . . . As the movement is now very different in different places, it may also have varied very much in intensity at different periods."[1]

In conclusion I will mention an analogous case, which clearly shows how little the changes in the proportion of land and sea can be of use to us as a measure of time. We know that the coast of Medoc in the Bay of Gascony is continually being encroached upon by the ocean. The ancient Noviomagus, which was swallowed up by the waves in the year 580 A.D., lies in ruins under the sea. The rock of Cordouan, on which was a lighthouse, was originally connected with the coast, it is now distant from it about three leagues. Since 1818 the rate at which the sea is encroaching has been accurately recorded. From 1818 to 1830 the sea gained 180 metres of ground. If we average this, we get 15 metres a year, and according to this the sea

---

[1] *Principles of Geology*, ii. p. 345. Cf. Leonhard, *Geologie*, ii. 89.

would have gained another 180 metres in twelve more years, that is, from 1830 to 1842. But it did not do this by any means, for instead of 180 metres it gained in those twelve years 350 metres, that is to say 29 instead of 15 metres a year, and from 1842 to 1845 it gained at the rate of 35 metres.[1] Who is to prove that the contrary may not have occurred in other instances of alterations in the face of the country, and that the alteration in former centuries was not much greater than in the last? The same holds good for the Niagara Falls, which have been used for measuring time. It has been observed that the Falls recede from 1 to 2 feet in each year, and it had been calculated that it took 35,000 years to form the gorge. Recent observations, however, show that latterly it has receded more than $3\frac{1}{2}$ feet in a year. Calculation is impossible, for it washes away both hard and soft strata, and nobody knows how great was the volume of water which came over the Falls 1000 years ago.[2]

4. In the Somme valley, near Amiens and Abbeville, human bones and implements have been found in gravel beds which do not lie near the present river bed, but on the slope of the hills round the valley, and are from 80 to 100 feet higher than the present river bed. I have already mentioned the discovery, and I shall return to it shortly; at present I am only concerned to find out whether the age of these gravel deposits can be calculated. They are covered by a layer of sand of about 6 feet thick, by a layer of clay of the same thickness, and by a layer of common alluvial soil.

[1] Ausland, 1862, 1032. See also Molloy, *Geology*, p. 47.
[2] Schaaffhausen, see *Archiv für Anthr.* viii. p. 270.

These three layers have therefore been deposited still later than the gravel bed, and when this gravel bed was deposited the valley must have had a shape quite different from the present. Since the valley assumed its present shape, a peat bed has been formed in it, which is in places 30 feet deep.[1]

We shall see later that this peat bed gives us no data for calculating how long the valley of the Somme has existed in its present shape. But is it possible to calculate the length of time during which the valley was changed to its present shape from that which it had when the gravel bed was deposited? If we are to assume, with Lyell and Vogt, that the Somme has gradually hollowed out the valley until it formed its present bed, as it is supposed that some rivers slowly but continuously hollow out their beds, a very long time must of course have elapsed since the valley had such a conformation that the gravel bed was deposited by the river. Lyell himself suggests the objection, that if we judge by the alterations which are still going on in the river beds, no period of time would be long enough to explain such a transformation of the valley. To this he answers, that it is more than probable that such alterations, together with elevations and subsidences of the land, took place in former times more rapidly than they do now. But if we assume that formerly other and more powerful causes existed, or that the present causes worked with greater intensity, then surely we entirely give up all hope of calculating time. The only possible formula for such a calculation is this. "The river deepens its bed, accord-

[1] Vogt, *Vorlesungen*, ii. p. 46 seq.

ing to present observations, at the rate of—let us say—
a foot a century ; the conformation of the valley shows
that the river bed lay formerly 100 feet higher than it
is now, therefore since then 10,000 years have gone by.
But the calculation is not correct, indeed any calculation
becomes impossible directly we admit, what according
to Lyell is "more than probable," that besides this
deepening of the river bed at the rate of one foot a
century, other causes may have been at work which
have altered the conformation of the valley; such as, for
instance, inroads of the sea, which, according to Vogt,
has evidently sometimes penetrated far inland in the
Somme valley, other inundations which may have
removed masses of earth and stone, upheavals which
have raised the sides of the river valley, or subsidences
by which its centre has been lowered. I am, of course,
not able to prove that such causes have really been at
work to alter the configuration of the Somme valley
in the course of about 4000 years ; I am not even
enough of a geologist to describe in detail the occurrences by which this alteration may possibly have been
produced in this time. But in order to be persuaded
that nothing here compels us to put the antiquity of
man many myriads of years back, it is quite enough
for us laymen to know first, that Lyell himself refrains
from making any estimate, because he admits that it is
possible, and even highly probable, that other forces
may have been at work here formerly besides the river
with its slow washing away of the soil ; and secondly,
that other geologists think that it is probable that
the conformation of the valley has altered in a shorter
time.

Thus one of the most eminent of English geologists, Professor Phillips, speaking at the meeting of the British Association in 1863, when this subject was discussed, while admitting that the discovery in the Somme valley proved the co-existence of man and the extinct mammals, added that he thought he could explain the fact that the deposits in which the proofs of this co-existence were found lie from 30 to 100 feet above the present river bed, without postulating such a long period of time as Lyell.[1] Further, we find the following quotation in a criticism of Lyell's book, published in an English periodical, and apparently written by a scientific man. "An estimate or conjecture of the greater antiquity of the gravels as compared with the peat may be formed on two grounds. First, by their elevation above the level of the valley which contains the peat, for this implies either an excavation of the valley below the level of the gravels since the date of their deposition by the waters of the Somme, or the elevation of what was once the river bed to the actual height of the plateau of St. Acheul. Either of these events, if we are to judge by what is now going on in the valley of the Somme, would require a period so long as to be practically incalculable. The river Somme could never excavate such a valley, nor is there any proof of upward or downward movement now in progress in its whole course. This method of observation obviously yields no other result but the rejection of all estimates which are founded upon the actual measures of natural forces in their vicinity. . . . Such confused gravel heaps prove, indeed, the force

[1] *Athenæum*, 19th September 1863.

and agitation of the water, but not the length of time consumed in the accumulation. Nor can a sure mode of computation be founded on the position which is occupied by the gravels, elevated as they are 80 or 100 feet above the river. If the river formerly ran at this high level and deposited the gravel there, and has since cut its way down to the actual channel, its action must have been formerly incomparably more violent than now, or the time to be allowed must be absolutely beyond all belief. But, in fact, if we may trust observations at St. Acheul, there is no necessity for supposing that it did cut down the valley; on the contrary, the gravel, sand, and loam appear to have been uplifted by an angular movement which affected the whole valley of the Somme, a movement which is part of a system of disturbances of late date parallel to and between the anticlinal axes of Boulogne and the Pays de Brai. . . . Nor is the problem of the age of the gravels thus rendered definite. For, as these movements were *partial* and irregular, they cannot be computed by the only formula yet proposed, viz. that deduced from the general and gradual elevation of Scandinavia."[1] Therefore the age of the deposits in the Somme valley also cannot be given in figures.

I will conclude by quoting an observation from a lecture "on the method of prehistoric inquiry," given at the Anthropological Congress in Copenhagen in 1869 by Schaaffhausen. "One of the most important, but at the same time most difficult of our tasks is the

---

[1] *Quarterly Review*, October 1863, pp. 400, 416. Cf. Fraas, *Die alten Höhlenbewohner*, Berlin 1873, p. 25; *Archiv für Anthr.* v. 478, viii. p. 268.

computation of time, and we cannot deny that even the estimates of the antiquity of certain discoveries or certain epochs which some eminent savants have attempted, have no scientific value. We have no certain measure of time with which to estimate these ages. The statement that the fragments of pottery found at a depth of 72 feet in the Nile mud are 24,000 years old, or Dowler's assertion that a human skeleton in the Mississippi Delta is 57,600 years old, or Agassiz', that human remains in the coral reef of Florida are 10,000 years old, even Steenstrup's calculation that the Scandinavian stone age is 4000 years old, all these rest on the most uncertain assumptions.[1]

[1] *Archiv für Anthr.* v. 118. Cf. same, viii. 269.

XXXV.

THE PREHISTORIC PERIODS.

The view that the antiquity of the human race goes back many thousand years is connected by some savants with the theory that man is developed from the "anthropoids" or from the apes who were the common ancestors of those of men. No doubt if man was not created by God as a being endowed with reason, but was evolved from the ape according to the laws laid down by Darwin, at least 100,000 years would be necessary in order to explain the difference between man as he exists now and his ancestors. After what I have said in a previous lecture I need not waste another word on this argument for an antiquity of many thousand years for the human race. Lyell, no doubt, does not quote this argument in his *Antiquity of Man*, but we find the following amongst his "geological" proofs:[1] Many thousands of years must have been required to raise man from his original barbarous and savage condition to the stage of civilisation to which the old Egyptian monuments, for instance, bear witness. Now this proof, if it is a proof at all, of the high antiquity of the human race, is at best historical, and not geological. I have already discussed in its general aspects the theory, that man

[1] See p. 413 seq.

existed originally in a condition of barbarism resembling that of the animals.[1] Another theory is, however, connected with this one, and this I must now discuss more in detail, because it has been brought forward very prominently in illustrating Primæval History, or Prehistoric Archæology, during recent years: I mean the distinction of a *stone* age, a *bronze* age, and an *iron* age.[2]

The Danish savant, E. C. Thomsen, who in the year 1837 brought into use this method of classifying northern antiquities,[3] is not its inventor. The Roman poet Lucretius declared that man first of all used stones as weapons, then bronze, and lastly began to work iron.[4] Several antiquaries in the last century[5] believed that the stone, bronze, and iron ages followed each other, but they attached no great importance to it. The theory of the existence of these three periods has attracted more attention in recent years, because implements of stone have been found and recognised in greater number and variety, and this was greatly due to the French savant Boucher de Perthes.

He announced in 1847, in a book on Celtic and

---

[1] See above, p. 175.

[2] Cf. *Chilianeum*, iv. 234, and the books there quoted.

[3] *Leitfaden zur nordischen Alterthumskunde*, Copenhagen 1837, p. 58. Cf. *Archiv für Anthr.* viii. 289.

[4] *De rerum natura*, v. 1282:—
    Arma antiqua manus, ungues dentesque fuerunt
    Et lapides . . .
    Posterius ferri vis est ærisque recepta,
    Et prior æris erat quam ferri cognitus usus,
    Quo facilis magis est natura et copia major.

[5] In the year 1752, Goguet distinguished between the stone, bronze, and iron ages in his book, *Origine della leggi*, etc. This, however, was not noticed again until 1863. Cf. G. Pigorini, *Le abitazioni lacustri, Nuova Antologia*, vol. xiii. 1870, p. 102.

antediluvian antiquities, that in the Somme valley, near Abbeville and Amiens, he had found human implements in deposits which must belong to the diluvial or quaternary period, because they contained the bones of mammoth and other extinct mammals; and that he had therefore obtained a proof that man had existed contemporaneously with those extinct animals, which, as we have seen, was then still denied by most geologists. Boucher de Perthes' book contains a variety of curious statements; Vogt calls him a meritorious, but excitable and very fantastic writer, and as a proof of his lively fancy he quotes Perthes' assertion that he had found antediluvian stone instruments for cutting the hair and nails. We can understand, therefore, why geologists and antiquarians at first took no notice of his discovery, or treated it as doubtful or as a joke.[1] Perthes was obliged, as Vogt says, simply to go begging from door to door with his discovery, attracting no attention, till at last a few of his neighbours, then a few Englishmen (first H. Falconer and J. Prestwich, then Lyell), noticed it, and confirmed the discovery. They then drew attention to it in periodicals and at meetings of scientific men; the subject attracted more and more attention in the following years, and at last Amiens, Abbeville, St. Acheul, Menchecourt, and other smaller places in the valley of the Somme, became regular places of pilgrimage, to which geologists and antiquarians resorted every year.[2] The discussion on Boucher's discoveries turned principally on the question whether they really proved that

---

[1] *Etudes relig.* 4 s. t. 1 (1868), p. 40. Baltzer, *Die Anfänge*, p. 88.
[2] Vogt, *Vorlesungen*, ii. 51

man had existed at the same time as the mammoth. Just as it was supposed formerly, in the case of bone caves in which human remains and animal bones had been found together, that the former had come into the cave later than the latter, so it was thought by many people that in the case of the deposits in the Somme valley the animal bones belonged to an earlier age than did the human remains; it was supposed that the beds of earth on which and in which the two classes of objects had been deposited at different times had been so tossed about by floods, and the strata so mixed, that the earlier and later deposits could not be distinguished in this *terrain remanié*, as the French call it.[1] It is now unimportant whether this theory is correct or the other, viz. that these deposits still remain in the original state, and that the bones of animals and stone implements are of the same age, because the belief now prevalent amongst geologists, that man existed in the diluvial or quaternary age, has been sufficiently attested by other facts.[2]

Very few human bones were found in the deposits of the Somme valley. At first none were found, and in his *Antiquity of Man*, Lyell wrote a long dissertation in which he tried to explain this strange fact.[3] Then a jawbone was found, which gave rise to many discussions, some of which were of a comic nature, and the suspicion that the savants had allowed themselves to be duped was never quite removed.[4] Later on

---

[1] Cf. Vogt, *Vorlesungen*, ii. 300. *Jahrb. für Deutsche Theologie*, viii. (1863) p. 56.
[2] See above, p. 280.
[3] P. 190.
[4] Cf. *Chilianeum*, iv. 325. Nadaillac, *L'ancienneté*, p. 76. *Etudes*, etc. p. 42.

Boucher found a skull, and this discovery was attested by a sworn declaration for greater security.

Vogt describes the flint implements, silex taillés, found in the Somme valley, in these words.[1] "They are remarkably rough in workmanship, and have evidently been flaked from the flint boulders which are found in the chalk of the district itself. Two boulders were knocked together till one split, and then from the fragments those were chosen which seemed most suitable for making the implements. Light blows were then given to the flint on both sides of the edge till it became more or less sharp. The so-called knives, or more accurately flakes, 'éclats,' are the least worked; these are thin sometimes rather long pieces, sharpened on both sides, running up to a more or less sharp point, and they therefore distantly resemble a knife blade. They were used for cutting meat and bark, for skinning animals, and other similar operations, as we learn from the worked bones, where the cuts made with these flakes can often be distinctly traced. Two other forms appear to be more worked, one of which rather resembles a lance-head and the other the point of a halberd. The lance-like form is the longer, they are found up to 8 inches in length, they are pointed at the end, at the broad part often much more massive and thick, so that the implement might have been held in the hand. The instruments in the form of an egg have generally been the most worked with little blows, and are sharpened all round; the blunt end was probably wedged into a piece of wood or horn, and there tied fast with bark or some other fibrous material."

[1] *Vorlesungen*, ii. 50.

Now are these peculiarly formed stones, which have been found in almost all countries since Boucher de Perthes drew attention to them, really human implements, knives, axes, and picks, or have they by chance been thus formed by nature to look like the work of human hands; are they, in fact, *Lusus naturæ?* Like many older writers, several modern savants have thought this probable.[1] Andreas Wagner probably believed it to the day of his death; he still asserted it in one of his last lectures in the Academy at Munich,[2] and in this lecture, among other things, he called attention to the fact that the workmen in the Somme valley, who might be considered to be as experienced on this point as the savants, and also less prejudiced, would not acknowledge the stones to be implements; and that the cuts in the bones and horns, said to have been made with these implements, might very well have been only rents and splits which had happened later. But Wagner certainly went too far. No doubt some of the objects which are supposed by many people to be of human fabrication, "implements" as they are now called, are naturally formed splinters of stone. Lipsius and Ebers, for instance, proved in 1870 and 1871, in the *Zeitschrift für Ægyptische Sprache und Alterthumskunde*, that the stone implements which French travellers said they had found in Egypt in 1869 were not manufactures;[3] and probably the same holds

[1] Probably Michele Mercati, writing in the second half of the sixteenth century (see his *Metallotheca*, printed in 1709), was the first to suggest that the so-called *pietre di fulmine* were in reality works of art, *pietre lavorate*. Cf. Pigorini, *Op. cit.* p. 100. Nadaillac, *L'ancienneté*, p. 2. *Archiv für Anthr.* i. 45.

[2] *Report of the Bavarian Academy of Science*, 1861, ii. p. 29.

[3] Cf. *Corr.-blatt der D. Gesellsch. f. für Anthr.* 1875, p. 20.

good of thousands of others which are preserved in collections of prehistoric antiquities.¹ Others are real works of art, but do not belong to the diluvial or quaternary period, but to the nineteenth century. The workmen at Amiens, when the search for flint hatchets became eager, set going a regular manufactory of them. It is not more wonderful that since prehistoric antiquities have come into fashion they should be fabricated, than that Roman antiquities should be fabricated in Italy and other places, as has been the case for a long time.²

But even if many stone implements are not works of art at all, and others not ancient works of art, there is no doubt that in recent years many thousands of implements have been collected which were similarly fashioned and used by men in primæval times, just as they are now made and used by savage peoples. If people choose to call the age in which a race had no metal implements, and made use of implements of stone, and also of wood, bone, horn, and such like, the stone age,—the name of "premetallic age" which has been most recently suggested is more correct,³—there is nothing to be said. But we must be careful to guard

---

[1] N. Whitley. (The flint implements from drift not authentic ; being a reply to the geological evidences of the *Antiquity of Man*, London 1865. Cf. Ausland, 1865, p. 683 ; 1869, p. 214.) He asserts that most of the stones in question are not works of art. His principal reasons for this are—1st, The "implements" are all flint; the real implements which were used in the stone age were made of serpentine, greenstone, etc. 2nd, They vary from a perfectly roughly-shaped flint to a completely almond-shaped implement; two thirds of the implements preserved in the Abbeville museum are evidently not manufactured. 3rd, They are found in thousands, that is, in quantities quite out of proportion to the very scanty population of those early ages.

[2] Cf. Vogt, *Vorlesungen*, ii. 45, 51.

[3] By A. Ecker, *Archiv für Anthr.* vii. 144, and *ibid.* ix. 47.

against two errors which many people fall into, and which have given rise to all kinds of erroneous ideas.

In the first place, we must not assign every stone or non-metallic implement to the stone age. For stone implements have been used together with those made of metal, on this side of the Alps as in other lands, down to the Christian era. "Spears with points of stags' horn," says Fraas,[1] "arrows with sharp flint heads, and especially the stone axe, stone chisel, and stone hammer, are found amongst the Germans often even down to the time of the Franks, and their like exist among a series of races who were well known to the historians of the classical age. According to Herodotus, there accompanied the army of Xerxes Ethiopians who were so savage that they only possessed weapons of stone and bone, and were dressed in the skins of wild beasts; they had long bows made of the ribs of palm leaves, and cane arrows with a pebble point; their javelins were pointed with the horn of a gazelle." Five hundred years later Tacitus mentions German tribes whom he calls Fenni, and of whom he says, "They have no (iron) weapons—their only means of attack is by arrows, to which, having no iron, they give a bone point." "The Homeric heroes," says Vogt, "who knew bronze, or rather copper, and iron, used in spite of this to hurl huge stones at each other's heads, and the sling was till not very long ago a legitimate weapon. It is proved by several facts that the stone implement, after it was no longer generally used and had been replaced by metals, was considered specially holy,—and that stone knives and stone axes were used at religious

[1] *Die alten Höhlenbewohner*, Berlin 1873, p. 30.

ceremonies, because it was supposed that the metals which required a good deal of human work were therefore to a certain extent unclean."[1] In Sweden Nilsson[2] says that with the exception of a few arrows of bronze, the missile weapons are all made of stone, and these are found beside very prettily worked swords and other bronze weapons. The metal was probably too costly to be generally used for missile weapons. Besides it is quite possible that among the ancient nations, in many cases only the leaders, the rich and mighty men, had metal weapons, and that the common soldiers, on the other hand, had for the most weapons of stone, bone, and horn, just as in the Middle Ages only the knights wore steel armour.[3]

The numerous "finds" of metal together with other implements do not therefore belong to the stone or premetallic age. Even if implements of stone and bone are found alone in one place, this by itself does not prove that they belong to an age when the metals were not yet in use in that region. This can only be considered probable when a great number of caves, graves, and other places in the same region afford no metal implements.

Secondly, we must not suppose that the date of the

---

[1] *Archiv für Anthr.* i. 8.   [2] *Die Ureinwohner*, etc. p. 89.
[3] *Home and Foreign Review*, April 1863, p. 485. Virchow, *Die Urbevölkerung Europa's*, Berlin 1874, p. 41. There is nothing surprising in the fact that at a time when bronze was known stone implements should still have been used. I have myself seen the natives of the island of Puynepet, in the Caroline Archipelago, hollowing out their canoes with stone hatchets, they being at the time in possession of European firearms. The bronze implements were no doubt articles of luxury, and could probably only be procured by rich and mighty men, while the implements for ordinary use were made out of stone and wood." See Hochstetter in the *Oesterreichische Wochenschrift*, 1864, p. 1612.

stone age can ever be exactly ascertained. Just as the Ethiopian and Germanic tribes I have mentioned had no metal implements at a time when other tribes had already possessed them for long, so the races of the middle and north of Europe may have come to possess metals at different times, some earlier, some later, and therefore the stone age of one people or country may have been contemporaneous with the bronze or iron age of another.

The bronze and iron ages cannot be distinguished as two consecutive periods in any case, but this is specially true of central and northern Europe. Many have supposed, with Lucretius, that brass or bronze was in use before iron, because it was more difficult to melt and work the latter.[1] Experts tell us that the last assertion is untrue; and the first, stated so broadly, contradicts historical facts.[2]

The negro tribes in the south and interior of Africa have a very simple and natural way of working iron,[3] and they make no use of the oxide of copper which is found in their country, because they consider that it is more difficult to work than iron. Among the ancients we always find that iron and brass were both in use to-

---

[1] Bronze is a mixture of copper and tin, in the ratio of 92 : 8 (medals), 90 : 10 (cannons), 80–90 : 10–20 (machines), 78 : 22 (bells). See Ausland, 1866, p. 418. In the antique bronzes the proportion is, on an average, 89 parts of copper to 11 parts of tin, besides which there are traces of iron, nickel, silver, lead, sulphur, and antimony. *Archiv für Anthr.* viii. 300. The suggestion that some discoveries of pure copper which have been made would warrant our supposing that a copper or brass age existed before the bronze age (see Büchner, *Die Stellung der Menschen*, p. 87) has met with but little support.

[2] Cf. Hostmann's careful discussion on both points in the *Archiv für Anthr.* viii. 293, ix. 197.

[3] *Archiv für Anthr.* x. 431.

gether from the oldest times. At any rate it cannot be
proved that a special bronze age, an age in which only
bronze was used, and which was followed by the use of
iron, existed in any country. Neither can it be proved
that a bronze age in this sense existed in northern or,
central Europe, and the descriptions given by Scandinavian savants of the expulsion in ancient times from
Scandinavia of the people who had stone implements,
by a people with bronze implements who came in from
Asia, and who in their turn were succeeded by a people
with iron implements,[1] is gradually being recognised
as thoroughly unhistorical. The numerous old bronze
objects which are found in northern and central Europe
are believed by the most trustworthy observers not to
have been manufactured in the country, but to have
been imported from other countries. It has been
proved not only that several of the Mediterranean
nations were skilled in the working of metals at a very
early stage, but also that they had commercial relations
with the northern peoples; the Phœnicians and their
colonies communicated specially with the countries on
the coast, perhaps up to the Baltic Sea: the Greeks with
the countries round the Black Sea and the southern
districts of the Danube on the one side, and with
southern Gaul on the other; the Etruscans, and later
the Romans, with southern and central Germany, partly
through Gaul, and partly over the Rhetian and Noric
Alps.[2] The Italian commerce with the north began,

[1] *Archiv für Anthr.* viii. 278, 303.
[2] Cf. besides the works of Nilsson, Rougemont, Pallmann, and others, especially Lindenschmit in the *Archiv für Anthr.* i. 56, 364; iii. 107, 122; iv. 11; viii. 161. Also A. Von Cohausen, i. 324. H. Genthe, vi. 237. C. Grewingk, vii. 98, 108. See also Virchow, *Ihering Die* 5

according to Lindenschmit, at least as far back as the fourth century B.C., and none of the bronze implements found in ancient Germany are apparently older than this.[1] Probably all the bronze implements which are found in Germany and Scandinavia are of southern origin; and if some of them were of home manufacture, this manufacture was probably connected with the commercial relations.[2]

At any rate, however widespread may be the idea that the stone, bronze, and iron ages were everywhere, or even only in central and northern Europe three consecutive periods, it is now looked upon as erroneous by the most eminent students of the subject. Lindenschmit says that this division is of no more use to us than the division of the products of nature into the mineral, vegetable, and animal kingdoms;[3] and Pallmann says that the persons it benefits are careless directors of antiquarian museums; it enables them to divide the antiquities according to the materials of which they

allg. Versammlung der D. Gesellschaft für Anthropol. zu Dresden, 1874, Brunswick 1875, p. 79. *Edin. Rev.* vol. cxxxii. (1870) p. 470. In the *Archiv für Anthr.* ix. and x. there is a lively discussion between Scandinavian and German savants on this subject.

[1] Hostmann, see *Archiv für Anthr.* viii. 306.

[2] "The few moulds and so-called foundries which have been discovered must not be considered to show that attempts were being made to discover how to mould bronze, but as decisive proofs that there existed a manufacture completely developed, the knowledge of which had been imported with the bronze implements; this, as we gather from analogous facts in the Middle Ages and in modern times, was in the hands of wandering artisans. When the braziers in the Middle Ages and the tinmen in modern days brought the industry of the towns to the villages and farmhouses, this relation between the industrial centres and the country population is a striking proof, it may even have been a survival, of the ancient trade between the cultivated states of the south and the barbarous countries and provinces."—Lindenschmit, see *Archiv für Anthr.* i. 364. Cf. viii. 306.

[3] *Archiv für Anthr.* viii. 173.

are made (stone, bronze, and iron), just like a bad librarian who classes his books according to their size (folios, quartos, and octavos); but for chronology nothing is gained by this classification.[1]

This *has* sometimes been the case in museums. Some years ago in Ireland, weapons of stone and bronze were found in the Shannon; no one noticed, when they were dug out, whether they were intermixed or whether the former were in a deeper and older, the latter in a more recent deposit, because the distinction between a stone and bronze age had not yet then been thought of. In spite of this, an Irish savant afterwards reconstructed a stone age and bronze age out of these materials, and he even hazarded conjectures as to the length of time between these two periods; whereas nobody can make out whether the implements really belong to different periods at all. Other museums have been formed, like that at Dublin, by the gradual collecting of objects, concerning whose discovery in many cases nothing certain is known. It would therefore be very wrong to assign all the stone implements to the stone age. The stone age, as I have shown, can only be said to include those implements which are known to belong to a time in which metals were as yet quite unknown in the regions where they were found, and if a stone age is proved to have existed in any region, this even would not give us any means of ascertaining, even approximately, its date. If I say "in the time of the emperors," this is a very inexact way of fixing a date, unless I add whether I mean the Roman or the German emperors. Just in the same way the stone age may

[1] *Die Pfahlbauten*, p. 76.

have lasted for centuries longer, or have occurred much later in one country than in another. Some savage peoples may be still living in the stone age.

We can trace the use of metals in central and north Europe as far back as a few centuries before Christ. The stone age, or rather the premetallic period, therefore here ends at a time which can only be called prehistoric relatively to the peoples who inhabited these regions.[1] The question when this period began is the same as the question as to when these lands were first peopled, and the stone implements give us no data for answering either.

[1] "If we call only those things *prehistoric* which occurred at a period of which we have no history, we shall get into great difficulties. If we begin history at the time when we have the first contemporary information, we get a very long way back. Egypt and India take us back to such early times that the student of Egyptian or Indian antiquities is much surprised to hear the period just before or even just after the birth of Christ called prehistoric. We do not ask, 'When does history as a whole begin?' but, 'When does history begin at any one special spot; when does day first break *there?*' Everything which lies before the dawning of any *local* history is without doubt prehistoric. The day of history passes just like any ordinary day. Just as the sun moves on, and at one spot on the earth it is still dark, while in another it is already broad daylight,—so it is with history. When it was broad noon-day over the most favoured countries of the earth, when culture had there reached a high stage of development, and government very complicated forms, there still existed in our land wild, unnamed tribes, of whom no one knew anything, whom no one has described, of whom history says nothing. They are prehistoric. And when we look at the different portions of our great country, when we ask when it was that the lands beyond the Elbe and the Oder were touched by the light of true history when the sun rose there, we shall find that this took place in the tenth and eleventh and even as late as the twelfth century; and we shall be forced to admit that things which are found in Germany, and belong to the eighth, ninth, and tenth centuries must, under certain circumstances, be called prehistoric. But if we imagine that only those events must be called prehistoric which occurred at a period when there was no history at all, when Egypt, India, and China did not exist, no doubt the space covered by the prehistoric period is reduced to a very small compass."—See Virchow, *Die 6 allg. Versammlung der D. Gesellsch. für Anthr.*, Munich 1875, p. 12.

Sir John Lubbock,[1] Worsaee, and others have divided the stone age into one, two, three, or four periods. Lubbock distinguishes between an ancient and a recent stone age, a palæolithic and a neolithic period. In the first it is supposed that roughly worked stone implements, and in the second polished stone implements, were used. To this Vogt rightly rejoins: " If we are to gather from the way in which the flint implements are worked, from their polishing and grinding, that there were different epochs in the stone age, we may be disregarding the principles of exact and accurate inquiry. No doubt with every step which man makes in comfort, he feels more and more the wish to make his existence beautiful and pleasant. Therefore he would probably take the roughly worked flint axe, and first work and chip out its edge, then grind and polish it, and work the horn with the knife, and he would do this the more diligently the more his situation and the struggle for existence gave him time for such occupation, which at first he might have considered useless. But just as in our present state of civilisation there are many countries in which a man's whole time is taken up in satisfying the first necessary wants of life, so the same difference must have existed, and was perhaps even more marked, in the earliest times; so that in one place civilisation had progressed, and implements were finely worked, while in a neighbouring region men were still content with the rough form. Is not this shown by the settlements of Concise on the Lake of Neuenburg on the one hand, and those of

---

[1] *Prehistoric Times.* Cf. *Archiv für Anthr.* viii. 249. For Worsaee see same, viii. 60.

central and eastern Switzerland on the other? If these settlements were situated above one another, if above the rough tools of Robenhausen we found the finely worked implements of Concise, we should unhesitatingly say that here were two different consecutive epochs of civilisation. As it is, these settlements may have existed exactly at the same time, although civilisation seems much more advanced in one than in the other.[1]

Others have asserted that the fact that some of the flints are coarsely and others well marked, or that they are hewn, polished, and bored through, cannot by itself be looked upon as a proof that they were made at periods far apart from one another;[2] and it has been asserted latterly that the difference in the manufacture of the flint implements is primarily caused by the difference in the material used. If flint or jasper is split, it produces flakes of more or less thin and knife-like form, and if these were shaped, other implements could be made out of them; crystalline stones, on the other hand, as gneiss, granite, deorite, etc., would have first to be polished. If this observation is correct, it quite destroys the theory that the age of hewn flint implements preceded that of polished flint implements.[3]

Further, a *megalithic* period is spoken of, that is, the period of large stone monuments, which have been called by the Celtic names of Dolmen, Menhir, Kromlech, etc. Such monuments, which are made of large stones placed on one another, or laid side by side, and under

---

[1] *Archiv für Anthr.* i. 17, xii. 273.
[2] Grewingk, see *Archiv für. Anthr.* viii. 82, 77.
[3] H. Fischer, see *Archiv für Anthr.* viii. 239.

which graves are usually found, have been discovered in France, England, Ireland, and North Africa, etc.[1] In the graves we find sometimes only implements of stone, sometimes of bronze also. The monuments no doubt are of different periods, and partly belong to the Christian centuries, therefore it is not right to speak of a special megalithic period.[2]

Lubbock, however, does not rely only on the difference in the flint implements in distinguishing between the first and second stone ages. According to him, one of the characteristics of the palæolithic period is that the mammoth, the woolly haired rhinoceros, the hippopotamus, and other animals then lived in Europe, whereas these had died out in the neolithic period. This leads me to the discussion of another division of the prehistoric time, besides the division into the stone, bronze, and iron ages. This division is based upon the animals whose bones have been found intermingled with human remains and implements, and which it is supposed were contemporaneous with the men who have left these remains. Lartet, for instance, and other French savants enumerate the periods of the cave bear (*Ursus spelœus*), the mammoth (*Elephas primigenius*), the two-horned rhinoceros (*Rhinoceros tichorrhinus*), the reindeer (*Cervus tarandus*), and the aurochs (*Bison europœus*).[3]

Let us for the present put aside the attempts which have been made to identify these four periods with the different stone ages, and let us look at them a little

---

[1] See illustrations in Baer's *Der Vorgeschichtliche Mensch.* p. 261 seq.
[2] E. Desor, see *Archiv für Anthr.* i. 261. J. Ferguson, see *Quarterly Review*, vol. cxxxii. (1870) p. 439.
[3] Quatrefages, *Rapport*, p. 187. Nadaillac, *L'ancienneté*, p. 22.

more closely. It is now pretty generally acknowledged that man existed in Central Europe at a period when it was inhabited by some kinds of animals which are now either quite extinct, or no longer exist there. But is the fact that human remains have been found, mingled sometimes with the bones of one animal and sometimes with those of another, sufficient ground for dividing the time during which man and the animals in question existed together on the earth into periods called after the separate kinds of animals? At any rate we must not imagine these periods to have been so clearly defined that, as Vogt expresses it, on the day of the death of the last cave bear the first mammoth was born. The reindeer and aurochs may no doubt have existed in the mammoth period; it is only called the mammoth period because in the period that followed the mammoth had died out, whereas the reindeer and aurochs still existed.

Let us begin our examination of the separate periods with the last two, which are called after still existing animals. The reindeer, the aurochs, the elk, the urus, the glutton, and other animals were formerly spread over the whole of Central Europe, but gradually withdrew, either to the north or to the mountain country, as the climate got milder and human cultivation spread more widely. The periods, therefore, during which these animals still lived in Germany, Belgium, France, etc., where their bones are found with human remains and works of art, are called the reindeer and aurochs periods. But many people think that the reindeer and aurochs periods cannot be distinguished from one another, and that the latter cannot be said to follow the former; for the bones of the aurochs and reindeer are often found together.[1] Further, it is hardly correct to call these periods prehistoric, for the reindeer certainly existed in Germany in the time of Julius Cæsar,[2] and it is said to have been hunted in Scotland in the twelfth century.[3] The aurochs, or more correctly the bison, which is still preserved in the forests of Poland, and is wild in the Caucasus, and was also found in the last century in Moldavia and Transylvania, existed in the sixth and seventh centuries in Germany, and probably as late as the eleventh in Switzerland.[4]

Reindeer bones are found in many places mixed with the bones of the mammoth, rhinoceros, and cave bear.[5] The bones of the mammoth and cave bear indeed are usually found together.[6] So that at any rate the four periods I have mentioned cannot be distinguished from one another chronologically.[7] We must admit that man existed in Central Europe at the same time as the animals in question, and we can at most add that in some districts the mammoth or the cave bear seems to have become extinct before the other animals. "In try-

[1] Vogt, see *Archiv für Anthr.* i. 23, 32, 127.
[2] Cæsar, *B. gall.* vi. 26 : Est bos cervi figura, cujus a medio fronte inter aures unum (geminum?) cornu existit excelsius magisque directum his, quæ nobis nota sunt, cornibus. Ab ejus summo sicut palmæ ramique late diffunduntur. Eadem est feminæ marisque natura, eadem forma magnitudoque cornuum. Cf. O. Fraas, see *Archiv für Anthr.* ii. 49, v. 191 ; and J. Fr. Brandt and Schaaffhausen, *ibid.* ii. 126, viii. 264. Ausland, 1870, p. 2.
[3] *Edinburgh Review*, vol. cxxxii. (1870) p. 457.
[4] *Archiv für Anthr.* ii. 126, viii. 265. The *aurochs, bos primigenius*, became extinct before the bison, and its name is therefore sometimes given to the latter.
[5] O. Fraas, see *Archiv für Anthr.* ii. 49.
[6] Vogt, see *Archiv für Anthr.* i. 23, 30. Nadaillac, *L'ancienneté*, etc. p. 31.
[7] *Edinburgh Review*, vol. cxxxiii. p. 459. Nadaillac, *L'ancienncte*, p. 24.

ing to imagine the former conditions of the earth's surface, and of the different animals and plants which live on it," says Schaaffhausen, "we often commit the error of separating by long periods of time things which are only separated by space. Very possibly the reindeer may have lived in Europe on high plains whose climate was cooled by the neighbouring glaciers, while the mammoth was eating young pine woods and juicy grass in the plains, and the woods resounded with the roar of the cave bear. But just as in primæval ages different natural conditions prevailed simultaneously even in different parts of Europe, . . . the civilisation of our race showed the greatest differences in those ages. While Phœnician colonies were flourishing on the Mediterranean, the last reindeer hunters may have been living in the Pyrenees, and while the first Phœnician ships were bringing amber from the Baltic coast, the inhabitants of that land may have been savages using implements of stone and bone."[1]

Quenstedt shows that we need not suppose that vast periods were necessary for the extinction of the animals in Central Europe. He says,[2] "The wild reindeer wanders to vast distances in the present day in Siberia; this is fortunate for the poverty stricken people, for they lie in ambush at the beginning of autumn when the shy herds are crossing the streams to the south, and gather in the bloody harvest for the whole winter. The instinct of the animal makes it more than likely that similar herds once penetrated as far as the home of the Celts and Germans, so long as

---

[1] *Archiv für Anthr.* v. 123.
[2] *Klar und Wahr*, pp. 149, 158. See above, vol. i. p. 397.

the population was scanty enough to allow of it. They would even appear again, together with tigers and wolves, if European culture were to perish. The unusual freshness of the skeletons makes us suppose that their date is rather late than early, especially as in Cæsar's time the German forests were a *terra incognita* to the Romans, and seemed to the Greek Tarandos to belong to the realm of fable. No doubt, one thousand years are no more to geologists than as a day from sunrise to sunset; but when we are approaching the time of civilisation, when it is a question not of the origin, but only of the disappearance of creatures which had been for a long time in existence, one thousand years may bring about enormous changes. When the French landed in Algiers in 1830, the officers hunted the Numidian lions even on the sea-coast; but these have long ago retired respectfully before the European guns to the farthermost parts of Juba's kingdom. Thirty years were sufficient entirely to destroy the sea-cow of Steller, which inhabited the desert island of Bering beyond Kamschatka, and which was a gigantic beast weighing 30 cwt., and very good to eat. If this happens in the course of a lifetime under our very eyes, what may not centuries do? Just as the inhabitant of the north longs for the warm south, even so does the unreasoning animal seek to leave its own country if it believes better food can be found elsewhere. No one is likely to suppose that the bears have for three centuries withdrawn from the fertile Suabian lands to the barren rocks of Davos and the Engadin, because they are more comfortable there. No, it is the last fastness from which they can still pursue the struggle for existence. If we were to suffer under pestilence and famine, troops of wolves would rush in upon us from the Polish and French forests. We may well believe that man saw the mammoth and destroyed him, if not by strength, by excess of cunning. It is only a question of the date. I have described above how easily animals withdraw from a place, and sometimes entirely die out; why should not this have been the case with the mammoth? If we look at the bloody bones, and the carcases which are found with the skin and hair still on them, in the frozen ground of Siberia, we shall hardly believe that they are hundreds of thousands of years old."

After all that has been said there can be no question of hundreds of thousands of years; and directly afterwards Quenstedt speaks of "a few thousand years." O. Fraas says that "there is no valid reason for placing the period in which the reindeer, mammoth, rhinoceros, and cave bear existed together with man in Suabia, farther back than the time when the kingdom of Babylon flourished, or when Memphis and the Pyramids were built."[1] The period named after the mammoth, cave bear, etc., may therefore be so far called pre-historic, because it precedes the time when we have certain historical information about Central Europe; but it is contained within the period about which we possess the historical documents of the ancient nations, and is therefore in this sense not prehistoric.

After what has been said, it is evident that a two-fold error is caused by the division of the prehistoric age in the following or any similar way. 1. The period

[1] *Archiv für Anthr.* ii. 50.

of the mammoth. 2. The period of the reindeer. 3. The period of polished flint implements. 4. The bronze period. 5. The iron period.[1] Or : I. The stone age. 1. Man fighting with the mammoth and cave bear; 2. Transition age from the period of the mammoth to that of the reindeer; 3. The period of the reindeer, or the period of the migration of the animals; 4. The period of polished flint implements (lake dwellings, Kjökken möddings, and stone monuments). II. The bronze age. III. The iron age.[2] On the one hand, this division may give us the false idea that the periods followed one another as did the periods of the kings, the republic, and the emperors in Roman history; and on the other, we may get the equally false idea that these periods, at any rate those before the bronze age, by far exceed the number of years of which ancient history gives a record, especially when estimates like the following[3] are added to the description given of them : "The first introduction of bronze into Europe is attributed to a people called Aryas or Arian, who entered the country from Asia about 5000 years ago. . . . The age of the reindeer period may for various reasons be estimated at about 10,000 years. . . . It would be difficult to give any guess at the age of this (the mammoth period), but we have every reason for supposing that 50,000 years would not be too much."

According to geological terminology the period called after the mammoth, cave bear, etc., belongs to the diluvial, post - pliocene, post - tertiary, or quaternary

---

[1] Thus A. Müller, *Die ältesten Spuren des Menschen in Europa*, Basle 1871.

[2] Thus W. Baer, *Der Vorgeschichtliche Mensch.*, Leipzig 1874.

[3] A. Müller, *Op. cit.* p. 46, 33, 25.

period.[1] Is there any reason for supposing that man existed in the previous, *i.e.* the tertiary period, or, to express it more clearly, that he existed in Europe before the so-called glacial period, which here forms the boundary between the tertiary and quaternary periods? Much has been said in late years about "*tertiary man*," the discussions have been very animated, and the existence of tertiary man has been very decidedly asserted by French savants, above all by the Abbé Bourgeois,[2] while it has been just as decidedly disputed by others. It is said in favour of the existence of tertiary man that human bones or implements have been found in deposits which belong to the pliocene, and even to the miocene periods.

Among these human skeletons, we may mention first the so-called fossil man of Denise; these are human bones which were found in 1844 in the neighbourhood of Le Puy en Velay, on the slopes of the extinct volcano of Denise, in a block of light porous tufa, which was supposed to have been thrown up during the last eruption of the volcano. Apart from other objections, it is very doubtful whether the last outbreak of the volcano did really take place in the tertiary period; the fact that the bones of the mammoth and rhinoceros have been found in the same region in similar blocks of tufa, would rather seem to point to the quaternary period. At any rate this discovery proves nothing.[3]

---

[1] See vol. i. 283, 387.

[2] Cf. *Contemporain*, 1872, Mai, p. 213.

[3] Quatrefages, *Rapport*, p. 189. Nadaillac, *L'ancienneté*, p. 189. There is another point worthy of notice in the history of the fossil man of Denise. Vogt says, see *Vorlesungen*, ii. 43: "When once people's attention had been awakened, and the great importance of the Denise discovery had

At Savona a skeleton was found in a bed of clay, which, judging from the shells found in it, must belong to the pliocene age; but the body was very probably buried there at a later time. In the year 1853, when a well was being dug in California, a skull was found buried 153 feet deep, under lava and volcanic ashes. But it has not been proved that the volcanic eruptions began in these regions in the pliocene age, as is asserted.

The existence of the bones of tertiary man has therefore not been proved.[1] Even those who assert his existence, rely principally on other traces of it, on flint implements which are said to have been found in miocene and pliocene strata at Thenay and St. Prest, and on the bones of tertiary animals, especially of the Halitherium and the southern elephant, *Elephas meridionalis*, on which it is said that marks have been found which must have been made with flint knives when the bones were still fresh. But, in the first place, it is doubtful whether the flints in question are really

been recognised, a good deal of cheating took place. There are still some blocks in the possession of different persons, in which the bones appear to be simply stuck in with plaster; and one of the most eminent of French savants, Bravard, informed the Geological Society of France that a clever workman had been surprised and exposed while manufacturing a block of this kind. After the discovery of this attempted fraud, some people tried to show that the original block had been also manufactured by a dishonest workman, but a careful examination has proved that this first block is genuine. We ought not to be surprised at occurrences of this kind. As soon as a discovery has been made, collectors flock to the place, Englishmen especially cause the prices to rise, indeed there are many quarries whose owners gain more by the sale of fossils than by selling the stone. The greater the competition the higher is the price, and the greater the temptation to fraud and illicit gain. The workmen then not unnaturally try to manufacture the desired articles, or even to produce new and more remarkable ones."

[1] *Revue Catholique*, new series t. iv. (t. xxx. 1870) p. 503. Nadaillac, *L'anciennete*, p. 177.

manufactured, and, in the second place, whether the strata in which they were found are really tertiary, and the marks on the bones, which, according to some, are cuts made by the hand of man, according to others, were caused by animals who gnawed the bones,[1] if, indeed, they were made when the bones were fresh, and are not of later date.[2]

These discoveries have been repeatedly discussed at the International Anthropological Congresses. O. Fraas perhaps expresses himself too strongly when he says that after tertiary man, half abortion and half monster, had seen the light at the Brussels Congress in 1872, he was buried at the Stockholm Congress in 1873.[3] But, however this may be, there is no doubt that the greater number of the most eminent savants think that man appeared, at any rate in Germany and in the north, after the glacial period. Some think that there are traces of his existence in the "interglacial" period,[4] that is, the age between the two glacial periods. In France, where there are no formations belonging to the

[1] Vogt, *Archiv für Anthr.* i. 20. Heer, *Die Urwelt*, p. 550. Cf. *Revue Cath.* p. 499. Nadaillac, *L'ancienneté*, p. 174. *Edin. Rev.* p. 443. *Corr.-blatt der D. Gesellsch. für Anthr.* 1875, p. 20; 1876, p. 19. Quenstedt, *Klar und Wahr*, p. 166. *Revue des Questions Historiques*, t. xix. (1876) p. 426.

[2] "It was asserted by an eager Frenchman that the bones of the elephants and rhinoceroses of the tertiary period were covered with regular streaks and furrows, which were evidently artificial, and showed that man must have existed long before the glacial period. One of the opposite party went to the museum where the bones were kept, and asked one of the attendants his opinion on the subject. He explained, to the delight of the sceptic, that the bones when first dug up and still soft were scraped with a knife in order to remove the earth which adhered to them, and that this caused the streaks."—O. Schmidt, *Das Alter der Menschheit*, p. 15.

[3] Ihering, *Die 5 allg. Versammlung der D. Gesellsch. für Anthr.* etc. Dresden 1874, p. 57. Cf. *Corr.-blatt der D. Gesellsch. für Anthr.* 1872, p. 92.

[4] Rütimeyer, *Archiv für Anthr.* viii. 133, ii. 220.

glacial period, it is thought, as I have said, that traces of the simultaneous existence of man and the southern elephant have been found. But even if this should be proved, there would be no grounds for supposing that the mammoth period was preceded by an elephant period, for the bones of the southern elephant have been found in several places mixed with the bones of the mammoth and other mammals, of which some lived after the glacial period and some are still in existence.[1]

Further, I may observe, that considering how uncertain is the whole division into periods which I have been discussing, the attempts which have been made to combine these periods with the Biblical history of man, and to place some of them before, others after the Noachian Deluge, are premature and hazardous. I do not think it likely that central and northern Europe was ever inhabited by man before the deluge, or that any of the traces of man which have been found there are antediluvian in the Biblical sense.[2]

Lastly, I must mention, besides this division into periods called after animals, another division which has been made specially in the case of Denmark, and which has reference to the growth of trees, namely, pine period, oak period, and beech period. In discussing this I can go into the question mentioned in my last lecture, namely, whether peat is of any use as a measure of geological time.

---

[1] Pfaff, *Schöpfungsgeschichte*, p. 631. *Revue Catholique*, new series, t. v (t. xxxi. 1871) p. 11.

[2] F. von Rougemont, *Die Bronze Zeit*, pp. 5, 304. He distinguishes the mammoth age, reindeer age, aurochs age (recent stone age), bronze age, and iron age; and he places the first, or the first two, of these before the Deluge.

There are next to no pine trees in Denmark now, and it is apparently long since pine forests existed there; at least we have no historical records of their existence. But a careful examination of the peat moors there shows that pines did formerly exist in Denmark. There are, besides the ordinary meadow bogs which are formed in and round the river basins in the damp low parts of the valleys, and the high bogs which are formed from mosses in the plains, peculiar little forest bogs, "skovmoose," which fill up deep hollows which have formed in the ground from various causes. Trees grew on the steep sides of these almost funnel-shaped hollows, and they gradually sank down and fell into the bogs. We find at the bottom of these bogs pines up to three feet thick, and sometimes, it is said, with several hundred rings; then evergreen oaks and hollies, which have also almost entirely disappeared from Denmark now; and then in the top layers, we come at last to oaks, birch, hazelnut, and alders. The beech, which now forms the Danish forests, is never found in the peat moors. So that it really seems as if we could distinguish in Denmark a pine, oak, and beech age. But will this enable us to determine the antiquity of the population of Denmark? Lyell says, "What may be the antiquity of the earliest human remains preserved in the Danish peat cannot be estimated in centuries with any approach to accuracy. . . . In the time of the Romans the Danish isles were covered, as now, with magnificent beech forests. . . . Yet in the antecedent bronze period there were no beech trees, or at most but a few stragglers, the country being then covered with oak. In the age of stone, again, the Scotch fir prevailed, and already there were human inhabitants in those old pine forests. How many generations of each species of tree flourished in succession before the pine was supplanted by the oak, and the oak by the beech, can be but vaguely conjectured, but the minimum of time required for the formation of so much peat must, according to the estimate of Steenstrup and other good authorities, have amounted to at least 4000 years; and there is nothing in the observed rate of the growth of peat opposed to the conclusion that the number of centuries may have been four times as great." [1]

Let us put aside the very doubtful attempt to identify the pine, oak, and beech ages with the ages of stone, bronze, and iron, and let us keep to the question of whether peat can be used here and in other places as a measure of time; whether by its aid we shall be able to determine the antiquity of the human race. This will only be possible if we assume beforehand that we know how quickly peat grows. If, for instance, we know that a peat bed increases by the thickness of 1 foot in 100 years, as it has been supposed to do on an average,[2] we could say that 3000 years would be necessary for the formation of a peat bed 30 feet thick, such as is found often in Denmark. This would be a simple calculation. But the matter is by no means so easy.

Boucher de Perthes thought that peat increased at the rate only of 3 centimetres, that is, a good inch, in a century. But if this is so, a bed 30 feet thick

---
[1] *Antiquity of Man*, p. 17.
[2] Oswald Heer. See Vogt, *Vorlesungen*, ii. 95.

would require such myriads of years for its formation that even Lyell says he hesitates to accept this chronometric scale.[1] But on what does Boucher rest his calculations? In French peat beds Roman antiquities are found which must be 1500 years old. But the depth at which they occur, and the thickness of the peat beds which lie over them, vary very much in different places. This must necessarily be the case. Sometimes the peat is so liquid that heavy objects sink into it, sometimes so tough and dense that they remain on the surface. Now Boucher found several flat earthen plates of Roman make in one place lying horizontally, so that they could not have sunk in far, and on this he based his calculation. But it is most arbitrary to draw a general inference from one single instance, and Lyell observes quite rightly that data for determining the age of peat beds can only be obtained by multiplying such observations and carefully comparing them. He adds that up to that time no careful observations had been made in order to determine what is the minimum time which is requisite for the formation of a certain amount of peat. Vogt speaks even more decidedly if possible about this subject on two occasions. "Up to the present time we have no data for determining the rate at which peat grows, for the calculations which people have tried to make rest on very uncertain foundations. There are no materials at present for calculating the vertical increase of peat; and after a great deal of correspondence and conversation with the men who are trying to determine it, I have not arrived at any single fact which would make the calculation easier."[2]

[1] *Antiquity of Man*, p. 156.   [2] *Vorlesungen*, ii. 131, 153.

But if, as Vogt says,[1] "a science which is to draw irrefutable conclusions must have mathematically certain premises," it is clear that no calculation ought to be attempted so long as those premises are absent. There is not even an immediate prospect of obtaining such premises, for all kinds of things have to be considered in calculating the growth of peat. Lyell says that peat-cutters tell him that they have never known any of the holes made in the peat to fill up; therefore they thought that peat did not grow at all. He adds that is not the case, but that it shows that the growth is very slow. Others say that in the East Frisian plains, ditches 6 feet deep grow up again in thirty years;[2] the peat is not of a very dense texture, but it may be obtained several times. Were we to found a calculation on this instance alone, we should find that the age of a peat bed of 30 feet, which Boucher de Perthes reckons at 30,000 years, was 200. Both calculations are undoubtedly wrong.

"One foot in thickness of highly compressed peat, such as is sometimes reached in the bottom of the bogs, is," as Lyell says, "obviously the equivalent of a much greater thickness of peat of spongy and loose texture, such as is found near the surface." Farther on he observes: "Differences in the humidity of the climate, or in the intensity and duration of summer's heat and

---

[1] *Vorlesungen*, i. 4.'
[2] Leonhard, *Geologie*, iii. 534. Quenstedt, *Epochen*, p. 793. Lesquereux has shown that in the Jura peat seldom grows less than 2 feet in a century, and may grow twice as much. He quotes one instance which shows that after the peat had been cut, new peat 6 feet deep formed in one place in 70 years, while in another place only 4 feet formed in 140 years In other places it has grown even faster, in one instance from 4 to 6 feet in 30 years.—Nöggerath, *Der Torf*, Berlin 1875, p. 16.

winter's cold, as well as diversity in the species of plants which most abound, would cause the peat to grow more or less rapidly, not only when we compare two distinct countries in Europe, but the same country at two successive periods."[1]

Even in the same country peat will grow in the same time, in one place 1 foot and in another 1 inch. It depends on the condition of the ground, and on the plants which occur in it. Some peat mosses in Scotland, described by Hugh Miller,[2] only date from Roman times; not only have quantities of Roman coins and other ancient remains been found there, e.g. a Roman kettle 8 feet under the surface, but also Roman axes sticking in the trees which are buried in the peat. Apparently the Roman soldiers cut their way here through forests; the trees they cut down decayed on the ground, dammed up little brooks, and so formed pools; the ground, deprived of air and light, could not support its former vegetation; thus watery, mossy bogs were formed, one generation flourished and decayed after another, and in the course of time a deep peat moss was formed.

Lyell himself in one of his earlier works has put together a series of facts which are unfavourable to the theory of a *general* very slow growth of peat : " In the

---

[1] *Antiquity of Man*, p. 156. Nöggerath, *Op. cit.*: "If the conditions under which peat can be formed are absent, for instance if there is no water and the moss dries up, the growth stops. No doubt the growth of peat did stop on some of the old moors in ancient times for this reason, on others it may only have been interrupted for several centuries. Thus Cuvier was justified in asserting that the growth of peat could not be used as a measure of time in order to estimate the antiquity of the present condition of the earth's surface."

[2] *Sketchbook*, p. 7.

same moss of Hatfield, as well as in that of Kincardine and several others, Roman roads have been found covered to a depth of 8 feet by peat. All the coins, axes, arms, and other utensils found in British and French mosses are also Roman; so that a considerable portion of the European peat bogs are evidently not more ancient than the age of Julius Cæsar. Nor can any vestiges of the ancient forests described by that general along the line of the great Roman way in Britain be discovered, except in the ruined trunks of trees in peat. Deluc ascertained that the very site of the aboriginal forests of Hircinia, Semana, Ardennes, and several others are now occupied by mosses and fens; and a great part of these changes have, with much probability, been attributed to the strict orders given by Severus and other emperors to destroy all the wood in the conquered provinces. Several of the British forests, however, which are now mosses, were cut at different periods by order of the English Parliament, because they harboured wolves or outlaws. Thus the Welsh woods were cut and burnt in the reign of Edward I., as were many of those in Ireland by Henry II. to prevent the natives from harbouring in them and harassing his troops. . . . In June 1747 the body of a woman was found 6 feet deep in a peat moor, in the Isle of Axholm in Lincolnshire. . . . In Ireland a human body was dug up, 1 foot deep in gravel, covered with 11 feet of moss."[1] In a peat moss at Gröningen, a coin of the time of the Emperor Gordian was found at a depth of 30 feet, and in the lowest part of the peat bogs in the Somme valley, which are

[1] *Principles of Geology*, iii. 205. Cf. Nöggerath, *Op. cit.* p. 24.

30 feet deep, a boat laden with bricks was discovered.[1] At Flensburg, in recent years, Roman remains were found, for instance, bronze shields ornamented with dolphins and heads of Medusa; these were at a depth of 10 or 11 feet.[2] In one of his books,[3] Lyell reminds us of the important fact, which he has already observed before, that in England and Ireland bogs have burst in historic times, and have emitted great quantities of black mud, which have spread like a stream of lava, and have sometimes overflowed woods and houses, and have covered them with a layer of mud 15 feet thick.

All these details confirm the following observation of Vogt's.[4] "Even although we may be able to explain tolerably in detail the botanical and chemical formation of peat, we have got no nearer to answering the question as to the rate at which peat grows within a certain time. We do not know in general how long a peat bed of about 1 foot in thickness would take to grow, nor have we obtained up to the present time any scientific data by means of which we can ascertain the rate of growth in any given time for any single peat moor. A little reflection will tell us beforehand that this growth must be different in different peat moors, and even that it must have varied in a given place at different periods." Consequently peat is of no use as a measure of time, and all the calculations as to the antiquity of man which rest on this, may be unhesitatingly classed as geological fancies.

[1] *Quarterly Review*, Oct. 1863, p. 378.
[2] *Home and Foreign Review*, Oct. 1863, p. 736.
[3] *Principles of Geology*, iii. 208.
[4] *Archiv für Anthr.* i. 13.

XXXVI.

LAKE DWELLINGS AND OTHER PREHISTORIC ANTIQUITIES.

PROBABLY no discovery in archæology or primæval history has attracted so much and such widespread attention, as that of the so-called Lake Dwellings. The literature on the subject is already enormous, although the discovery is hardly thirty years old. In order to ascertain how far the lake dwellings can help us in calculating the antiquity of man, we must first shortly recapitulate the facts about them, and in doing this we must separate poetry from fact, and trustworthy observations from arbitrary assumptions.

In January 1854 the water in the lake of Zurich sank lower than it had done for centuries, 1 foot lower than it did in the year 1674, when the water was said to have stood lower than it ever did before. The inhabitants of the shores made use of the large tracts which lay dry for buildings. Amongst others, some landowners at Obermeilen tried to reclaim a piece of land from the lake, by erecting a square of wall in the bed of the lake, and then filling up the walled-in space with earth, which was dug up from the lake bed in two different places. The workmen had first of all to remove a layer of yellowish, grey mud, $1\frac{1}{2}$ feet thick; underneath this they found a stratum of black muddy earth from 2 to 3 feet thick. In this stratum implements of flint, bone, and horn of different kinds were found, pieces of stags' horns, bones of animals which had been pierced, etc., such as had been fished and dredged up from the bottom of the lake in former years; also potsherds, nutshells, decayed grass and leaves, and suchlike, lastly the heads of thick wooden piles, of which a great number stood in rows in the ground, 1 to 1½ feet apart, and which had become so soft that they could easily be cut through with the spade. The schoolmaster of the place called the attention of antiquaries in Zurich to this discovery. The latter, and among them more especially Ferdinand Keller, made wider and more careful investigations, and it was soon discovered that these were the traces and remains of old human dwellings, which had been erected on the piles driven in to the bed of the lake, and which for this reason are called Pfahlbauten, also lake dwellings.[1]

In the course of the next few months the traces of similar dwellings were found in several other Swiss lakes, for instance, in those of Bienne, Neufchatel, Geneva, etc. At the present time about 200 lake dwellings are known to exist in Switzerland, for which many thousand piles have been used. In the course of the next few years the traces of lake dwellings were discovered in other countries, in Southern Germany, in North Italy, in Mecklenburg, Pomerania, etc.[2] For some years they were regularly the fashion. "The lake dwelling fever," says Lindenschmit,[3] "spread far

---

[1] In French, constructions, stations or habitations lacustres; in Italian, abitazioni lacustri or palafitte; and from this in French (see Desor), palafittes.

[2] Pallmann, *Die Pfahlbauten*, p. 56.   [3] *Archiv für Anthr.* i. 52.

beyond the antiquaries amongst whom it originated, and reached even into the circles of the bureaucracy, so that the discovery of lake dwellings was recommended and ordered as something affecting the reputation of the country." At any rate many people supposed that their country was inferior to others, so long as it could not produce the traces of lake dwellings. So far did it go, to give an instance, that a Viennese paper triumphantly announced that Austria was no longer shut out from the ranks of the countries in which lake dwellings had been found, as traces of the latter had been discovered at Olmütz, and that not in a lake, but in a river, a fact which was hitherto unparalleled; although it was true that no piles had been found, but only several kinds of implements and tools, bones of animals, etc., and a few beams of wood in a horizontal position. This shows that Lindenschmit was not far wrong in saying that in consequence of the general fever some savants suffered from an intermittent weakness of sight and of judgment; a lake dwelling without piles reminds us of Hamlet with the Prince of Denmark omitted.

The Swiss savants Ferdinand Keller, Rütimeyer, Heer, Troyon, Morlot, Desor, and the Germans Hassler, Lindenschmit, Hochstetter, Franz Maurer, Moriz Wagner, Pallmann, and others have taken a leading part in the scientific examination of the lake dwellings, and of the questions to which their discovery gave rise. The following observations are founded on their investigations.

The discovery of the lake dwellings created all the more sensation because not the smallest recollection of their existence had been preserved in Switzerland, where they are most numerous; they are not mentioned by the old writers, not even in the account given by the Romans of their incursion into Switzerland in the last century before Christ. The fact that the remains of the lake dwellings were not discovered before, can be explained by two things; first, the dwellings erected on the piles have quite disappeared; and then some of the piles themselves are covered with bog—as in those places where the water of the lakes has receded in the course of ages—and some with clay, sand, mud, or calcareous tufa, or they lie several feet, sometimes 30 feet, deep below the surface of the water.

After the lake dwellings had once been discovered, numerous analogies to them were soon found. Herodotus writing in the fifth century before Christ says, that about fifty years before his time the Persian general Megabazus failed to subdue a Thracian tribe, because they dwelt in the middle of the Lake Prasias, in huts which stood on high piles, and which were only connected by a narrow bridge with the mainland. If any of them married he had to obtain three new piles in order to increase the size of the dwelling. The children were fastened by a cord round their feet, lest they should fall into the lake. Empty baskets were let down through trap doors by cords, and by this means the fish which abounded in the lake were caught, and they furnished food for the inhabitants, and also, as Herodotus assures us, for the horses and beasts of burden. The Arabian geographer Abulfeda, writing in the fourteenth century, speaks of a lake in Syria in which Christian fishermen lived in huts built of wood and resting on piles. The celebrated English discoverer of the ruins of Nineveh, Layard, found lake dwellings among an Arab tribe living in the marshes of the Euphrates. Other travellers have found similar dwellings in our century amongst the Negroes of the Ischadda Lake in Central Africa, amongst the Papuans of New Guinea, the Dajahs of Borneo, and in other places.[1]

These recorded instances, and the researches made on the spot, prove that on these piles in the Swiss and in other lakes there stood in olden times whole villages of huts, which were reached from the land either by narrow bridges or in boats, and which therefore afforded to their inhabitants a certain protection against enemies and wild beasts. On the other hand, savants are still uncertain whether these huts were the real and only regular dwelling-places of those who built them, or whether they were only used as temporary places of refuge in danger, or as store-houses for the safe keeping of grain and other kinds of food, of implements, etc.[2] Only conjectures can, of course, be made as to the nature of the structures which were erected on the piles, as only the piles themselves are preserved. Beams and boards were laid on the upright piles; the walls of the huts built on them were probably formed by upright poles through which willows were woven; this framework was probably plastered over with clay. The gaps in the floor may have been filled up with rushes, over which a coating of clay was spread. The roof was probably

[1] Pallmann, *Die Pfahlbauten*, pp. 52, 70. Virchow, *Hünengräber und Pfahlbauten*, Berlin 1866, p. 28. Hochstetter, see *Oesterreichische Wochenschrift*, 1864, p. 1608.

[2] Cf. M. Wagner, see Ausland, 1867, p 418. Lindenschmit, see *Archiv für Anthr.* ii. 351.

made of straw, twigs, or bark. We can only form conjectures as to whether the huts were round or square, how large they were, what were the internal arrangements, and other similar questions. The pictures of these villages which we find in certain books on the subject [1] must be looked upon as truth interwoven with fiction, just like the landscapes of the coal and other primæval periods, with which popular works on geology are sometimes ornamented. In one recent book [2] we even find as a frontispiece, a picture of a fire in a lake village, painted in bright colours, the only historical authority for this picture being the fact that some partially burnt piles and other objects have been found; this no doubt would point to the conclusion that the lake dwelling in question was destroyed by a fire which was either accidental, or caused by an enemy's hand.

We can get no trustworthy information about the history of the inhabitants, as we have no data to go upon. On the other hand, we can get a more or less clear idea of their mode of life from the different objects which have been found near their dwellings, and which have been carefully examined by antiquaries. The builders of the lake dwellings cultivated the ground and bred cattle. Archæologists have been able to ascertain, from the grains and ears preserved in a charred condition, what were the special kinds of wheat and barley which they grew. The grain was probably preserved in large earthenware jars, of which several fragments have been found. The grain, which was very

---

[1] See Staub, *Die Pfahlbauten;* Lyell, *Antiquity of Man;* Baer, *Der Vorgeschichtliche Mensch.*

[2] Le Hon, *L'homme fossile.*

possibly roasted beforehand, was probably ground between round stones, polished on one side, which were laid in pairs next to one another. Of these a great number have been found. Besides the grain, charred apples and pears have been found, also the stones of sloes, nut-shells, and beech-nuts, and the remains of raspberries and blackberries. Besides this the inhabitants of the lake dwellings could get fish and the flesh of wild and domestic animals. The remains of cattle, sheep, goats, and pigs have been found, also the bones of dogs, who appear to have been the companions of men even in these early times. Of the wild animals, the bones of the bear, the aurochs, the bison, the wolf, the wild boar, the red deer, the fallow deer, etc., have been found.[1] The bones and horns of animals were made into all kinds of implements, even into spear and arrow heads; all kinds of stuffs and cords were made from flax; vessels from wood and clay; hatchets, knives, hammers, and also ornaments, from stone, bronze, and iron.[2] In all the larger collections of antiquities we find a more or less rich selection of these curious things. Modern ingenuity has no doubt taken advantage of the love of antiquities to seize upon this branch of archæology; the antiquities of the lake dwellings have been artificially imitated like other antiquities, and we cannot always be sure that what is shown as a relic of the period of lake dwellings, is not the work of a man who is still numbered among the living.[3]

[1] Pallmann, *Die Pfahlbauten*, p. 95.
[2] See plates in the otherwise valueless work of Staub, *Die Pfahlbauten*, and in many other books.
[3] In making the railway at Concise, near the lake of Neufchatel, a lake

I have just said that in consequence of the entire absence of information concerning the inhabitants of the lake dwellings, nothing certain can be known about their history. Notwithstanding this, however, many efforts have been made to fill up the gap by hypotheses. Sometimes these hypotheses are asserted with such boldness, that some of those who are not conversant with the subject might be led to believe that they were historical statements. Some writers describe as graphically as if they had been present how the first builders of lake dwellings migrated from Asia into Switzerland; how after they had lived a long time in their huts on the lakes, they were attacked by another people of Iberian race coming from the east; how the latter destroyed the lake dwellings partly by fire, and then settled down themselves on the lakes; how these Iberians had to give way to the Celts, and the Celts to the Helvetians, etc.[1] All this is not history, it can hardly be called even a historical romance, it is simply a fancy picture which rests on much less certain and weaker foundations than did the piles of the lake dwellings.

It is not wonderful that the first news of the discovery of the lake dwellings should have surprised

dwelling of the stone age was found, in which enormous masses of stags' horns were discovered heaped up in all stages of manufacture. When the workmen, who had at first not noticed the discovery, found that antiquaries pounced upon it, like hawks on chickens, they first raised the prices, and when the implements they had discovered were nearly all gone, they replaced them with other stags' horns. Many antiquaries were deceived in this way. Herr Troyon, the Curator of the Lausanne Museum, bought a whole collection of these articles and put them in the museum, where they remained until the fraud was detected by some other archæologists. Vogt, *Vorlesungen*, ii. 43.

[1] Schleiden, *Das Alter des Menschengeschlechts*, p. 14. Troyon, see Vogt, *Vorlesungen*, ii. 133, 153.

every one, and that in the first moment of surprise and wonder the importance and significance of the discovery should have been exaggerated. It seemed as if all at once a new people had appeared amongst those known in history; a people of a peculiar kind, with no connection with the nations of history, and belonging to a time before the Egyptian pyramids and the great Assyrian monuments, a time preceding all historical records. The progress of inquiry has taken away most of what is surprising and peculiar in the discovery. As I have shown, lake dwellings have existed in other places and in other times, nay more, they still exist. It is now generally acknowledged that the lake dwellings of Switzerland and the surrounding countries belong to the recent period; they were surrounded by the same animal and vegetable world which now exists in those countries, or which did exist there not many centuries ago. The few human skulls which have been found in the lake dwellings, and which are supposed to be the skulls of their inhabitants, do not differ in any essential degree from the skulls of the present inhabitants of those regions.[1] Virchow even asserted at the meeting of the Society of Natural Science at Munich in 1877, that as far as could be gathered from the skulls found up to the present time, the brain development of the lake-men was not only not below the average brain development of the present inhabitants of the same regions, but often exceeded it considerably. The inhabitants of the lake dwellings must therefore simply be classed among the nations

---

[1] Vogt, *Vorlesungen*, ii. 145, 175. Pallmann, *Die Pfahlbauten*, p. 98 His, see *Archiv für Anthr.* i. 61.

whom we know from other sources to have been the oldest inhabitants of Central Europe, however impossible it may be for the present to ascertain more accurately what was their nationality.

Of course people have attempted to include the lake dwellings in the scheme of the stone, bronze, and iron ages. In most of the lake dwellings no metals have been found, in some, especially in Western Switzerland, bronze has been found, in a few cases iron. But here it is even more difficult than elsewhere to show that the three periods were consecutive in time; it is quite possible that in one part of Switzerland metals were being used at the same time as stone implements were in use in another part; and even if no metals are found in a lake dwelling, it does not necessarily follow that its inhabitants knew of none.[1]

But let us turn to the question which is the most important for our purpose, namely, that of the antiquity of the oldest lake dwellings. How far do they help us in estimating the antiquity of man?

On this subject Prof. Rütimeyer of Basle, whose name I have mentioned before among the Swiss savants, and who is among those who have most carefully examined the lake dwellings, speaks as follows.[2] "With reference to the question, usually the first to be put by the public, as to the length of time which has elapsed between the period just discovered in

---

[1] "I must admit that I am inclined to agree with those who hold that the fact of bronze being found in some dwellings and stone in others proves, not that they were of different date, but that their inhabitants were of different rank."—Hochstetter, see *Oesterr. Wochenschrift*, 1864, p. 1612. See above, p. 307, note 2.

[2] *Die Fauna*, etc. p. 239.

the existence of our race and the present time, I believe that we shall have to withhold our decision for some time, or at any rate that it will be necessary to limit it to merely relative statements. Some of the direct statements as to time which have been made hitherto, are open to the strongest objections. My observations give me only very uncertain conclusions with reference to the relative computation of time. They lead me to place the beginning of the last, and in some ways illimitable period,—that is, the iron period,— at a relatively very late, probably not prehistoric age. On the other hand, there is every reason for ascribing a long duration to the two preceding epochs; but even these must not be measured by the elastic standard of *geological* periods." Other Swiss savants, however, are not so prudent and reserved. Troyon makes the following calculation. In the neighbourhood of Yverdon there exists in the middle of the moor an island of rock about 400 feet high, at the foot of which piles, with stone axes, have been discovered under from 8 to 10 feet of peat. This pile work is about 5500 feet from the lake. On the banks of the lake, on a sandy heath which lies across the moor, lies Yverdon, the Roman Eburodunum. According to Troyon, the lake must have washed the walls of this town in the time of the Romans; it is now 2500 feet distant. But if the lake has taken about 1500 years to retire 2500 feet, it must have taken 3300 years to retire 5500 feet from the pile work. This, therefore, dates from between 2000 and 3000 years B.C.

But another Swiss savant, Gillieron, gets the number of 6000 years from a similar calculation, also based on the gradual retiring of the lake of Bienne. Vogt observes,[1] I think quite rightly, that both calculations rest on an incorrect foundation, as the rate at which a lake retires cannot be calculated from the horizontal distance, but only from the decrease in the depth of the water. He might have added, that calculations based on vertical subsidence are quite uncertain, because we do not know whether the rate at which a lake has diminished has been the same in all centuries as in the last, or whether some special causes, such, for instance, as the formation of a new, or of a larger outlet, may not have produced a sudden subsidence of as many feet as might have previously taken a thousand years.

The calculation of the age of the lake dwellings made by Morlot is that which is best known. In the neighbourhood of Villeneuve, on the Lake of Geneva, the bed of a torrent called La Tinière was cut through by railway works. The greatest height of the cutting above the rails is $32\frac{1}{2}$ feet. The structure of the bed, which is completely exposed by the cutting, appears to be quite regular. At different depths three different layers of ancient vegetable soil can be distinguished, which formerly formed the surface of the bed. The highest of these layers is from 4 to 6 inches thick, and lies at a depth of 4 feet under the surface, pieces of Roman tiles and a Roman coin were found in it. The second layer is 6 inches thick, and lies at a depth of 10 feet, a few fragments of vessels made of unvarnished pottery and a bronze hairpin were found in it. The lowest layer is from 6 to 7 inches thick, and lies at a depth of 19 feet under the surface, in it rude pottery,

---

[1] *Vorlesungen*, ii. 152.

charcoal, and broken bones of animals were found. Morlot ascribes the highest stratum to the Roman age, the middle to the bronze age, the lowest to the stone age. The Roman age in Switzerland was at least thirteen, and at most eighteen centuries before the present time. Now, if the brook has made a deposit 4 feet thick since this time, it follows, provided that the deposit has proceeded at the same rate since the earliest ages, that the bronze layer has an antiquity of at least 2900, and at most 4200, and the stone layer an antiquity of at least 4700, and at most 7000 years. But there are very weighty objections to this calculation. In the first place, is the discovery of a few fragments of unglazed pottery and one bronze hairpin enough to warrant our ascribing the middle stratum to the bronze age? Vogt only says that "possibly" the lowest layer may belong to the stone age; there are no implements of flint or horn, which usually characterize this age; and as for the bones, Rütimeyer, probably the most competent authority in what concerns the fauna of the lake dwellings, expressly says that they are the bones of animals which in no way differ from the present races of animals, but which do differ from those of the lake dwellings of the stone age; and for this reason he believes the bones to be very recent. Lastly, Vogt adds that it is even doubtful whether the highest layer really belongs to the Roman age; and yet this is the foundation of the whole calculation. You see, therefore, that everything which is assumed in the calculation to be a known quantity, becomes on closer examination merely $x\ y\ z$, and this alone would invalidate the whole calculation. But there is one more thing to which the late Andreas Wagner[1] has called attention, and which is the more important because Vogt, who usually contradicts him wherever it is possible, on this occasion adopts his argument almost word for word.[2] It is this. Morlot concluded from the regularity of the bed of La Tinière that it had been regularly formed. But in spite of all apparent regularity, the deposits of a mountain stream can never be really and properly regular; one single exceptional flood caused by a storm may bring down more material in one day than do many centuries of regular deposits, and this material will, in consequence of its weight, be deposited at the sides just as regularly as if it had been gradually washed down.

Morlot's whole calculation therefore rests on premises of which none is even moderately certain, and therefore a conclusion can no more be obtained from them than from an equation of unknown quantities. It is only just to Morlot to say that he looked on his own calculation as only a doubtful experiment. All the savants who have considered it speak just as decidedly against it as does Vogt.[3] In spite of this, several modern books refer to it,[4] as well as to the above-mentioned [5] calculation of the antiquity of the Nile deposits, and they are occasionally taken as a model for other

---

[1] Bedenken über einige neuere Versuche, das Alter der europäischen Urbevölkerung zu bestimmen, see *Reports of the Bavarian Academy of Science*, 1861, ii. p. 29.

[2] *Vorlesungen*, ii. 149.

[3] M. Wagner, see *Report*, etc. p. 430; also Ausland, 1867, p. 462. Leindenschmit, see *Archiv für Anthr.* i. 53. Quatrefages, *Hist. de L'homme*, ii. 22.

[4] Desor, *Die Pfahlbauten*, p. 130. Le Hon, *L'homme fossile*, pp. 116, 140.

[5] See above, p. 275.

calculations.¹ I have consequently been obliged to discuss them in detail, and to prove their untrustworthiness, and also to show expressly that all the most competent savants acknowledge that they prove nothing.

After all that has been said, we see that Lyell was quite right in asserting that the efforts of Swiss archæologists to ascertain the age of the lake dwellings were confessedly imperfect, and mere attempts, but I do not understand why he should think that they deserve notice and are full of promise. Vogt rejects them all, and says in conclusion,² "The *only trustworthy* means for calculating time would be found in the vertical increase of peat in those regions in which lake dwellings are buried in the peat." He repeats this on a later occasion. " I cannot refrain from saying again and again, that peat mosses, and peat mosses *alone*, can give us the means of ascertaining the real date of the lake dwellings."³ But, as I have shown in my last lecture, and as Vogt himself unhesitatingly admits,⁴ there are no data for ascertaining the rate of the vertical growth of peat.

Recently, people have begun to doubt whether the antiquity of the lake dwellings is nearly as great as it was asserted or supposed to be. Hochstetter⁵ says it is very likely that they date from the last thousand years B.C.; Franz Maurer⁶ puts them between the eighth and fifth centuries; Pallmann⁷ in the last

---

[1] Similar calculations may be found in the *Archiv für Anthr.* iii. 157, 159, 358, and 362.
[2] *Vorlesungen*, ii. 153.   [3] *Archiv. für Anthr.* i. 13.
[4] See above, p. 328.   [5] *Oesterr. Wochensch.* Dec. 1864, p. 1610.
[6] *Ausland*, 1864, p 913.   [7] *Die Pfahlbauten*, pp. 13, 161.

four centuries B.C.; Hassler,[1] with whom O. Fraas[2] agrees, thinks that most of the more recent lake dwellings date from the third century B.C., and of the older ones he says, "There is absolutely no reason for going back before the year 1000 B.C., and least of all when dealing with the more or less deep peat beds and layers of rubbish under which the lake dwellings are partly buried. For it might be easily proved that no calculations of time can be based on them, and this because their origin and formation is influenced by the most different circumstances, and is quite different in different places. But if there is nothing to make us go back more than 1000 years B.C., many circumstances point to a more recent period." Here, therefore, we have a number of savants who, without any theological bias, for scientific reasons, and mostly independently of each other, have come to the conclusion that the lake dwellings date at farthest from the year 1000 B.C. I will make one more quotation from what I might call a semi-official article in the *Augsburg Allgemeine Zeitung*,[3] in which, in the name of geologists, all responsibility for the calculation of time from the lake dwellings is renounced. "Ferd. Keller," it says, "the man who most thoroughly investigated this subject, never attempted to give any estimate of their age in figures, because there are absolutely no scientific data for such a calculation. For

---

[1] *Deutsche Vierteljahresschrift*, 1865, 1 Heft, p. 80.

[2] *Vor der Sündfluth*, p. 469. Virchow thinks that the lake dwellings of North Germany belong to the seventh, eighth, and ninth centuries A.D., or even to a later age. Ihering, *Die 5 Allg. Versammlung der D. Gesellsch. für Anthr.*, Dresden 1874, p. 80.

[3] 1864, 30 Dec. No. 365 Beil.

the same reason neither Desor, nor the clever Petersburg academician von Baer who has studied the primæval age of the human race in Europe more minutely than any one else, nor Lyell, nor any of the Danish antiquaries, has ever dared to hazard a hypothesis as to the number of centuries or thousands of years which have elapsed since they existed. Even Morlot's attempt to make a geological calculation of the antiquity of the lake dwellings has been found, on closer examination, to be quite unsatisfactory. What are we to say to the easy hypotheses and thoughtless combinations made by men who have never visited the Swiss places where the discoveries have been made, but who, on the strength of Keller's investigations, have set up bold and fantastic theories as to the age and origin of the lake dwellings, and trumpet them forth to the world? This is in truth scientifically worthless, and can only tend to introduce confused ideas among those of the educated public who do not read the original works of the above-mentioned savants. Not long ago Ferd. Keller expressed not unreasonable irritation at the way in which even eminent German periodicals took up such stuff." After all these statements we may unhesitatingly reject the assertion that the lake dwellings prove that man is of greater antiquity than the Biblical chronology will allow, for it has been already repudiated by science. Unfortunately the results of sober inquiry are accepted by the general public much more slowly than are the fabulous descriptions of the lake dwellings which were spread abroad when they were first discovered. In the year 1875, Virchow, speaking at the Anthropological Meeting at Munich, complained of this. He says, "What mischief have not the lake dwellings done, inasmuch as people believe that every lake dwelling must at least date from the year 4000 B.C. This erroneous belief may be a mere common opinion, and not the fault of any one single savant, but at all events it is undeniable that there is a popular tendency to place every lake dwelling before the period of the oldest traditions. This overlooks the fact that even now large and numerous tribes live in lake dwellings, that they existed in many places in Europe in historical times, and that some of the Wendish towns were lake dwellings even in the eleventh and twelfth centuries. It is simply asserted, without qualification, that all lake dwellings must date from the same period, probably from about the year 4000 B.C."[1]

I may mention incidentally another class of erections somewhat similar to the lake dwellings, which are found in Ireland, and are there called Crannoges. These are small islands in the Irish lakes, of lime and gravel, which were dry in summer, but flooded in winter; they were strengthened by palisades, and in some cases by walls, and were used in dangerous times as places of refuge and concealment. They are now mostly under water, as the water in the lakes has risen, it is supposed in consequence of the destruction of the forests and the increase in the peat. Hardly any stone or bronze implements are found in the crannoges, those found are mostly of iron or bone, and there are some remains of still existing domestic

[1] Kollmann, *Die 6 Allg. Versammlung der D. Gesellschaft für Anthr.*, Munich 1875, p. 13.

animals. This alone would show that these erections are not old. But we have historical evidence that they were used as late as between the ninth and fourteenth centuries. They do not bear therefore upon the question of the antiquity of the European population.[1]

Some other prehistoric remains of a different kind have been found on the northern coast of Denmark; these are heaps of shells which lie some feet above the present level of the sea, and are 3, 5, and sometimes 10 feet high, 1000 feet long, and from 150 to 200 broad. These are not natural shell banks formed at a time when the level of the sea was higher; for we find only a few kinds of shells, all of full size, and species are intermingled which do not live at the same depth in the sea. Besides, the shells are mixed up with the bones of animals, rough stone implements, coarse pottery, charcoal, and ashes. These things were evidently left by men who lived here, and who threw together the shells of the shell-fish they had eaten, the gnawed bones of animals and other refuse. Northern savants have therefore very properly called these heaps Kjökken-möddings, Kitchen middens. No human bones have been found in them. The shells are those of still existing shell-fish, and the bones those of still existing mammals and birds. The heaps therefore belong to the recent period.[2]

We cannot ascertain what is the exact age of the kitchen middens. Lyell and others[3] think that they

---

[1] Cf. *Edin. Rev.* July 1862, p. 173. Ausland, 1862, p. 994. Pallmann, *Die Pfahlbauten*, p. 53.

[2] Vogt, *Vorlesungen*, ii. 112. Büchner, *Die Stellung des Menschen*, p. 53. Similar heaps have been found in France, North America, and Brazil: *Archiv für Anthr.* ii. 321, iii. 153, 161.

[3] Cf. O. Schmidt in the *Oesterr. Wochenschrift*, 1863, ii. 387.

must be very old, because the oysters and other shells are not so numerous or so large now in the Baltic as they seem to have been formerly, and the cause of this is supposed to be the decrease of salt in the Baltic, which is produced by the gradual narrowing of the inlets which connect it with the salt Atlantic Ocean. The kitchen middens therefore are the product of a time when these narrow parts of the sea allowed more salt water to pass in, and this must be a long time ago. But it is impossible to calculate how long ago.[1] Vogt will not allow that this argument of Lyell's is valid. He says that the diminution in the saltness of the Baltic would not explain the diminution in the shells; the Romans succeeded in transplanting oysters to the sweet-water lakes near Naples, and the cockles and mussels, whose shells are also found in the kitchen middens, flourish in brackish water, and even in waters which periodically become quite sweet. The reason for the diminution of these shell-fish must therefore be found elsewhere. Vogt thinks that it is to be found in the slow alteration and transformation of the sea-bed; this has been shown to be the case with the oyster beds, and is principally caused by animals which overgrow the oyster beds and gradually destroy them.

Vogt observes that the black-cock is one of the birds whose bones are found, and observes that this bird no longer exists in Denmark, because the pines, whose young shoots form its principal food in spring, are no longer found there. Therefore the kitchen middens must date from a time when the pine was very common in Denmark. I am not enough either of an ornitho-

[1] See above, p. 202.

logist or of a sportsman to say with certainty whether black-cock cannot live without pine shoots. But it does not sound very probable; at least in my old home, when I was young, there were fewer pines and more black-cock than there are now, as the former have been largely planted, and the latter have been decimated by sportsmen.

As in the kitchen middens and lake dwellings, we can also ascertain from the remains in the bone caves and other places what was the food of men in ancient times. The implements show what kinds of tools they made and used, the graves how they buried their dead. So that in this way we can collect materials for the history of the culture of the earliest centuries in which Central Europe was inhabited. After all I have already said, I need hardly repeat my warning not to believe everything stated in popular books and pamphlets about primæval history. It is only too easy to draw very definite conclusions from very uncertain premises, and to found general descriptions on single observations. Because occasionally skulls of oval form, and bronze swords with small handles have been found in graves, it is said that the people who lived during the bronze age belonged to the races with oval skulls, had small hands, and were therefore of small stature. Such general statements are, of course, soon seen to be arbitrary, as on further search round skulls and swords with large handles are found.

There is another error into which people are apt to fall in this matter. The descriptions given by travellers of so-called savage races are often without further ado transferred to the so-called prehistoric races. No doubt in the lower stages of civilisation the ancient races resembled the present uncivilised races in many ways; they made implements of stone, horn, wood, they lived by hunting and fishing, etc. So that an examination of the conditions of the present savage races may be of great use in giving us some idea of some aspects of the life of the ancient inhabitants of Central Europe; we can, for instance, gather what was the use of certain implements, how they were made and handled, and so on. But, apart from such points, it is arbitrary simply to transfer all the conditions which are now found amongst savage races to the so-called prehistoric peoples. And yet in descriptions of what is called primæval history, we often find statements as to the religious beliefs, the morals, and social arrangements of men in the stone and bronze ages, which are based simply on travellers' accounts of the Fiji islanders, Hottentots, etc.[1] For these things cannot be ascertained from stone implements and the bones of animals. It is still worse, as I have already said,[2] to arrange the present savage races in a series, beginning with the most barbarous and ending with the most cultivated, and then to transfer this series to primæval times, so that the most barbarous are given as the type of the oldest races, that is, the men of the so-called palæolithic or tertiary age, the rather more cultivated as the type of the men of the neolithic or mammoth age, etc. There is no need to prove that such a proceeding cannot be called scientific. And it is plain from such descriptions as these, that primæval history is still a very young science. As inquiry proceeds, these

[1] Cf. *Archiv für Anthr.* viii. 271.   [2] See above, p. 176.

early theories will be cast off, criticism will be more freely used, and greater soberness and reticence will prevail.

A passage in a paper in the *Archiv für Anthropologie*,[1] from which I have on different occasions quoted with approval, will show us how ingenuously people still write about primæval history. The author says quite naturally, " In deciding what is the relative age of deposits and their contents, we are sometimes guided by the doctrine of the progressive development of organisms. In consequence of this the Neanderthal skull is supposed to be older than the Engis skull. And this is confirmed by the fact that the latter in its general shape much resembles several skulls found in old German or Celtic burying-places, but that up to this time no human skull has been found which can be compared to the Neanderthal skull. At any rate it shows a much lower organization than do the human remains found in the quaternary strata. Considering these facts, may we not hazard the hypothesis that in the Neanderthal skull we have the type of the man of the tertiary period?" A single incompletely preserved skull, whose age cannot be accurately ascertained, and which is probably a diseased formation,[2] is to represent the earliest form of skull, simply because it bears out the theory that man has developed from a pithecoid form.

One more example. It is well known that some of the most barbarous races are cannibals. Now, as according to the theory I have mentioned the first men must have resembled the most barbarous savages, it would not be surprising, says, for instance, Le Hon,[3]

[1] *Archiv für Anthr.* v. 118. [2] See above, p. 149. [3] *L'homme fossile*, p. 48.

if we found signs that the men who inhabited Europe in the tertiary or in the oldest diluvian period were cannibals. And if this is probable *à priori*, of course a prehistoric (urgeschichtlicher) historian who is worthy of the name will find proofs of this. And accordingly Le Hon gives us the following. 1. Children's bones have been found which bear signs of having been gnawed by human teeth. Why the teeth must have been *human* is more than I can say. 2. Human bones have been found which appear to have been broken in order to extract the marrow, as is the case also with the bones of animals. Le Hon is honest enough to add that it is not quite proved that the bones were broken on purpose. 3. Human remains have been found in the so-called kitchen middens. But, of course, it cannot be proved that they were thrown away as kitchen refuse, and did not get in among the shells and bones of animals in some other way.

Such things as these belong not to prehistoric history, but to prehistoric nonsense. But what becomes of these proofs of the low condition of man in the mammoth age, when real works of art are produced which are said to belong to that time, drawings scratched on slate or ivory, on bits of reindeer horn, on mammoths' bones, etc.? It is true, no doubt, that some of these prehistoric works of art have been made by living artists. Lindenschmit proved that two drawings on animals' bones, which were said to have been found in 1875 at Thayingen in Switzerland, and which were believed to be genuine by several archæologists, were simply copied from the drawings in a child's book which was published in 1868, and the forgery was subsequently acknowledged.[1] Some other pieces also are of very doubtful antiquity.[2] But many of these drawings are evidently genuinely old. The question however is, how old?[3] If they belong to one of the so-called prehistoric periods, no doubt the men who lived in that period cannot have been so barbarous and savage as is often supposed. Ranke in discussing this point rightly observes, " Recently many of the results of exact science have seemed to show that the original inhabitants of Europe were not autochthonous savages, but immigrants who brought with them to a new country the culture and civilisation of a happier ancestral home."[4] Schaaffhausen thinks that the works of art which have been found in France could hardly have been produced without the influence of a cultivated people, perhaps the Phœnician or Greek colonies on the coast of the Mediterranean ; but he adds rather ruefully, that this assumption would much diminish the antiquity of these objects, which up to this time has been believed to be very great. And not only the

[1] *Archiv für Anthr.* ix. 173, 269.
[2] In the *Archiv für Anthr.* viii. 270, Schaaffhausen says: "An ivory plate found by Lartet, engraved with the picture of a mammoth, bears no signs of forgery, such as may be detected on other drawings on stone which were exhibited in Paris in 1867 ; but the circumstances under which this picture of the mammoth was found were such that one could hardly help suspecting a forgery." The workmen in the cave of La Madelaine knew that Lartet was coming with a stranger to visit the cave on a certain day. When he appeared with Falconer, they brought him five pieces of a mammoth's tooth, which he put together, and the engraved picture then appeared. The appearance of the mammoth was well known in France, because in a French periodical Adams had just described the one found on the Lena, with its skin and hair still preserved.
[3] A. Ecker, "Ueber præhistorische Kunst," *Archiv für Anthr.* xi. 133. Cf. *Corr.-blatt. der deutschen Gesellschaft für Anthropologie*, Oct. 1877, p. 103.
[4] *Anfänge der Kunst*, Berlin 1879, p. 30.

antiquity of these objects, but also of the whole mammoth and reindeer age; for the mammoths' bones and reindeer horns on which the drawings are scratched, and the other objects which have been found in the same deposits as the works of art, cannot be thousands of years older than the latter.

The theories of the so-called prehistoric science will be greatly modified by the progress of inquiry. At present much is still uncertain. It is the more to be lamented that this period is now-a-days made the subject of popular descriptions, which in the nature of things are only too much calculated to spread erroneous beliefs. "It is a difficult matter," says Ecker, "to popularize a young science which is in the midst of its development, and in which so much is still a matter of dispute, and what our Nestor, K. E. v. Baer, says, in his autobiography, about the subject in general must be specially applied to this science. He says, 'I have always believed that science ought to be popularized; but now that this is being done, and all that has been discovered and ascertained is being ground in countless mills, it seems to me that these mills are like the bone-mills in which the remains of living organisms are ground up into shapeless powder, which is then used to manure the fields and to produce nourishment for the people. The object is undoubtedly good; but it is only too easy for untrue, that is unwholesome, matter to get into the powder, and it then becomes irrecognisable, as all witness of its origin is lost;' and," adds Ecker, "every savant will admit that in the sketches of primæval history, however carefully they may be made, 'unwholesome matter will get into the powder,'—every savant at least who knows what confusion the words stone age, bronze age, etc., have created in many brains."[1]

In fact, we may fairly say with Virchow[2] that the common accounts of prehistoric times are scientific fictions, just as mythology is popular fiction. And they are perhaps harmless enough when they are presented in the shape of historical romance.[3] But we sometimes find such accounts, containing more romance or "scientific fiction" than history, thus recommended to "educated people of all ranks."[4] In the last century many attempts were made to lift the dark veil which covers the primæval history of mankind; but they were all in vain, as all data were still wanting. But just as our earth has written her own history on herself, so to her we owe also extensive revelations of the primæval history of mankind. It is true that it is only on stones and bones that we can discern the traces of the existence of man, and of his activity at a period long before the first beginnings of history and legend. These dumb and yet eloquent witnesses of a period which not long ago was hidden, have opened before our wondering eyes a new world of which we had no suspicion. The birth pangs of the new ideas were very severe, for it was soon seen that

---

[1] *Archiv für Anthr.* vii. 114.
[2] *Die Urbevölkerung Europa's*, Berlin 1874, p. 4.
[3] A historical novel of the reindeer period is advertised in the Paris *Polybiblion*, March 1872, p. 91. It is called *Solutre ou les chasseurs de rennes dans la France centrale*, par Adrian Cranille, Paris Hachette, 1872, pp. 200–8 et 10 gravures.
[4] Prospectus to W. Baer's book, *Der Vorgeschichtliche Mensch.*, Leipsic 1874.

they would bring about a revolution in the theories which had hitherto obtained concerning the world and life. But fortunately science will suffer no unassailable dogmas. The new truth has made a way for itself in spite of all hindrances and objections, etc. etc. And the book which is to show "educated people of all classes" the errors in "the theories which have hitherto obtained, concerning the world and life," and which announces the "new truth which has at length made a way for itself," that is, which asserts the theory of descent and the pithecoid theory, the doctrine of the stone, bronze, and iron ages, etc., as if they were unassailable dogmas, is furnished with several pictures and engravings in order to illustrate the text, such as "Man fighting in the flint age," "Arrangements for a festival in the stone age," "The first artists of the reindeer age," and so on; pictures of which Ecker justly says, "Even if the sober inquirer does not object to them, they are only too much calculated to give wrong ideas to unscientific people, and it is for the latter, not for earnest inquirers, that the book is written."

In conclusion, I return once more to the question of the age of man. You may say, if the calculations which have been made directly and indirectly by geologists are really so untrustworthy as you claim to have proved that they are, how is it possible that savants, who in their separate branches are just as great authorities as Lyell, believe that geological inquiry has shown that men must be about 100,000 years old? I answer, it is not possible, but neither is it true. Many of the older savants have attempted to ascertain by means of geology what is the antiquity of the human race. In one of his earlier works Lyell says that it was presumptuous of those savants to attempt the solution of such a complicated problem without having collected numerous data. Lyell himself hesitated a long time before he published his book on this subject, and he never denied the difficulty of ascertaining the antiquity of man by geological means. While he was occupied in writing his book, Morlot imparted to him his calculation as to the age of the lake dwellings which I have already mentioned, and in doing so he observed that he knew very well that this was only a first imperfect and rash attempt, which had no value in itself so long as it was not confirmed by other similar attempts. Lyell wrote back to him, "Some one must have the chivalry to begin."[1] He therefore thought that the task of numerically estimating a geological period was so difficult, and gave so little hope of an assured result, that not only learning, cleverness, and prudence, but also chivalry was wanted before the first step in this slippery path can be taken. For this reason Lyell himself is far from considering the investigations described in his book as being conclusive, or as furnishing a valid and assured result. He repeats over and over again, that many more separate observations must be made before full knowledge can be attained; that all the estimates of the antiquity of man quoted by him are only indefinite and experimental, and that the time has not yet arrived when geologists can come forward with any assured conclusion. I quote the testimony of another eminent English geologist. Professor Phillips,

[1] *Bibliothèque universelle*, Geneva 1862. *Arch.* xiii. 313.

speaking at the meeting of the British Association held at Bath in 1864, said that there was the greatest difficulty in obtaining trustworthy results as to the time which has elapsed, and that this occurred where it was least expected, namely, in the case of the deposits of the last geological period, that in which the history of man falls. It is therefore, he adds, self-evident that this field of inquiry must be very carefully trodden, and that in investigating facts and choosing measures of time all possible care must be taken before we can say that the human period, even in our regions carefully as they have been examined, is known through the natural phenomena, and before geology can assert that man lived on earth at a period much before that fixed by history and tradition.[1] In the following year he spoke at the meeting at Birmingham, and I give an extract from his speech: "Let us not expect or devise for them (these questions) a very quick, or at present a very definite settlement. Deep shadows have gathered over all the earlier ages of mankind, which perhaps still longer periods of time may not avail to remove." He then enumerates a series of questions which must be considered, and continues: "Before replying finally to these questions further researches of an exact nature are desirable. . . . When these are completed, some future Lyell, if not our own great geologist, may add some fresh chapters to the *Antiquity of Man*."[2] I have given you many quotations from the works of German savants, containing warnings against uncertain and

---

[1] *Athenæum*, 24th Sept. 1864, p. 405.
[2] *Athenæum*, 9th Sept. 1865, p. 343.

exaggerated geological calculations. I will add to these the declaration with which Pfaff closes his inquiries into this subject. "All the figures which are taken from natural measures of time, and which are given as estimates of the antiquity of man, are most uncertain; the most trustworthy do not exceed 5000 to 7000 years."[1] K. G. v. Baer speaks in the same way in his last work, and says that the antiquity of man is very likely no greater than might be supposed from the Biblical narratives.[2]

You see I may safely assert that the assertion that geologists believe they have proved that man has existed from 50,000 to 100,000 years on the earth is incorrect. Geologists who deserve the name of thorough inquirers, and who confine themselves to the limits of their science, do not assert this. They are extremely prudent and modest in their assertions. No doubt we often see it said now-a-days that geologists have proved that the human race is 100,000 years old, or at any rate much older than the Bible says it is, or than has hitherto been thought possible; but the principal people who find pleasure in making this assertion, and in repeating it with all kinds of variations, are, first, men of science who, when they are treating matters of science in a popular form, invariably mix up their religious and philosophical views with them, and who speak the more bitterly about the Bible the less they know and understand it; among these I place Vogt and Schleiden. Then we find that this assertion is made by people who have not studied earnestly either natural science or history or theology, but who think they are qualified

[1] *Die neuesten Forschungen*, p. 76. [2] *Studien*, p. 412.

to explain scientific questions to educated people of all classes by popular writings, in pamphlets and magazines. Now as boldness of assertion generally stands in inverse ratio to the extent and thoroughness of knowledge, we find that in this literature many things are said to be certain scientific conclusions which real savants have either never asserted, or do not now assert, or do not yet assert, but only regard as a hypothesis. And thus we find those writers unhesitatingly making the boldest assertions with reference to the antiquity of mankind, whereas the leaders of science still consider it a proof of chivalry to utter even hypotheses on this question.

I admit unhesitatingly that very eminent geologists think that the present state of the inquiry seems to show that the Biblical estimate of time is probably too short. But they do not consider that the researches which have only just been begun on a comprehensive scale, and which the investigators themselves say are very difficult and complicated, are in any way at an end, and we must therefore wait to see whether the researches will continue to bear out what now seems probable to geologists, or whether other results will be obtained. I have shown you that the theologian may safely admit that the so-called Biblical chronology is too short, and that the first appearance of the human race may be dated hundreds and even thousands of years before the year 4000 B.C. The question here is not so much of a contradiction between the Bible and natural science, as of one between the chronology assumed in history and "prehistoric" chronology. And I think I am justified by an argument from analogy in confidently expecting that the progress of research will be favourable to historical chronology.

When the results of geological inquiry were first compared with the Mosaic Hexæmeron, the former seemed to confirm the latter in an accurate and remarkable manner, and the fossils gave irrefutable proofs of the Deluge. But after this first period of harmony between theologians and geologists, there followed another period of bitter enmity; the former geological theories were found to be untenable, and the newly obtained geological results seemed to be in hopeless contradiction with the Bible. Now we are living in the third, and to all appearance the last period, one of honourable peace; theologians do not claim to find in the results of geological inquiry a striking confirmation of the Biblical record, but they can prove that these results in no way contradict the statements of the Bible when these are rightly understood. The boundaries of both sciences have been now fixed, this was omitted or was probably impossible before; but it has been shown that if the two sciences will meet each other openly, the boundaries and limits of both can be decided in a manner satisfactory to both.

I think that the question of the antiquity of mankind will have a similar fate. Cuvier and his followers thought they had found geological proofs of the accuracy of the Biblical chronology; that was the first period. Their views proved erroneous, and we are now living in the second period, in which there seems to be a hopeless contradiction between the theories of geologists and not only the Biblical statements, but also the views on the antiquity of the human race held by historians and believed to be admissible by exegetes. May we not expect in this case also a third period, in which the progress of research will show that although we must not expect geology to confirm the so-called Biblical chronology, geologists will not be able to dispute the chronology which is historically vouched for and admitted by the Bible?

At all events we, as true Christians, know that all contradictions between Nature and the Bible are only apparent, and are caused by the mistakes of men of science or of exegetes; and that although learned men may not yet have succeeded in removing these apparent contradictions, yet the teaching of the Earth's strata can never really gainsay that which is gathered from the leaves of the Bible.

THE END.

INDEX.

Abbeville, ii. 293, 301.
Aeby, ii. 105, 123, 138, 139, 147, 148, 149, 174, 213.
Agassiz, i. 79, 369; ii. 240, 188.
Alix, ii. 145.
Alluvium, i. 283, 384.
American race, ii. 192, 203 ff.
Amiens, ii. 293, 301, 305.
Ampère, i. 3, 78.
Amphioxus, ii. 126.
Anatomy, comparative, ii. 106.
Andrias Scheuchzeri, i. 263.
Angels, fall of the, i. 119, 121, 318.
Animals, creation of the, i. 136, 157, 313 ; ii. 2, 32.
—— and plants, i. 313, 338 ff.
—— classification of, i. 100, 449 ; ii. 95.
—— extinct, i. 390 ff.
—— in the ark, i. 407, 446 ff.
—— primæval, i. 269 ff., 319.
—— separate creations of, i. 284, 448.
Anthropoid, ii. 122, 236.
Anthropology, ii. 176, 266. *See* Man.
Anthropomorphism, i. 101, 102.
Anti-geologists, i. 84.
Ape, ii. 117, 121 ff. passim.
Ararat, i. 408, 416.
Archæology, ii. 266.
Ark, i. 446 ff.
Astronomy, i. 189 ff.
Augustine, S., i. 44, 45, 101, 102, 106, 130, 139, 141, 146, 152, 162, 163, 183, 451 ; ii. 2, 126, 245, 246.
Aurochs, period of the, ii. 316.
Australian race, ii. 209, 210.
Autogeny, ii. 2.
Azoic period, i. 282, 341.

Bacon, i. 72.
Baer, K. L. von, i. 78 ; ii. 14, 66, 109, 110, 189, 216, 232, 358.
Baer, W., ii. 321, 359.
Baltzer, i. 105, 139, 184, 294, 360.
Bara, i. 103, 135.
Basalt, i. 212.
Bastian, ii. 9.
Bathybius, ii. 11.

Beech age, ii. 325, 327.
Bellynck, i. 415 ; ii. 258.
Beringer, i. 260.
Bert, P., ii. 145.
Bertrand, i. 267.
Bible and nature, the, i. 23, 189 ; ii. 366.
—— does not teach science, i. 29 ff., 89, 218 ff.
—— phraseology of the, i. 33, 98, 409, 458.
Biot, i. 78.
Bischof, G., i. 57, 62, 77, 216, 247, 291 ; ii. 20.
Bischoff, Th., ii. 141.
Blainville, i. 78.
Blumenbach, ii. 192, 193.
Böhme, Jakob, i. 120, 147.
Boker, i. 168, 169.
Bone breccias, i. 380.
Bone caves, i. 378 ff., 391 ; ii. 302.
Bourgeois, ii. 322.
Brachykephalous, ii. 198.
Brain, ii. 134, 141, 158.
Breadth, index of, ii. 198, 199.
Brewster, Sir D., i. 80.
Brongniart, A., i. 57, 78.
Bronn, H. G., ii. 29.
Bronze age, ii. 300, 308, 310, 311, 321.
Buch, L. von, i. 214.
Büchner, ii. 169.
Buckland, i. 31, 79, 167, 288, 311, 325, 371, 378.
Buffon, i. 237 ; ii. 40.
Bunsen, i. 104 ; ii. 250.
Burmeister, i. 54, 55, 61, 210 ; ii. 15, 129, 186, 201, 229.

Cainozoic period, i. 283, 336, 338, 377.
Cambrian system, i. 282.
Camper, Peter, ii. 293.
Cannibalism, ii. 355, 356.
Carboniferous period, i. 282, 290, 305, 334, 344, 346.
Caucasian race, ii. 182, 192, 201, 206, 207, 208, 214, 215, 217, 220.

Cauchy, Aug., i. 78.
Cave bear, i. 337.
—— hyæna, i. 337.
Cell, ii. 13.
Chalmers, i. 28, 79, 167, 311, 401.
Chaos, i. 111, 224, 312, 326.
Chateaubriand, i. 250.
Cheirotherium, i. 256.
Choyer, i. 32, 221.
Chronology, biblical, i. 191; ii. 252, 364, 365.
—— geological, i. 191, 290, 382; ii. 264.
Chrysostom, S., i. 142, 196.
Claudius, i. 83.
Concordistic theory, i. 183, 330–347.
Convulsionists, i. 210, 288.
Conybeare, i. 79.
Copernicus, i. 74.
Coprolites, i. 144, 269.
Cornelius, i. 63.
Cosmogonies, heathen, i. 20, 21.
Cosmogony, Mosaic, i. 21, 22, 97 ff.
Cotta, i. 286, 306.
Craniology, ii. 197.
Crannoges, ii. 350.
Create, i. 103, 104.
Creation, Mosaic account of, i. 16 ff., 89–102, 172, 154 ff.
—— centre of, ii. 236.
—— second account of, i. 159.
Cretaceous system, i. 283.
Crystallization, i. 14.
Cuvier, i. 3, 382; ii. 35, 43, 95, 267.

DARWIN, i. 295; ii. 22, 44 ff. passim, 122, 123, 124, 137, 153 ff. passim, 170, 171.
Daubeny, i. 81.
Davy, Sir H., i. 80.
Day and night, i. 124, 133, 166, 203.
Days, six, i. 94, 95, 161 ff., 192, 294–376, 398.
Deism, i. 238.
Delitzsch, i. 21, 102, 104, 121, 138, 202, 227, 405, 431, 448; ii. 250, 263.
Deluc, i. 78, 237, 382; ii. 267, 268.
Deluge, i. 222, 378 ff. passim, 403–461.
—— fossils caused by the, i. 258, 262, 294, 295.
Denise, fossil man of, ii. 322.
Descent, theory of, ii. 28–120.
Deutinger, i. 55, 244.
Devonian system, i. 278, 283.
Dillmann, i. 22, 195, 406.
Diluvial, ii. 302, 321.
Diluvium, i. 283, 376 ff. passim.
Dinotherium, i. 270.
Dolichokephalous, ii. 198.
Dolmen ii. 314.

EARTH, axis of the, i. 437.
—— formation of the, i. 209, 210, 229–253.
—— nucleus of the, i. 213, 231.
—— a spheroid, i. 229, 246, 436.
—— upheaval and depression of the, i. 439; ii. 287 ff.
—— flattening of the, i. 229, 246, 436.
Ebrard, i. 333, 345, 449.
Egypt, ii. 275 ff.
Elephant period, ii. 325.
Elk, i. 337.
Elohim, i. 104, 160, 161.
Embryo, ii. 107, 108.
Engis skull, ii. 147, 355.
Entozoa, ii. 9.
Eocene or Eogene, i. 278, 377, 398.
Eozoon Canadense, i. 287; ii. 103.
Ereb, i. 168, 169.
Erratic blocks, i. 382.
Ethiopian race, ii. 182, 192, 208, 210, 214.
Euler, i. 76.
Evening and morning, i. 124, 168.
Evolution. See Theory of Descent.
Evolutionists, ii. 40 ff.

FABRE d'Envieu, i. 327; ii. 151.
Fabri, ii. 117.
Facial angle, ii. 193 ff.
Faraday, i. 80.
Firmament, i. 125.
Fleming, John, i. 79, 383.
Flint implements, ii. 302 passim.
Flood, legends of the, i. 404.
Flourens, ii. 8.
Foraminifera, i. 272, 287.
Formation, i. 212, 278.
Fossils, i. 212, 254–293, 295, 296, 319, 334 ff.; ii. 274, 355, 362.
—— footprints, i. 256; ii. 286.
—— raindrops, i. 257.
Fraas, i. 62, 78, 239, 254; ii. 174, 278, 320.
Fracastoro, i. 262.
Frohschammer, i. 144; ii. 13, 16, 78, 93, 161, 163, 181.
Fuchs, J. N. von, i. 77, 216.

GALILEO, i. 75.
Ganges, delta of the, ii. 283.
Gastræa, ii. 101.
Generatio æquivoca, ii. 1, 31.
Giebel, C. G., i. 139, 342, 453; ii. 122, 240.
Glacial period, i. 388; ii. 322.
Glaciers, i. 387.
Gneiss, i. 213, 282.
God, nature of, i. 64.
—— Spirit of, i. 113 ff., 319.

Goethe, i. 265 ; ii. 43.
Goppert, i. 292.
Gorilla, ii. 122, 130, 133, 134, 139, 141, 145, 151, 160, 175.
Granite, i. 213.
Gratiolet, ii. 144, 145.
Greenough, i. 246, 385.
Gregory, S., of Nyssa, i. 140, 143.
Grimm, ii. 241.
Guadeloupe, fossil man of, i. 272; ii. 285.

HÆCKEL, i. 61; ii. 10 ff., 24 ff., 47, 48, 69, 70, 88, 90, 96 ff., 126, 165 ff.
Hamberger, i. 120, 147.
Haneberg, i. 179.
Harvey, ii. 3.
Hassler, ii. 348.
Heaven, i. 126.
—— and earth, i. 105.
Heer, i. 77.
Height, index of, ii. 198, 199.
Hengstenberg, i. 70, 146, 167, 311.
Herodotus, ii. 336.
Herschel, Sir J., i. 86, 199, 229.
Heterogeny, ii. 1.
Hexæmeron, explanation of, i. 89 ff. *See* Creation and Days.
His, ii. 113.
Hitchcock, i. 79.
Hochstetter, ii. 238, 307, 347.
Hoffmann, ii. 36, 65.
Horner, ii. 275.
Huber, i. 63 ; ii. 62, 81, 115.
Human race, age of. *See* Man.
Humboldt, A. von, i. 49, 53, 375 ; ii. 187, 212.
Hutton, i. 214.
Huxley, i. 51, 55, 256 ; ii. 8, 12, 20, 71, 72, 131 ff., 145 ff., 179, 228.
Hybridation, ii. 37.
Hylæosaurus, i. 271.
Hypsikephalous, ii. 198.
Hyrtl, i. 77.

ICHTHYOSAURUS, i. 270, 336.
Ideal theory, i. 184, 205, 348-375.
Iguanodon, i. 271, 336.
Induction, ii. 118.
Infusoria, ii. 6 ff.
Inspiration, i. 14 ff., 409 ; ii. 251, 254.
Instinct, ii. 82, 83.
Iron age, ii. 300 ff. passim.

JAMESON, i. 80, 383.
Jaw, ii. 196.
Jazar, i. 103.
Jehovah, i. 160.
Jom, i. 168, 169.
Jura, i. 278.
Jura limestone, i. 283.

KANT, i. 229.
Kaulen, ii. 219.
Keerl, i. 221, 225, 314, 319, 323.
Keil, i. 104, 149, 167, 294 ; ii. 182.
Keller, ii. 335, 348.
Keppler, i. 37, 74.
Kircher, Athanasius, i. 258.
Kjökken möddings, ii. 351 ff.
Knobel, i. 104.
Kurtz, i. 19, 24, 29, 41, 70, 118, 173, 174, 199, 311, 313, 318, 322 ; ii. 248.
Kutorga, i. 299, 300.

LAKE dwellings, ii. 332 ff.
Lamarck, i. 237 ; ii. 41.
Land and Sea, i. 128.
Land animals, i. 100, 135 ff.
Language, ii. 219, 220, 221.
Laplace, i. 229.
Lartet, ii. 357.
Latham, ii. 200.
Lateran Council, fourth, i. 108.
Laurentian system, i. 282, 287 ; ii. 103.
Leonhard, i. 77, 210, 354, 391, 441.
Lepus Darwinii, ii. 69, 70.
Lias, i. 278, 283.
Light, i. 123, 124, 196, 198 ff., 316, 317.
—— existence of, before sun, i. 201, 202.
Lindenschmit, ii. 291, 310, 335, 356.
Linnæus, i. 138 ; ii. 33, 121.
Literal interpretation of six days, i. 165, 204, 245, 294-310, 398.
Lombard, Peter, i. 30 ; ii. 3.
Lotze, i. 240 ; ii. 116.
Lubbock, ii. 171, 312, 313.
Lucæ, ii. 105, 138.
Lucretius, ii. 300.
Lüken, i. 20, 404 ; ii. 188.
Lusus naturæ, i. 259 ff.; ii. 304.
Lyell, i. 52, 209, 275, 283, 391 ; ii. 149, 267, 287, 294, 326, 361.

MABILLON, i. 414 ; ii. 257.
Macculloch, i. 79.
Mädler, i. 77, 200, 203.
Maillet, de, ii. 41.
Malay race, ii. 192, 199, 208 ff. passim.
Mammoth, i. 254, 261, 271, 280 ; ii. 301, 315, 357.
Mammoth period, ii. 315, 316.
Man, antiquity of, i. 295, 383, 390 ff.; ii. 265-298, 360 ff.
—— creation of, i. 139 ff.; ii. 126.
—— fossil, i. 272, 273, 296 ; ii. 285, 322.
—— races of, ii. 191 ff.
—— tertiary, ii. 321.

VOL. II.   2 A

Mankind, unity of, ii. 178, 181-245.
Mantell, G., i. 80, 240, 267, 373.
Martin, i. 26, 75, 78; ii. 9, 25, 180.
Mastodon, i. 337.
Maurer, F., ii. 284.
Mayrhofer, i. 105, 120.
Megalithic, ii. 314.
Megalosaurus, i. 271, 336.
Meignan, i. 237, 337; ii. 258.
Mesokephalous, ii. 198.
Metamorphic rocks, i. 214, 341.
Meyer, B., i. 63; ii. 73.
Meyer, H. von, i. 78, 391; ii. 122.
Mezozoic, i. 282, 335, 336, 338.
Mica slate, i. 213, 282.
Michelis, i. 50, 105, 120, 187, 357; ii. 39, 114.
Microcephalous idiots, ii. 143.
Migration, law of, ii. 63.
Miller, Hugh, i. 79, 84, 174, 325, 334, 399, 440, 441, 459.
Miocene, i. 283, 377, 398; ii. 323.
Mississippi, delta of, ii. 283.
Moigno, Abbé, i. 318, 419.
Molasse, i. 336, 378, 399.
Moleschott, ii. 134.
Molloy, i. 331, 337; ii. 271.
Monera, ii. 10 ff.
Mongolian race, ii. 192, 195, 196, 205 ff.
Morlot, ii. 344, 345, 361.
Müller, Joh., i. 77; ii. 38, 190, 219, 224.
Müller, Max, ii. 165, 219.
Murchison, i. 80, 210, 287.
Mutzl, i. 168.

NATURAL science, task of, i. 48-68.
—— misuse of, i. 7, 61, 239; ii. 172, 173, 358, 363.
Naumann, i. 268.
Neanderthal, ii. 147 ff., 355.
Nebulæ, i. 200.
Nebular hypothesis, i. 230, 231, 247.
Negro, ii. 182, 209, 211 ff. passim, 229, 231.
Neocene or Neogene, i. 283, 378.
Neolithic period, ii. 312.
Neptunism, i. 207-228, 248.
New Hollanders, ii. 210.
Newman, i. 30, 59.
Newton, i. 74.
Niagara, ii. 293.
Nicolas, i. 3.
Nile, ii. 275 ff.
—— delta of the, ii. 281.
Nilsson, ii. 307.
Nöggerath, i. 254, 270; ii. 329, 330.

OAK period, ii. 325, 327.
Oken, ii. 18, 188.

Oligocene, i. 283.
Omalius d'Halloy, i. 415, 416.
Ontogeny, ii. 107.
Organisms, pedigree of, ii. 88, 99, 100
Orthognathous, ii. 196.
Orthokephalous, ii. 198.
Owen, i. 80; ii. 188.

PALÆOLITHIC period, i. 282; ii. 312.
Palæontology, i. 208, 253, 277-293, 312 ff.; ii. 101.
Palæozoic period, i. 282, 283, 334.
Pallmann, ii. 309, 334, 339, 341, 347, 351.
Pantheism, i. 238.
Paradise, i. 144, 155, 156, 309, 310.
Pasteur, ii. 6 ff.
Peat, growth of, ii. 327 ff.
Pelvis, ii. 199, 219.
Pererius, i. 110.
Permian system, i. 278, 283, 346.
Peschel, ii. 171, 191, 211, 227.
Petavius, i. 110, 244.
Peter, S., i. 221, 222.
Peter Lombard. *See* Lombard.
Pfaff, i. 77, 182, 216, 332, 419, 456; ii. 114, 362.
Phillips, i. 395; ii. 295, 361.
Phylogeny, ii. 108.
Pianciani, i. 85, 110, 168, 190, 243, 244, 304, 412, 413, 435, 436.
Pine period, ii. 325.
Pini, Hermenegild, i. 188.
Pithecoid theory, ii. 177, 366.
Plants, classification of, i. 99.
—— creation of, i. 129 ff., 284, 313, 315, 339; ii. 2, 32.
—— existence of, before sun, i. 204.
—— primæval, i. 268 ff.
Platykephalous, ii. 198.
Pleistocene, i. 283, 377.
Plesiosaurus, i. 269, 337.
Pliocene, i. 283, 377, 398; ii. 323.
Plutonism, i. 207, 228.
Polythalamaceæ, i. 272.
Porphyry, i. 213.
Post pliocene, i. 283, 378.
Post tertiary, i. 283, 378.
Pouchet, ii. 6.
Prasias, lake, ii. 336.
Preadamite men, i. 273, 329.
Prehistoric age, ii. 320, 358.
Premetallic age, ii. 305.
Prichard, i. 80, 448; ii. 140, 187, 231.
Primary, i. 278.
Primæval and present world, distinction between, i. 272, 324, 376, 402.
Prognathous, ii. 196.
Pterodactylus, i. 269.

INDEX.

QUATERNARY, i. 283, 386; ii. 302, 322.
Quatrefages, de, i. 78; ii. 23, 37, 40, 144, 175, 236.
Quenstedt, i. 57, 78, 219, 257, 259, 274, 290, 305; ii. 17, 318.

RACE, ii. 36.
Rask, ii. 247.
Raumer, K. von, i. 77, 120, 220, 311.
Recent, i. 283, 377.
Redi, ii. 5, 8.
Reindeer period, ii. 315, 358.
Reptiles, i. 336.
Restitution, theory of, i. 117 ff., 311–329, 385, 401.
Retzius, ii. 196, 197.
Rocks, primitive, i. 277, 278.
—— sedimentary, i. 277.
—— stratified, i. 212, 277.
—— transition, i. 277.
Römer, F., ii. 102, 325.
Rougemont, F. von, ii. 325.
Rudimentary organs, ii. 74 ff.
Rütimeyer, ii. 112, 342.

SABBATH, i. 19, 94, 95, 153, 175 ff.
Saint Prest, ii. 323.
Saint-Hilaire, G., ii. 43.
Saurians, i. 271; ii. 43.
Savage races, ii. 171, 177, 353.
Schaaffhausen, ii. 124, 128, 273, 297, 317, 357.
Scheuchzer, A., i. 262, 263.
Schlegel, Fr. von, i. 120.
Schleiden, i. 4, 49, 60; ii. 284.
Schleiermacher, i. 70.
Schmerling, i. 391.
Schubert, H. von, i. 77, 120, 311, 323, 432; ii. 270.
Schultz, i. 308, 357.
Secchi, i. 203.
Secondary, i. 278.
Sedgwick, i. 79, 386, 417.
Selection, natural, ii. 5 ff. passim.
—— sexual, ii. 55 ff. passim.
Semper, ii. 15, 44, 113, 114.
Serres, M. de, i. 3, 78.
Silberschlag, i. 264.
Silliman, i. 79.
Silurian system, i. 278, 283, 287, 341; ii. 102.
Sin and death, i. 144, 322.
Skin, colour of the, ii. 191, 192, 230.
Skulls, human, ii. 193 ff., 213, 232.
—— of man and ape, ii. 132 ff.
—— primæval, ii. 147 ff., 355.
Smith, J. Pye, i. 80, 85, 279, 327.
Smith, W., i. 279.

Solar system, i. 230, 231.
Sorignet, i. 294.
Soul, human and animal, ii. 161 ff.
Spallanzani, ii. 6.
Species, ii. 32 ff. passim.
—— human, ii. 186.
Speech, ii. 163 ff., 200.
Spontaneous generation, ii. 1–31.
Stalagmite, i. 273, 379.
Stars, i. 133, 194 ff., 316, 319.
Steenstrup, ii. 327.
Steffens, i. 77.
Stiefelhagen, i. 20, 404.
Stone age, ii. 300, 306, 307, 310 ff.
Strauss, Fr., i. 192, 193, 195; ii. 9, 10, 47, 146, 157.
Suarez, i. 110, 200.
Sun and moon, i. 35, 133, 195.
Sweden, ii. 286, 287, 290, 291.

TELERPETON Elginense, i. 286.
Teliosaurus, i. 337.
Telliamed, ii. 41.
Tertiary, i. 278, 283, 377, 393.
Tertullian, i. 258.
Thohu wabohu, i. 111 ff. passim, 223, 314, 324, 384.
Thomas Aquinas, S., i. 37, 39, 44, 102, 109, 146, 153, 163, 196, 322; ii. 3.
Thomsen, ii. 300.
Tiedemann, ii. 134, 189, 212, 223.
Tinière, la, ii. 344.
Triassic system, i. 278, 283, 334, 344, 345.
Trilobites, ii. 162.
Troyon, ii. 340, 343.
Tuttle, Hudson, ii. 45.

ULRICI, i. 63, 202; ii. 9.

VALROGER, ii. 151, 257, 262.
Varieties, ii. 36.
—— of human race, ii. 186.
Veith, i. 294.
"Vestiges of the Natural History of Creation," i. 237; ii. 44, 125.
Virchow, ii. 35, 135, 146, 349.
Vogt, i. 144, 217, 237, 247, 394; ii. 44, 48, 123, 129, 142, 168, 284, 302, 303, 313, 328, 329, 332, 345, 347.
Volcanoes, i. 211, 216.
Voltaire, i. 265.
Vosen, i. 117, 146, 179, 309, 311, 370.

WAGNER, A., i. 77, 120, 216, 220, 311, 384; ii. 188, 304, 346.
Wagner, M., ii. 62, 63, 64.
Wagner, R., i. 77; ii. 188.
Waitz, ii. 135, 218, 223, 226, 237, 241.
Wallace, ii. 45, 156.
Walworth, i. 184, 360.

Waterkeyn, i. 79, 184.
Waters, i. 125, 427 ff.
Week, i. 176 ff. passim.
Welcker, ii. 199.
Werner, i. 216, 277.
Westermayer, i. 105, 120, 122, 311, 318.
Whewell, i. 57, 79, 85.
Wiseman, i. 9, 10, 50, 63, 167, 374, 378 ; ii. 234.
Woman, creation of, i. 147 ff.

Woodward, i. 262.
Worsaee, ii. 313.

XENOPHANES, i. 257.

YEAR, meaning of, in first ages, ii. 247.

ZITTEL, i. 262.
Zöckler, i. 221, 337, 345.

www.ingramcontent.com/pod-product-compliance
Lightning Source LLC
Chambersburg PA
CBHW031418230426
43668CB00007B/351